AF709046

BEFORE THE MARKET

The Political Economy of Olympianism

D. N. Wang

Before the Market

The Political Economy of Olympianism

D. N. Wang

COMMON GROUND RESEARCH NETWORKS 2018

First published in 2018
as part of the New Directions in the Humanities Book Imprint
doi:10.18848/978-1-61229-902-0/CGP (Full Book)

Common Ground Research Networks
2001 South First Street, Suite 202
University of Illinois Research Park
Champaign, IL 61820 USA

Copyright © D. N. Wang 2018

All rights reserved. Apart from fair dealing for the purposes of study, research, criticism, or review as permitted under the applicable copyright legislation, no part of this book may be reproduced by any process without written permission from the publisher.

Library of Congress Cataloging-in-Publication Data

Names: Wang, D. N., author.
Title: Before the market : the political economy of Olympianism / D.N. Wang.
Description: Champaign, IL : Common Ground Research Networks, 2018. | "First published ... as part of the New Directions in the Humanities Book Imprint."--Title page verso. | Includes bibliographical references and index.
Identifiers: LCCN 2016026211 (print) | LCCN 2016031134 (ebook) | ISBN 9781612299020 (pdf) | ISBN 9781612299006 (hardback : alkaline paper) | ISBN 9781612299013 (paperback : alkaline paper) | ISBN 9781612299020 (ebook)
Subjects: LCSH: Greece--Economic conditions--To 146 B.C. | Economics--Philosophy--History--To 1500. | Greece--Commerce--History. | Markets--Political aspects--Greece--History--To 1500. | Markets--Social aspects--Greece--History--To 1500. | Greece--Politics and government--To 146 B.C. | Greece--Social life and customs--To 146 B.C.
Classification: LCC HC37 (ebook) | LCC HC37 .W276 2017 (print) | DDC 330.938--dc23
LC record available at https://lccn.loc.gov/2016026211

Cover Photo Credit: Kamila Czubaj

To my grandfather, father, and their generations of Chinese intellectuals.

Table of Contents

Timeline of Ancient Greece
(All dates BCE unless otherwise noted.)

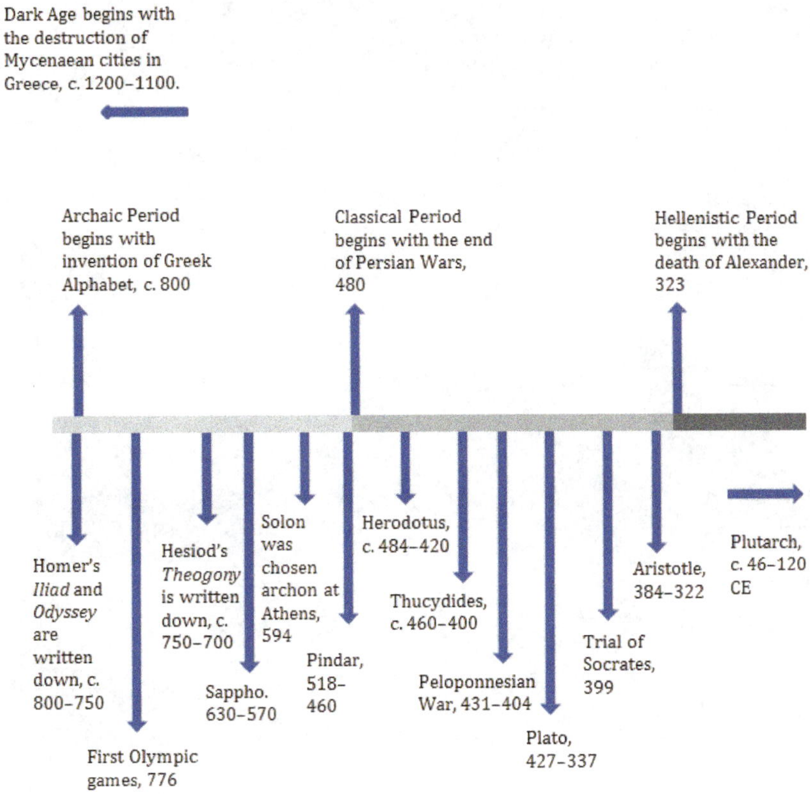

PROLOGUE

Listening to the Silenced

The tendency for historians to reflect the view of victors is common not only in biographies of "great men" and stories of war and conquest, but also in studies of institutions and cultures. In other words, the convenience and payoff of attending to winners at the expense of their distractors can also distort accounts of everyday life and society.[1]

Two sweeping modern entities dominate how we imagine social organization: the global market economy and the territorial nation-state. The global market economy thrives on private ownership, capital accumulation, and free commercial exchange, while the nation-state enforces territorial sovereignty, exclusive citizenship, and internal hierarchy. Many commentators have accepted as a given that the best future of humanity is tied to these two systems, but the veracity of that conclusion is by no means certain.

In this project, I have explored what lies outside the bounds of the market and the state. To illuminate other configurations, especially historical ones that have been obscured by time and neglected by contemporaries, we must look into the debris beneath our current civilization and conduct a meaningful conversation between the past and the present.[2] For the ancient Greeks, to whom I specifically turn for this mission, the market and the state were at best vague and not at all concepts they used to analyze their lives. However, examining their societies through this lens not only casts a new light on them, but also on what is plausible and desirable for us. Through balanced two-way dialogue, a mindful interchange that resists the gravitational pull toward "history by the victors" becomes possible across time and space.

What exact relevance does a study of ancient economy hold for readers in 2017? Hailed as the cradle of the West, ancient Greece casts a long shadow in human history for ushering in the dawn of European civilization. The assessment of Greek antiquity is therefore critical for evaluating subsequent historical developments.[3] From this point of view, what sorts of economic principles and practices the Greeks adopted or

[1] For example, Chakrabarty's *Provincializing Europe* highlights the way in which conventional European historical analysis marginalizes non-Western and nonmodern ways of human existence, an awareness that reflects the broad concerns of subaltern and postcolonial theories at large.

[2] The goal is to balance "past-oriented history" and "present-oriented history." The former, also termed as "history of the past," refers to studying history for its own sake and in its own context. The latter, also known as "history of the present," is exemplified by Foucault, who highlights the archaeology and genealogy of concepts in order to deconstruct modern phenomena. See Michel Foucault, *The Birth of the Clinic: An Archaeology of Medical Perception* (New York: Vintage Books, 1994).

[3] The importance of ancient Greece can be seen in chronological surveys of European economic history, e.g., Neil J. Smelser and Richard Swedberg, *The Handbook of Economic Sociology* (Princeton: Princeton University Press, 1994).

favored are questions of enormous consequence. Did Greek antiquity, as many argue, display all signs of a nascent market system, lacking only the necessary technology and scale to enable something akin to modern capitalism? If so, then the whole of Europe's past, when stripped of temporary political and social vagaries, can be seen as a steady march—albeit with long pauses and disruptions—toward an ever-expanding market order. On the other hand, if some other economic system prevailed in ancient Greece at the birth of Western democracy, then the meteoric rise of capitalism in recent centuries amounts to a major divergence. As the first piece in a chain of dominoes, the questions about the ancient Greeks can uphold or impugn the received wisdom about the best political, social, and economic organization for societies all around the world.

Especially now in the aftermath of the 2008 financial meltdown, the underlying sense of collapse and decay in the global economy shows no signs of abating. The situation is compounded by related and equally pressing crises in politics, social welfare, and ecology. In this troubling time when everything we know seems to be falling apart, radical thinking, the kind that breaks with tradition and brings about a paradigm shift, is all the more necessary. Yet the greater the need for immediate remedies, the more necessary it is to search the full spectrum of human existence for concrete guidance. This study was conceived to be a purposeful step in that direction. Based on the lessons of ancient Greece, it constructs a new model of political economy and identity formation that speaks directly to the crises at the heart of modernity. The rationale and principles of this new system put the logic of market and the state firmly on the defense by exposing the ways in which the moral foundation of these two ruling entities runs counter to a number of cherished democratic and progressive values. With historical illustrations, this study supplies convincing rhetoric for meaningful system-wide change and personal transformation. Equally significant is the feasibility of implementing this alternative vision, since the experience from the past contains practical guidance for achieving prosperity and wellness without market and state institutions, and for forging a collective identity that transcends territory, ethnicity/race, and class. As it turns out, when we insist on seeking out the enfeebled voices, our repository of solutions and answers expands, along with the imagination and courage for realizing them. This enhanced capacity to confront challenges and improve our common lot is something that all of us, including the elites, stand to gain from.

PART I

Olympian Economics

CHAPTER 1

The Ancient Economy and Cultural Analysis

WHAT SCHOLARS HAVE SAID SO FAR

How the ancient economy should be characterized has been at the center of a contentious and enduring debate that first sprung up in the late nineteenth century.[4] The famous Bücher-Meyer Controversy of the 1890s already posed the question of whether a true market economy existed in ancient Greece. On one side of the argument, Karl Bücher argued that the ancient economy was "primitive," in the sense that it never developed beyond the level of isolated, self-sustaining households. On the other hand, Edward Meyer and Michael Rostovtzeff, scholars known as the "modernists," cited extensive evidence on trade and commerce to assert that the ancient economy, especially during late antiquity, was essentially a smaller and earlier version of modern capitalism.[5] To the modernist school, the economy of the ancient Mediterranean, despite existing more than two millennia earlier, differed from modern capitalism only in degree, not in form. The disagreement raged on fiercely during its day without being allayed and it polarized scholarly opinions into those two camps in the decades that followed.

Fifty years after the Bücher-Meyer dispute, the anthropologist and historian Karl Polanyi rekindled the debate by introducing the "substantive" and "formalist" distinction. Polanyi labeled non-Western, noncapitalist, preindustrial societies as "substantive," in that their economic activities are "embedded," i.e., made subservient to a variety of social, cultural, and communal functions. By contrast, modern, market-dominated economies are "formalist," because they remove extra-economic considerations from the rationalized pursuit of financial interest. With regard to the ancient economy, Polanyi classified Classical Athens as primarily substantive, drawing much protest from his modernist and formalist critics.[6]

The modernist/primitive and formalist/substantive dispute largely subsided after the publication of Moses Finley's *The Ancient Economy* in 1973, which quickly established itself as the new orthodoxy. Finley marshaled extensive evidence to demonstrate that the ancient economy was deeply embedded in a great number of political and social frameworks, particularly those that defined the civic life in the *polis*—the Greek city-state. It was not until nearly a decade after Finley's death that newer viewpoints emerged in the 1990s. This time, however, the juxtaposition of the

---

[4] For an excellent review of previous scholarship, see Heidi Michelle Sherman, "Barbarians Come to Market: The Emporia of Western Eurasia from 500 BC to AD 1000" (PhD diss., University of Minnesota, July 2008), 5–21.

[5] Michael Ivanovich Rostovtzeff, *The Social & Economic History of the Hellenistic World* (Oxford: Clarendon Press, 1941).

[6] See Karl Polanyi, "On the Comparative Treatment of Economic Institutions in Antiquity with Illustrations from Athens, Mycenae, and Alalakh," reprinted in *CITY INVINCIBLE: A Symposium on Urbanization and Cultural Development in the Ancient Near East* (Chicago: University of Chicago Press, 1960), 334–37.

ancient and modern economies itself became suspect. To someone like Ian Morris,[7] the demarcation of Greece and Rome from their contemporary civilizations was problematic in light of the emerging evidence indicating both internal diversity within as well as extensive ties with the greater Mediterranean region.[8] Furthermore, the conception of Greco-Roman antiquity itself betrays a colonial discourse that treats the West as exceptional.[9] Morris' solution was to embrace New Institutional Economics, a branch of economic thinking that, as its name suggests, focuses on how institutions condition economic choice. On that basis, Morris proposed that we clear away geographic divisions in order to apply across the board quantitative methods derived from the social sciences. At the same time, Leslie Kurke, a proponent of New Historicism, also took issue with the application of literary sources in the older works.[10] To Kurke, texts operate as fields of representation: they do not contain information about material reality, but only the maneuvers of signs and symbols. According to this theory, written sources reveal only the semiotic negotiation and manipulation conducted in specific performative and ritualized moments, not patterns and features of the real economy.[11] Given these powerful critiques and pushbacks, the comparison of ancient and modern economies can resume only after breaking new theoretical ground.

METHODOLOGY: CULTURE, DISCOURSE ANALYSIS, AND IDENTITY

To address the issues raised by Morris and Kurke, I employ cultural analysis in this study of the ancient Greek economy. My approach takes its cue from the cultural turn, an intellectual movement that stressed the formative power of "culture" in the way it shapes interrelated meanings. This important shift, which has swept through the humanities and the social sciences, has sent reverberations in the works of Clifford Geertz, Michel Foucault, Pierre Bourdieu, Hayden White and others.[12] As one of its

---

[7] There is a special type of gratitude reserved for one's PhD advisor, and I want to take this opportunity to express mine for Ian Morris. Although it will become clear that we think so differently about the world and the Greeks, the book would not have been possible without him.

[8] At one end, Liverani emphasized the heterogeneity of societies in the Near East. At the other end, Horden and Purcell rejected territorial divisions in the Mediterranean or even distinct periods for that matter. Mario Liverani, "The Near East: The Bronze Age," in *The Ancient Economy: Evidence and Models*, ed. Joseph Gilbert Manning and Ian Morris (Stanford, CA: Stanford University Press, 2005), 47–57; Peregrine Horden and Nicholas Purcell, *The Corrupting Sea: A Study of Mediterranean History* (Oxford: Blackwell Publishers, 2000).

[9] For assumptions of European superiority in scholarship, see Joseph Gilbert Manning and Ian Morris, "Introduction," in *The Ancient Economy: Evidence and Models* (Stanford, CA: Stanford University Press, 2005), 7ff.

[10] See Ian Morris, "The Athenian Economy Twenty Years after the Ancient Economy," review of *Athenian Economy and Society: A Banking Perspective*, by Edward E. Cohen, *Classical Philology* 89, no. 4 (1994): 351–52.

[11] For the theoretical framework of New Historicism, see C. Dougherty and L. Kurke, eds., introduction to *Cultural Poetics in Archaic Greece: Cult, Performance, Politics* (Cambridge, UK: Cambridge University Press, 2003), 1–12.

[12] See Clifford Geertz, *The Interpretation of Cultures: Selected Essays* (New York: Basic Books, 1973); Michel Foucault, *Discipline and Punish: The Birth of the Prison*, 1995; Pierre Bourdieu, *Outline of a Theory of Practice* (Cambridge, UK: Cambridge University Press, 1977); Hayden White, *Metahistory: The*

scholars George Steinmetz put it, there is a "general assertion of the constitutive role of culture;"[13] in other words, culture generates society's economic infrastructure and institutional structure rather than the other way around.[14] On this basis, I argue culture fashions human reality by issuing a series of "truth statements." A truth statement comes into existence through language, and must be comprehended and enacted by the audience. For example, a statement like "God is dead," or "All men are created equal, that they are endowed by their Creator with certain unalienable rights," is meaningless if not articulated in words and taken as true. It is to be differentiated from a fact, such as that of the Earth rotating around the sun, which may be said to be independent of human interpretation. Often, the most consequential truths for society, like the previous ones about God and men, are neither derived from facts nor can be proven in a strict scientific sense. Consequently, a truth statement is inevitably perspectival, polyvalent, and permutable. The unearthing of these kinds of systematic pronouncements, ones that govern social, political, and economic activities collectively as an entire culture, is the core offering of this book.

As a body of interlocking truths, culture is primarily located in the ideational realm, and thus cannot be dealt with using traditional empiricist and positivist methods. In this light, the sizable number of poetic texts that have survived from ancient Greece—while devoid of hard facts about real individuals and events—convey rich information about cultural operations. Scholars like Foucault and Said have successfully directed attention to how truth claims embedded in discourse and representation can structure reality.[15] In particular, they demonstrated two ways in which specific modes of thinking shaped the course of society. In *The History of Sexuality*, Foucault delineated how notions from scientific authorities regulated and disciplined the sexual behavior of the modern individual. In *Orientalism*, Said illustrated how exotic, imaginary Western accounts of the Middle East legitimized European conquest. In both cases, "the real" was created through concepts and ideas: the former by an epistemological regime, and the latter by the fantasies of an inferior *other*. Through these examples, we can see the potency of cultural truths in molding historical events.

Scholars of economic history are wont to emphasize tangible and quantifiable factors[16]—such as climate, technology, population,[17] commerce, and institutions—

Historical Imagination in Nineteenth-Century Europe (Baltimore, MD: Johns Hopkins University Press, 1973).

[13] George Steinmetz, *State/Culture: State-Formation after the Cultural Turn* (Ithaca, NY: Cornell University Press, 1999), 4.

[14] Ian Morris, "Hard Surfaces," in *Money, Labour and Land*, ed. Paul Cartledge, Edward E. Cohen, and Lin Foxhall (London: Routledge, 2002), 15.

[15] In this sense, discourse (à la Foucault) may overlap with ideology, which occurs more frequently in everyday language but often in an explicitly political context. The more precise definition of ideology given by Terry Eagleton is a good proxy for how I conceive of discourse: as something that "promot[es] beliefs and values congenial to it, naturalizing and universalizing such beliefs to as to render them self-evident and apparently inevitable; denigrating ideas which might challenge it; excluding rival forms of thought, perhaps by some unspoken but systematic logic; and obscuring social reality in ways convenient to itself." See Terry Eagleton, *Ideology* (London: Verso, 1991), 5–6.

[16] Marx famously placed material conditions above all other considerations.

[17] See Karl Gunnar Persson, *An Economic History of Europe: Knowledge, Institutions and Growth, 600 to*

precisely at the expense of neglecting cultural forces.[18] At the analytical level, these materialist and materialistic explanations either assume that society robotically follows a path set by nonhuman determinants, or limit the responses to the calculation of rational self-interest. In the first group, elements that *cannot* be predicted or fully controlled, such as climate change,[19] population movement, and technological progress are treated as primary causes, while the decisions and reactions of society are discounted, despite their obvious significance.[20] In the second group, economic outcomes are attributed to the preferences of an individual who engages in utility-maximizing calculus, a core assumption derived from methodological individualism.[21] Methodological individualism treats humans as autonomous, self-serving individuals who want infinite things, ignoring second-order considerations like group identification and differentiation as well as cultural inflections of desires and needs.[22] The problem with this model is that in reality the "I" varies greatly depending on that person's sense of the *self* in relation to historically contingent categories and perceptions. Even when transaction costs are introduced to complicate the rational pursuit of self-interest as in New Institutional Economics, the essence of *homo economicus*—an economic man of material appetite and entrepreneurial ambition—does not alter. This perspective, however, is by no means the only one. Consider Buddhism, for example. A Buddhist sees a car not as a vehicle but as a pile of metal ready to rot and decay, and the desire for such transient objects not as the pursuit of utility but the cause for suffering and misery. The person imbibing these Buddhist truths would thus define subject-object relationships through false desire and attachment, rather than utilitarian selection and trade-off. Yet by taking inherent changeability out of human nature, neoclassical, neoliberal and New Institutional Economics automatically deny the validity of any cultural truth that differs from the ones that undergird the model of *homo economicus*. Overall, the above approaches fall victim to the perennial trap of either leaning too much on given conditions by ignoring the human component, or too much on fixed agency from presupposing a universally valid, economically incentivized, materially insatiable being from *tabula rasa*.

---

the Present (New York: Cambridge University Press, 2010).

[18] For example, New Institutional Economics, or NIE.

[19] See Jared Diamond, *Guns, Germs, and Steel: The Fates of Human Societies* (New York: Norton, 2005).

[20] For example, in the case of technology, Eugene Rice argued that although both Europe and China had access to gun powder, the political reality in Europe enabled new inventions of weaponry. In other words, technology itself is a product of social outcomes, not the other way around. See Eugene F. Rice, *The Foundation of Early Modern Europe, 1460-1559* (New York: Norton, 1970), 15.

[21] Darley Jose Kjosavik detailed the influence of methodological individualism in the social sciences and charged that new institutionalism "leaves many of the core assumptions of mainstream economics unscathed." See Darley Jose Kjosavik, "Methodological Individualism and Rational Choice in Neoclassical Economics: A Review of Institutionalist Critique," *Forum for Development Studies* 2, no. 2 (2003): 232.

[22] The apologists would try to stretch the definition of utility broad enough to include nonmaterialist incentives like altruism and moral values. However, what is materially profitable and politically convenient is often directly opposite of what is good for the whole and what is ethical. When preferences can be tweaked to designate completely different things, utility maximization becomes a moving target that is unfalsifiable.

By contrast, the cultural framework I propose strikes a balance between structure and agency. At the most basic level, there is no question that truth claims are issued by humans—these statements are always being contested, modified, and transformed by us rather than stand alone as self-evident facts. As a result, any *a priori* assumption about the *self*—such as the rational pursuit of utility—must be shelved. Yet at the same time, truth-making is a thoroughly collective and interdependent phenomenon that takes place in the social world, which, to some extent, is also constrained by physical laws. As such, cultural truths can never simply be made by a single person or isolated individuals in an entirely fantastical manner. Via this conceptualization, the cultural approach accommodates both the enormous creative power of human beings as well as the imposing contours of their environment.[23]

Based on this individual-system dialectic, I further devised a three-part formula of *culture*, *identity*, and *action* for economics. As stated, culture exercises power by assigning meaning to, or forging truth for, a broad array of subjects, objects, and their relationships. When this happens systematically and holistically, the culturally conditioned world becomes real, natural, and all-encompassing. In the example above, a serious Buddhist aspires to detach himself from the material world and avoid doing harm to any life, setting him or her apart from individuals who follow other beliefs. In economic terms, the Buddhist would forgo consumption even if prices drop, choose ethical jobs that may not pay well, and denounce violence despite setbacks and defeat. When enough people become Buddhists in this way, their actions crystallize into corresponding patterns in institutions and infrastructure. Using this line of analysis, we can see how cultural truths translate into identity categories, which then produce concrete results on the ground. Moreover, since the meaning of an identity—such as a Buddhist, a socialist, or an American (with regard to wealth distribution, race relations, and foreign policy, etc.)—can always be contested, it becomes possible to explore why sometimes labels are unstable, actions inconsistent, and results unpredictable, lending further dynamism and fluidity to the cultural model.

Another major benefit of this approach is that, by relating culture to identity and linking idea to action, literary material can be used once again for political economy,[24] for there is always some "truth" behind what humans do. To implement this method, we need to treat source materials as reflective of a larger body of cultural discourse that structures each historical epoch.[25] As Foucault argued in *What is an Author*,

---

[23] In stating this, I flip the Marxian view that culture is the superstructure that rests on the economic base.

[24] I use "political economy" because it is a term used by other scholars who wish to challenge the assumptions of the classical school of economics.

[25] For examples of this kind of discourse analysis, see Dipesh Chakrabarty, *Habitations of Modernity: Essays in the Wake of Subaltern Studies* (Chicago: University of Chicago Press, 2002); Joan Wallach Scott, *Only Paradoxes to Offer: French Feminists and the Rights of Man* (Cambridge, MA: Harvard University Press, 1996); and White, *Metahistory*. It must be noted that, discourse analysis, by being predominantly linguistic-based, has often been accused of "los[ing] touch with the hard surfaces of life" in neglecting the less spoken dimensions of material reality. See Morris, "Hard Surfaces," 15, citing Geertz, *The Interpretation of Cultures*, 30. To avert this risk, we must also track the often silent omnipotence of political exclusion and economic limitation that are invisible in the text precisely because they rob the voices of those they impact. In the ancient Greek context, those operations stem from an elaborate body politic that dictates one's membership, status, and function both within the larger community as well as in relation to other groups on the basis of gender, class, and place of birth. When we do not lose sight of this

writers do not direct economic and social mainsprings; quite the opposite, larger cultural truths determine what is feasible, thinkable, and speakable for them in the first place. For example, when we read the work of Hesiod, we can claim that the poet/text uses an array of literary techniques and strategies to thematize self-sufficiency. But a Foucaultian reading would turn this around: society's idea of self-sufficiency was so prominent and well-defined that for Hesiod to ignore it or to discuss it in any other way was unimaginable. Following this line of thinking, the traditional inquiry on the intent, genre, and style of a particular author or text becomes unsatisfactory, and is therefore not the focus of this study. Similarly, the pure pursuit of "what did the ancients say" also errs, because both the meaning and verisimilitude of a truth statement hinge on the active interpretation of the audience and their society at large.[26] Since my end goal, in particular, is to discover inspiration for a new economic system, what matters are not so much self-standing facts that disclose the past—which we hardly possess in any case—but extant narratives and what to make of them and their popular perception.[27] This radical departure from empiricist, materialist, and past-oriented approaches is no doubt subject to critique, both theoretically and due to any deficiencies in my adoption. Nevertheless, most literary scholars have declared the texts and authors referenced here too disparate to be part of any common discourse/culture. This hypercritical stance has prevented applicable social and economic paradigms from being developed out of antiquity, and the void has been filled by universalist modern models that gladly do away with the ancients altogether.[28] Given this state of affairs, my method, for all its sins, is still meritable in making the most use of ancient evidence. At the same time, the deliberate engagement with compelling questions from the present could very well yield fruitful results.

In employing this particular cultural framework, this project also departs from New Historicism and universalist history, methods of studying the ancient economy advocated by Leslie Kurke and Ian Morris, respectively. As stated before, through the relationship established for idea, identity, and action, the "smokescreen" of linguistics that obscures material reality can be lifted, overcoming Kurke's concern that the texts are impenetrable. At the same time, the introduction of contingency and alternatives at the onset of European civilization nullifies geographic essentialism that treats the

---

configuration, the inconspicuous but significant patterns of power relations—the hard surface of life—will be exposed.

[26] This position is very similar to what Roland Barthes advocated in "The Death of the Author," in *Image, Music, Text*, trans. Stephen Heath (New York: Hill and Wang, 1977), 142–48.

[27] The method of discourse analysis relegates issues of the text, such as transmission, dating, authorship, literary genre, etc., to the background, although the most up-to-date findings in these areas, when relevant, will be incorporated.

[28] For example, when Edward Harris applied a universal definition of ownership—one that is extremely modernistic—to all societies, he did not prove how people actually understand it, for interpretations of formal laws are not the same as actual belief systems. See Edward Harris, "Did Solon Abolish Debt-Bondage?" *The Classical Quarterly* 52, no. 2 (2002): 427–28; Edward Harris, "Homer, Hesiod, and the 'Origin' of Greek Slavery," *Revue des etudes anciennes* 114, no. 2 (2012), 345–66; Edward Harris, "The Legal Foundation of Economic Growth," in *The Ancient Greek Economy: Markets, Households and City-states*, ed. Edward Harris, David Lewis, and Mark Woolmer (New York: Cambridge University Press, 2016), 119. The two specific conclusions—that Solon did not abolish debt-bondage but enslavement for debt and that slavery was already fully developed in Homeric society—will be addressed in the corresponding sections.

West as an intrinsic, immutable entity. In particular, the primary Greek cultural system presented in this book resonates strongly with particular facets of early non-Western and preindustrial societies as well as specific trends in the contemporary age, demolishing the boundaries that divide the West from the rest and antiquity from modernity. This dramatic disruption of traditional categorization removes the basis of Eurocentrism that prompted Morris to seek salvation in economic universalism. At the same time, the fundamental specificity of culture forestalls any application of a fixed logic, such as that of New Institutional Economics, to all periods and places indiscriminately.[29] With these maneuvers, the newly constructed methodological apparatus clears the objections against the attempt to historicize capitalism, so the old project can now proceed with renewed vigor.

A Three-way Struggle

Using the formulation of culture, identity, and action, this book suggests that not one, but three cultural systems of truths emerged in ancient Greece. For easy identification, I call them Olympianism, Polisism, and Oeconomism. In Olympianism, a multitude of special and unique beings shape the world in which humans, as inherently fragile and interdependent creatures, learn to inhabit together. In Polisism, those who are born as native male citizens glorify and immortalize their city through practicing the politics of egalitarianism and solidarity. In Oeconomism, autonomous and disaggregated individuals pursue utility maximization in competition against one another. In manifestation, Olympianism stimulates robust, dense, rhizomic social relations; Polisism promotes equality among male citizens; and Oeconomism incites the self-interested choices of individuals. Whereas the philosophies of Polisism and Oeconomism give rise to the territorial sovereign state and the free market, respectively, the vision of Olympianism fosters communal organization that bypasses state and market institutions. At the heart of this non-state and non-capitalist constellation lies the distinctive idea that human identity ought to be constantly fashioned through collaborative and reciprocal action. Such a formulation of a protean and evolving human nature rejects the role of "essentialized" attributes acquired at birth that distinguish "us" from "them," and of wealth inherited or won from winner-take-all gambits.

With this characterization, it should be kept in mind that the three distinctive systems existed as regimes of human-made truths, not as assemblages of absolute and infallible laws, and by that very nature, they were vulnerable to contingency, corruption, and complication when transported to the realm of actual practice. The gap between what these truths were intended to be and how they fell short in reality,

[29] Both theoretical tendencies have, in fact, been accused of aiding renewed colonialist and imperialist narratives. As Margaret Jane Radin put it, "Overstressing context-transcendence in trying to build a cross-cultural theory of human nature could be a form of modern Western cultural imperialism." See Margaret Jane Radin, *Contested Commodities* (Cambridge, MA: Harvard University Press, 1996), 77. Douglass North, the father of New Institutional Economics, has also been accused of conducting "cliometric imperialism." See Alain Bresson, *The Making of the Ancient Greek Economy*, trans. Steven Rendall (Princeton and Oxford: Princeton University Press, 2016), 21.

though important, is a separate consideration. The fact that variegated truths existed conterminously due to the concurrence of multiple cultures is already one major reason why the historical reality of ancient Greece does not neatly map onto any one coherent discourse.

With this qualification, I propose that the dispensation of Olympianism was strongest in the pre-*polis* period stretching from the late Iron Age to the Archaic Age (900–480 BCE, before the Classical era). With the movement toward rationalization propelled by the Ionian Enlightenment, a "disenchantment of the world" was effected due to new scientific modes of thinking, eviscerating Olympianism from the sixth century onward. The upheaval in thoughts and beliefs is evident in the sources from the second half of the fifth century onward,[30] and it energized the other two contending cultures of Polisism and Oeconomism. Roughly speaking, while all three cultures—Olympianism, Polisism, and Oeconomism—competed intensely during the fifth and fourth centuries, each of them was more supreme in the periods roughly corresponding to the Archaic (700–480 BCE), Classical (480–323 BCE), and Hellenistic Ages (323–30 BCE), respectively; readers can reference the timeline in the beginning of the book as needed. Again, this chronological progression is only a rough guide. It reflects general tendencies rather than the neat conformity of every single historical occurrence; in other words, there is room in this thesis for some heterogeneous strands to be interspersed in each period. Yet notwithstanding some minor inconsistencies, this model of cultural contestation is better able to account for the composite and heterogeneous economic reality than any singular world view that does not easily accommodate variation and deviation. In addition, this holistic approach integrates myriad aspects ranging from the literary, religious, institutional, political, and social into the study of economics, highlighting overarching connections that would otherwise be overlooked in expositions confined to a single subject. Capitalizing on these strengths, this book sets up the stage of the three-way cultural contestation and presents Olympianism as the hero for an alternative model of political economy.

Time and Space: Sacred Chronology and Geography

A brief and generalized review of Olympian metaphysics is due before we begin a detailed analysis of its political economy. The exercise involves first examining the notions of time and space in the world of gods and heroes. Owing to the tales of divine and extraordinary beings, the temporal and spatial world experienced by the Greeks can be called "sacred,"[31] that is, special and enduring. When time and space are special, they are unique and extraordinary, the opposite of homogeneous or

[30] See Jan Bremmer, "Atheism in Antiquity," in *Cambridge Companion to Atheism*, ed. Michael Martin (New York: Cambridge University Press, 2007), 12–9.

[31] The expression of "sacred time and space" came from Mircea Eliade, *The Sacred and the Profane* (New York: Harper & Row, 1959), 20, 22. However, the "sacred" should be differentiated from the use by Renee Girard, who gave it meaning from nineteenth century literature and the Judeo-Christian tradition. It is also to be differentiated from the use in Agamben's *homo sacer*, which originated from a Roman concept. By contrast, the sacredness of Olympianism I want to establish lies precisely in its universality: there is no inner and outer group, and no victim sacrifice.

prosaic; when they are enduring, they are all-encompassing and everlasting, the opposite of myopic and ephemeral. Greek mythology established the sacredness of the universe by rendering chronology and geography in vivid narrative terms and incorporating them into the stories of extraordinary beings.[32] In everyday life, religious festivals and rituals continuously reenacted these truths by commemorating days and places presented in those tales. This phenomenon of sacred metaphysics, which can only be conveyed discursively and experientially, and not grasped numerically or rationally, is a major cornerstone of the Olympian dispensation.

In addition to being special and unique, time and space in the Olympian culture also evince themselves as expansive and boundless. In the *Iliad*, the poet tells the Muses: "you are goddesses, and are present and know/have seen all things, while we hear only fame but know/have seen nothing at all."[33] Even though mortals are short-lived and short-sighted, this self-awareness helps them develop greater temporality and spatiality by fathoming the existence of higher beings. In the Homeric epics, for example, the gods regularly examine human affairs from multiple angles, even across the political divide. As a result, readers are also equipped with a synoptic and all-seeing vantage point when they can successfully identify with the divine perspective. This transcendent coverage, a product of imagination and faith, forces a diverse and broad range of views onto the audience.[34]

Besides observing outward phenomena from all sides, the immortals also screen the human interior to scrutinize thoughts, intention, and desire. For example, in Hesiod's *Works and Days*, an army of invisible ministers serving the goddess Justice travel up and down the earth in order to report men's iniquitous thoughts and ruinous intent to Zeus (248–260). This special mind-reading power also guards future promises like oaths and vows, which rely on sincerity and truthfulness. In Book 3, for instance, Agamemnon calls on Zeus, who sees and hears all things, to ensure the fidelity of sworn pledges (*Il.* 3.275–280).[35] When the gods observe penetratingly and constantly, they put the inner thoughts and feelings of the mortals under constant watch, so that one's heart and mind must always remain pure and righteous.

---

[32] The point was made by Richard Seaford, *Cosmology and the Polis: The Social Construction of Space and Time in the Tragedies of Aeschylus* (Cambridge: Cambridge University Press, 2012), 2. I will soon corroborate this feature on my own.

[33] *Il.* 2.484–486 translated by Alex C. Purves in *Space and Time in Ancient Greek Narrative* (Cambridge and New York: Cambridge University Press, 2010), 6. Also, in Book 11 of the *Odyssey*, the hero calls out to Helios, "who sees all things, and listens to all things" (109). All other passages of the *Iliad* are taken from Richmond Lattimore unless otherwise specified; see Homer and Richmond Lattimore, *The Iliad* (Chicago: Chicago University Press, 1951). Hesiod also invokes the gods with similar phrasing in his *Works and Days*: "The eye of Zeus sees all and notices all things" (267–69), translated by Purves, *Space and Time in Ancient Greek Narrative*, 4. The same belief also influences Solon, who states that "Zeus looks upon the end of all things" (Fragment 13.17), translated by Purves, *Space and Time in Ancient Greek Narrative*.

[34] In Book 20 of the *Iliad*, Zeus directly watches Greek and Trojan soldiers fighting each other from above (20.21–23). In several other scenes, the gods pay close attention to the fate of heroes on the both sides simultaneously. For example, in Book 15, Zeus looked onto Trojans and from mount Ida (15.4–7). The transcendence of political divisions makes it easier to attend to the voice and experience of the other side.

[35] Other examples are too numerous to be cited here, but for a detailed discussion of the way the Greeks swore oaths to the gods, see Alan H. Sommerstein and Isabelle C. Torrance, *Oaths and Swearing in Ancient Greece* (Berlin: De Gruyter, 2014).

The immortals transcend the limits of not only space, but also time. Their eternal presence produces a temporality that is extensive and abiding. By conversing with the Muses, Hesiod, a struggling farmer in a Boeotian village, reckons history from the genesis of the cosmos to his own days, incorporating a chronological range that is truly "epic." His mythical tales instantiate how humans can extend the conception of time from the birth of the universe to present-day affairs for a temporal range that far exceeds the duration of a single life.

Furthermore, in Greek religion, mortals descend to a grim but permanent realm below after they perish on earth. This belief essentially prolongs the duration of human consciousness indefinitely. The life beyond, however, does not bestow blissful redemption as in the Judeo-Christian tradition. Instead, the Greeks deemed their time on earth most precious and dear, and its loss inconsolable.[36] In the famous scene in which Odysseus meets Achilles in the underworld, the latter laments that he would rather live as a hireling than reign among the dead as king (*Od.* 11.489–92). The utter gloom of the afterlife steers Olympianism away from other-worldly speculations and toward the immanence of here and now. On this point, Finley remarked that "the Homeric heroes loved life fiercely, as they did and felt everything with passion, and no less-martyr-like characters could be imagined."[37]

The Relation of the Sacred to the Economy, Contrast with Commodification, and Impact on the Political

The economic and political ramifications of sacred time and space are enormous. Generally speaking, when unique time and space configure the universe, they endow everything within, from plants, to animals, to humans, and to the whole biosphere, with those qualities too. By being unique and special, entities in the Olympian world cannot be reduced to prosaic physical matter or biological functions, nor subsequently measured and numerated in standardized units that vary only in quantity—the *sine qua non* for market transactions.[38]

---

[36] In the poem from Anacreon of Teos (born c. 575 BCE), death casts the darkest shadow on life:

> Not much time is left
> of sweet life now, and so
> often I sob in dread
> of Tartaros. For Terrible
> is Hades' cove and awful
> the road down, for certain
> it is that he who descends
> does not come up again.

Barbara Hughes Fowler, *Archaic Greek Poetry: An Anthology* (Madison, WI: The University of Wisconsin Press, 1992), 185.

[37] M. I. Finley, *The World of Odysseus*, 2nd ed. (Middlesex: Penguin Books, 1979), 113.

[38] Gifts belong to this category, because they "have a value that is unrelated to their price in the market, because there is no market for goods whose value derives in part from their individual history of gift-exchange." See Robin Osborne, "Archaic Greece," in *The Cambridge Economic History of the Greco-Roman World*, ed. Walter Scheidel, Ian Morris, and Richard P. Saller (Cambridge: Cambridge University Press, 2007), 301.

To fully work out the implications, I explore what the antipode of the sacred world would be like. This antithesis to the sacred metaphysics of Olympianism would be *universal commodification*, a conceptual scheme developed by Margaret Radin to describe the system in which everything would be priced and commodified:

> Commodities are socially constructed as objects separate from the self and social relations. Universal commodification assimilates personal attributes, relations, and desired states of affairs to the realm of objects by assuming that all human attributes are possessions bearing a value characterizable in money terms, and by implying that all these possessions can and should be separable from persons to be exchanged through the free market.[39]

In summary, Radin identified three corollaries that make universal commodification possible: alienability, commensurability, and fungibility. Alienability is the separation of something (such as an entitlement, right, or attribute) from its holder so that the thing can be sold and bought in the market place.[40] Commensurability, in its broadest sense, is the idea that the values of all things can be arrayed on a single scale that varies only in quantity.[41] Fungibility assumes that things can be fully interchanged in monetary terms without any effect on the holder.[42] These three suppositions are necessary for universal commodification, the philosophical scaffolding of the free market.

The truths of Olympianism, however, reject all three premises of universal commodification. Sacred entities, in that they are not just the sum of biological and molecular processes, cannot be commensurated via abstract arithmetic. By being unique and invaluable, they cannot be sold or bought via commercial alienation. Last but not least, the attributes of and relations between sacred beings are not fungible, in the sense that they cannot be traded without altering the holders.

Aside from economics, the truth about boundless time and space affects politics as well. Because the gods can mete out penalties anywhere and anytime, one should always act righteously, overcoming greed and violence that bring only short-term gains. The concentration on *this life* propels actors to fight for solutions here and now, although with an interesting duality. On the one hand, since no satisfying afterlife awaits, the Greeks embraced sensual pleasures like love, comfort, and play, however fleeting, rather than spurn them for another realm.[43] In the same way, no moral condemnation was directed at activities that elicit and stimulate laughing, crying, and excitement, such as feasting, athletics, and chariot-racing; on the contrary, emotional

---

[39] Radin, *Contested Commodities*, 6.

[40] Ibid., 16–17.

[41] Ibid., 91. Cf. Aristotle, *The Nicomachean Ethics*, trans. H. Rackham (Cambridge, MA: Harvard University Press, 1999), 5.8.1132b31–1133b28.

[42] Ibid., 118.

[43] I shall quote Augustine who aptly highlighted the difference with Christianity: "But what do I love when I love my God? Not material beauty or beauty of a temporal order; not the brilliance of earthly light, so welcome to our eyes; not the sweet melody of harmony and song; not the fragrance of flowers, perfumes, and spices; not manna or honey, not limbs such as the body delights to embrace." See Augustine and R. S Pine-Coffin, *Confessions: Saint Augustine* (New York: Penguin Books, 1961), 211.

effusings were considered expressions of piety and humanity.[44] On the other hand, the eternal court of time does not permit unscrupulous hedonism, for the current moment will be followed by many in the future. Since humans do not know their fate until the very end—as the story of Croesus in Herodotus illustrates[45]—they must practice circumspection and prudence. In this way, adherents of Olympianism would tackle present issues head on without losing sight of long-term consequences.

In the remainder of this book, I shall demonstrate how Olympian actors treasure things for their rich, unique association rather than quantified, abstract utility; undertake moral actions that overcome short-term, tangible loss and gain; and struggle to solve immanent problems here and now. These manifestations underscore the force that sacred time and space exerted on the ancient Greeks who bought into the metaphysical, ontological, and sociological truths of Olympianism. Moreover, for someone immersed in this culture, experiential knowledge of extraordinary beings, instead of abstract reason, begets wisdom. Therefore, success attends those who revere the gods, obey their teachings, and practice introspection under their gaze. Conversely, tragedy falls on those who act arrogantly, defy divine wishes, and commit hubris. In these ways, deities who meddle in human affairs act as the ultimate *other* via their transcendence of time and space and their widespread ties to all beings. By constantly taking into consideration the voices and interests mediated by the immortals, members of the Olympian world develop an outlook of ecumenism and conviviality, i.e., principles of universal inclusion and mutual thriving, which will be discussed in great detail in Part II. This Olympian identity stands in stark contrast to the human agent postulated by utilitarianism, methodological individualism, and modern secularism. The rest of the book is devoted to explicating this unique *self* as well as the actions and outcomes it engenders.

INCOMPLETE PROGRESS

As already stressed, Olympianism, like any other cultural system, was neither monolithic or uniform, nor always consistent or incorruptible. The sources that embody the cultural truths of Olympianism also condone troubling sentiments of patriarchy, domination, and exploitation that contradict the core Olympian principles of universal inclusion and mutual thriving.[46] While it is wrong to turn a blind eye to its defects, we would also err in the other direction by writing off Olympianism wholesale because of them.[47] For instance, the awareness that Greek democracy

[44] Herbert W. Parke, *Festivals of the Athenians* (Baltimore, MD: Johns Hopkins University Press, 1977), 13.
[45] See Herodotus, *Histories*, Book 1. The brief version is roughly as follows. Croesus, the rich and powerful king of Lydia, expected Solon, a Greek statesman, to name him as the happiest man in the world. Solon, however, stated that he was unable to judge until the end of someone's life. Later, Croesus was captured by the Persian king Cyrus and finally understood the wisdom of Solon.
[46] The degradation of women is conspicuous in the poetic texts attributed to Hesiod and Simonedes, and, also to a lesser extent, in Homer's *Iliad*. I will discuss slavery and militarism of ancient Greece in depth later in this book.
[47] Josiah Ober, *Democracy and Knowledge: Innovation and Learning in Classical Athens* (Princeton, NJ: Princeton University Press, 2008), 24. Ober believed that while it is important to acknowledge the unjust exclusion of slavery and women, the Greek system has much to teach us about the equality of native male

excluded women and legitimized slavery, while significant, has often only helped to downplay the failings of modern society. At the same time, equating Athens with a quintessential slave society, though accurate to some degree, has also obscured the industriousness of Athenian free farmers and independent artists who made their city a home of quality artisanal production (see Chapter 3). Given these implications, while the dark side of Olympianism will not be ignored, it should also not be allowed to diffuse criticisms of modernity or diminish the faith in a better system.

With the above caveats, Olympianism itself arguably supplies the most effective means for problematizing and eradicating slavery, patriarchy, and imperialism from within. This position stems from a deep appreciation of the two key Olympian discourses of ecumenism and conviviality. In their coherent and mature state, ecumenism and conviviality advocate the most complete program of inclusivity and mutual thriving. From this perspective, Olympianism contrasts sharply with Polisism, which feeds on the exclusion of out-groups, and market, which pits individuals against one another. We should therefore bear in mind that, even though conviviality and ecumenism suffered in practice, they are unequivocally superior to the other two systems in design.

The Search for Alternatives: Mauss, Polanyi, and Finley-cum-Weber

While I present Olympianism as a viable challenge to the model of the free market, it is not the first time concerted efforts have been made to discover noncapitalist modes of economic organization from places distant or remote from the modern West. Marcel Mauss, Karl Polanyi, and Moses Finley, seminal figures in economic history, have all made important contributions on this front. Specifically, Mauss pointed out the omnipresence of gift giving in the Pacific Northwest, Polynesia, and Melanesia.[48] To him, the exchange of gifts initiates and reciprocates goodwill, a process that enhances social solidarity in those societies. Polanyi, on the other hand, underscored the primacy of redistribution and reciprocity alongside market exchange in a number of ancient civilizations.[49] In Polanyi's model, shared values, common tradition, and mutual obligation often overshadow conventional economic calculation. Finley, the only ancient Greek historian in the trio, was influenced by the other two. With regard to ancient Athens, Finley put emphasis on status, arguing that the civic ideology of the *polis* dictated the behavior and decision-making of citizens.[50] In essence, all three scholars pioneered case studies outside of the theoretical ambit of modern economics.

---

citizens.

[48] Mauss was influenced by Malinowski's study of the Kula ring on the Trobriand Islands off the east coast of New Guinea. Both Mauss and Malinowski, as economic anthropologists, believed that premarket economies should be studied on their own terms.

[49] See Karl Polanyi, "On the Comparative Treatment," 329–50.

[50] Finley appreciated Max Weber's way of understanding Western modernity through its own distinctive logic, and as a result, he paid more attention to the uniqueness of the social organization of Greek city-states. See Sherman, "Barbarians Come to Market," 17.

However, in so far as pure economic analysis is concerned, the portrayals of the ancient Greek economy as gift-based, substantive, or status-centered are vulnerable to counter-evidence, such as solid market behavior and profit-driven activities in trade, finance, and banking.[51] Indeed, scholars confirm three somewhat conflicting trends in the ancient Greek economy: the deployment of redistributive and regulative policies by the state,[52] the expansion of the free market along capitalist lines,[53] and the endurance of customs and modes of behavior that embody the archaic mode of reciprocity.[54] As it has already been argued, the perplexing patchwork of heterogeneous features cannot be reconciled by mere additional facts and data; their concurrence can only be clarified through more illuminating theory. In this sense, the important nexus between culture and economics was not forged in Mauss, Polanyi, and Finley.[55] Moreover, written before intellectual negation and relativism fully disputed the essences of society and knowledge, the works of Mauss, Polanyi, and Finley failed to highlight how language indeed introduces fluidity and tension in power relations and social categories. One consequence is that these scholars, who were essentially social scientists seeking to analyze premodern, ritualized societies through a secular lens, did not take it upon themselves to consider how theological discourses might bear upon economic and political norms. At the same time, they also did not always show special sensitivity toward slaves, foreigners, and women in accordance with the tenets of anti-imperial, subaltern, and feminist studies. For these reasons, prior explorations of alternative economies are no longer sufficient for the current age of postmodernism and late capitalism in which the old foundation of modernity has been shaken while new outlooks have yet to offer a unified body of positive claims.

By contrast, the approach that I devised for mapping out culture, identity, and action amends the shortcomings mentioned above. Instead of employing a single and sometimes non-Greek concept as did the aforementioned scholars,[56] a comprehensive cultural system derived from the Greek sources is being constructed to illuminate distinctive economic patterns and behaviors. The analysis further corrects for the imbalances in older scholarship by taking the experience of marginalized groups seriously, and by disavowing any unquestioned acceptance of contemporary benchmarks of progress. It goes without saying that any gain made by this historiography owes a great debt to those who bravely preceded me and those who

[51] See Edward Cohen, *Athenian Economy and Society: A Banking Perspective* (Princeton, NJ: Princeton University Press, 1992). Cohen was one of Finley's greatest critics, but he confused "substantive" with "primitive." The former describes the nature of the economy and the latter refers to scale. See Morris, "Athenian Economy Twenty Years after," 354.

[52] See "City Finance and Public Ownership" in Chapter Two.

[53] For example, Op. Cit. Rostovtzeff.

[54] See Ian Morris, "Gift and Commodity in Archaic Greece," *Man* 21, no. 1 (March 1986): 1–17; Gabriel Herman, *Ritualised Friendship and the Greek City* (Cambridge: Cambridge University Press, 1987).

[55] Weber, who influenced Finley, was probably most interested in culture, for he wanted to "emphasize the unique characteristics of ancient culture." See Morris, "The Athenian Economy Twenty Years after," 353.

[56] Mauss, for example, derived the paradigm of gift largely from observations on the life in the Pacific Northwest.

have gone out of their way to support me.[57] It is my hope that by combining the best of cumulative insights and original thinking, this book will be the catalyst for propelling the human vision forward in the twenty-first century.

OLYMPIANISM AND ITS SOURCES

As already stated, the foundation of Olympianism rests upon the truth that divine beings provide order and meaning to the universe.[58] In other words, individuals under the influence of Olympianism make sense of their lives through the stories of the gods and heroes. As a result, authors who present the gods preeminently are preferred over those who distance themselves from this faith. As examples of the latter category, Thucydides hardly brought up traditional deities; the thinkers of the Ionian Enlightenment developed explanations of the natural world without the Homeric gods, and some authors like Xenophanes even subjected the ideas about immortals to rational inquiry.[59] In this way, none of them would be good purveyors of Olympianism. Moreover, the mere invocation of the gods does not even necessarily guarantee a thorough identification with religious truth. Forensic speeches and philosophical writings of later periods mentioned the immortals in passing, but

[57] This is a very appropriate place to thank Ian Morris, Rush Rehm, and Michael Shanks, my teachers at Stanford who agreed to be on my dissertation committee so that I could conduct the preliminary research of this book as my PhD project. This rather unconventional project for Classics would have died in its infancy had they chosen to not give it a chance. I also want to thank Simon Springer, whom I asked to serve on my PhD committee out of my sheer interest in anarchism and critical geography. As a total stranger until then, Simon has demonstrated what solidarity and mutual aid on the Left would look like by never tiring of answering my requests big and small, with fascinating political debates interspersed throughout. Last but not least, I want to once again tell Max Preglau, my PhD committee member from Austria, that I feel so lucky to have him in life as a mentor and friend. Through the years since we came to know each other, our paths have crossed at Stanford, Innsbruck, and Shanghai with many happy memories that are dear to my heart. Finally, I want to thank my supervisor ChangGang Guo at Shanghai University. With mounting pressure to meet specific publication quota, hardly any other boss would have been as patient and indulgent of me, for I have been fixated with this book and have not published much to date.

[58] Before proceeding further, I shall once again stress that this particular take on Greek religion—a word that is misleading in itself—derives primarily from early Greek sources. The common image of the Greek gods in popular culture rests on the whole body of continuously produced myths that span more than one thousand years, and a significant portion of them was created by the much later Hellenistic or Roman authors. While we could turn to some common topics and motifs in authors like Ovid or Apollodorus, the specific narratives themselves would in all likelihood project or at least blend in cultural elements of later times (see discussion on sources). For this reason, I shall limit myself to dealing with Homer, Hesiod, and the lyric poets, while incorporating some basic information from later myth.

[59] These fragments of poetry are attributed to Xenophanes:
But mortals suppose that gods are born,
wear their own clothes and have a voice and body. (Fragment 14)
Ethiopians say that their gods are snub-nosed and black;
Thracians that theirs are blue-eyed and red-haired. (Fragment 16)
But if horses or oxen or lions had hands
or could draw with their hands and accomplish such works as men,
horses would draw the figures of the gods as similar to horses, and the oxen as similar to oxen,
and they would make the bodies
of the sort which each of them had. (Fragment 15)

offered mostly human-based explanations for social and political events.[60] These "secularized" narratives, while valuable for other purposes, are less serviceable for rendering the Olympian dispensation.

As a result, the task of documenting Olympianism falls largely on epic, lyric, drama, myth, and selected early historical works. These texts constantly engaged with the divine and sacred elements in earnest, and were "simply following...the normal way of arriving at the truth."[61] In this body of texts, Homeric epics and the Hesiodic poems carry the greatest weight because they are extensive and also closely overlap with Olympianism chronologically.[62] As for Archaic poetry, only the longer pieces will be consulted to verify broad cultural tendencies,[63] since most of it survives in fragments.[64] Besides epic and archaic poetry, drama and myth will be parsed for their mythological and religious renditions.[65] In terms of historical writing, only Herodotus passes the test: although the father of history sometimes seeks for answers in human behavior, his axiological lessons nevertheless confirm the overwhelming power of the gods.[66] Chosen more on the basis of content and nature rather than dating and genre, this selection is optimal for outlining the culture of Olympianism.

Overview of the Book

The rest of the book is divided into two parts. Part I discusses the Olympian model of political economy. Part II details its cultural truths. As specific cases are being brought to bear, the tension and fragmentation from the three-way cultural struggle, in

---

[60] In this sense, per Charles Taylor's *A Secular Age* (Cambridge, MA: Belknap Press of Harvard University Press, 2007), Greek society effectively became secularized in the fifth century by the virtue of people being able to *not* believe in the gods.

[61] Paul Veyne, *Did the Greek Believe in Their Myths? An Essay on the Constitutive Imagination* (Chicago: The University of Chicago Press, 1988 [First published 1983 in French]), xi.

[62] The use of epics in this way underlines my belief that these orally composed poems are tied to a broader set of cultural issues. In contrast, literary scholars who study how the epics were orally composed often conclude that these poems cannot convey meaning or thought because of a strict adherence to the form. See introduction to Dean Hammer, *The Iliad as Politics: The Performance of Political Thought* (Norman: University of Oklahoma Press, 2002), 1–18.

[63] Archaic poetry and Homeric epics are often seen as being closely related. The usual dating for Archaic poetry is the seventh through the fifth centuries, and for Homer as late as the eighth century. Most importantly, it is now believed that the traveling bards recited Archaic poetry together with the epics.

[64] The collection of Archaic poetry is large and diverse, and some selection is always necessary. I generally focus on the ones featured in Morris and Donlan for social analysis. See Ian Morris, "Antithetical Cultures," in *Archaeology as Cultural History: Words and Things in Iron Age Greece* (Malden, MA: Blackwell, 2000); Walter Donlan, *The Aristocratic Ideal and Selected Papers* (Wauconda, IL: Bolchazy-Carducci, 1999).

[65] The entire body of mythology presents a different problem. While the gods always take center stage in this genre, the loose collection of stories spans more than a millennium and incorporates cultural influences from later historical conjunctions, e.g., a large number of myths came from Ovid of the early Roman Empire.

[66] According to Lloyd-Jones, the work of Herodotus is "pervaded by the characteristic features of the archaic Greek outlook; notably a conviction of the all-powerfulness of the gods and the insignificance of man, and a belief that the gods maintain the universal order of justice by chastising not only mortals who offend against each other but also mortals who infringe by word or action their own peculiar prerogatives." See Hugh Lloyd-Jones, *Justice of Zeus*, 2nd ed. (Berkeley, CA: University of California Press, 1983), 59.

which Olympianism eventually lost out to Polisism and Oeconomism, will be highlighted.

The study of political economy begins with Chapter 2, which investigates the discourse on property in ancient Greece. I focus first on the distribution of land and argue that the paradigm of *kleros* favors distributing land widely for the purpose of sustaining a community of self-standing peers. In this tradition, equitable possession of land was critical for establishing identity and developing rootedness as well as forging bonds with kin, community, and nature. This cultural truth reveals that Olympianism did not assume an isolated, disembedded *homo economicus* who pursues private property rights against the claims of hostile rivals. Tracing the fate of *kleros* in the Archaic and Classical periods, I examine the historical episodes involving land tenure, such as the emergence of debt bondage before Solon and the commercialization of real estate beginning in the fifth century BCE. These instances reflect the advent of commodifying forces against the resistance of the older Olympian dispensation.

Next, I turn to "the commons," a term that designates—in defiance of economic convention—norms that guided the use of natural resources for open access and long-term sustainability.[67] In the Olympian culture, transcendent beings endow humans with natural resources out of benevolence. As divine gifts, their ownership dervies from subsistence fulfillment, labor expenditure, and group well-being. The idea of the commons stipulates that those in the community are rightful stakeholders and stewards of the common pool of wealth. I then locate this concept in the management of natural resources and the administration of public funds in fifth century Athens. Last, I consider how the practice of liturgy, driven by similar values, was confounded by the commodification of knowledge toward the fourth century.

Chapter 3 explores labor through the Olympian paradigm of *homo faber*—man who reaches the ranks of the gods and the heroes by achieving technical excellence, artistic creativity, self-discovery, and social purpose through his work. To elaborate on this cultural truth, I first emphasize the imperative of performing self-directed labor in the sense of not working for another. This necessity calls on society to create abundance and security and to eliminate deprivation and compulsion. Under this general principle, *homo faber* controls productive instruments, takes charge of conception and execution, and interacts with the community. In Classical Athens, the ideal of *homo faber* can be correlated with a large number of craftsmen, sole proprietors, small business operators, and yeoman farmers who flourished as democratic citizens and primary producers. Their success became possible in an economic environment defined by low barrier to entry, horizontal specialization (rather than vertical integration), open access to resources and technology, direct channels of exchange, and the freedom of itinerancy.

The end of Chapter 3 highlights the insidious impetus to replace self-production with surplus extraction through the practices of rentierism, imperialism, and slavery in Classical Athens. These institutionalized forms of violence betrayed the legacy of *homo faber* and *kleros*/commons. The rise of the market and the state, with their

[67] I am aware that the commons is typically associated with concept of the "tragedy of the commons." The ancient Greek example I deploy will challenge this interpretation in later sections.

rapacious appetite for cheap labor and capacity to deny out-groups equal consideration, exacerbated ancient Greece's proclivity to discriminate against women, slaves, and nonnatives. Nevertheless, for the local male population, the Olympian heritage impeded or slowed the commodification of land, labor, money, and knowledge, as well as the state's monopoly use of force to facilitate the market order.

Chapter 4 argues that Olympianism presaged the rise of democracy in a short interlude that highlights the fundamentals of Athenian politics. It then forwards the provocative view that this darling child of Greece blatantly betrayed the ideals of conviviality and ecumenism that gave birth to it. While the Athenian state upheld native male egalitarianism, it did so by excluding ascriptively determined groups of women, slaves, and foreigners from the city-wide polity of kinship, solidarity, and symbiosis.

Part II shifts from economics to culture in order to chart the truths that sustained the former. The philosophical core of Olympianism propagated inclusion and mutual thriving through ecumenism and conviviality. These two ideals, though often imperfect in practice, provide a panacea to the in-group and out-group division and the zero-sum competition that characterize the duopoly of the state and the market.

Chapter 5 elaborates on the concepts of ecumenism and conviviality as a way to delineate the ontology and sociology of Olympianism. Ecumenism refers to the potential of all people to have inalienable worth, rights, and entitlements as valuable and precious subjects before the gods. Conviviality refers to the cultural norms and social conditions that underpin the phenomenon of feasting. Ideally speaking, the communal feast, as part of ritual that pays homage to the divine, promotes inclusion, multiplicity, egalitarianism, and plurality among the participants. In perfect conviviality, the self and alterity coalesce so that individuals achieve a symbiotic convergence. Although in the ecumenical, convivial world, injurious conflicts can break out, the seeds of strife lie in the struggle for equality and recognition. Such violence should be differentiated from the invisible kind engrained in hierarchy, which either suppresses discontent or internalizes inequality for superficial peace.

Next, I introduce the concept of *agon*—a type of contest that unveils identity through intersubjective recognition. The agonistic ethos, which underpins a series of activities like combat, athletics, and symposiastic gatherings that epitomize Greek aristocratic life, unites the individual with the community, rather than dividing them. Reevaluating the Archaic period through poetry and other evidence, I maintain that the prominence of *agon* rationalized actions that exemplify democratic virtues: the performance of service and sacrifice, pursuit of individual excellence, protest of corrupt power, and tolerance of diversity.

In Chapter 6, I test the doctrines of Olympianism against a set of extant sources to conclude that women, enemies, slaves, foreigners, and the poor—groups otherwise marginalized vis-à-vis elite Greek men—are given formidable voices through the religious discourse in early literary representation. In particular, the acceptance that everyone creates and suffers fate collectively (although not in the same manner) debunks economic individualism that attributes responsibility solely to the downtrodden. After the treatment of marginal groups, I turn next to the dynamic between mass and elite in the body of Olympian literature. With a close reading of the epics, I reject the abiding consensus that warrior-princes exercised domination by claiming descent and favor from the gods. To establish my point, I revisit the episode of Thersites; the relationship among the people, the warriors, and the chief commander; and the role of the masses. Using the lens of conviviality and ecumenism, I maintain that Greek religion placed checks on "the best and the beautiful" while enabling dissenting voices from below. These ecumenical and convivial truths guided social relations between middle and peripheral, mass and elite groups, solidifying the ground for democratic interaction and solidarity.

The undeniable Olympian roots of Athenian politics dismantle the standard account that Greek democracy broke free from an elite-dominated past weighed down by religion and "tribalism," nor do they support the view that the march toward the duopoly of the state and the market constitutes progress. These seismic ruptures upset the notion that history advances through a series of successive stages that are inevitable and unidirectional.[68] Moreover, the restored vision of Olympianism casts profoundly doubts on the legitimacy of global capitalism and the nation-state, the modern heirs to Oeconomism and Polisism. For those who truly believe another world is plausible and paramount, that future could very well begin with a hard look at the past.

---

[68] This generalization, in fact, applies to Marx, Durkheim, and, to a lesser extent, Weber.

CHAPTER 2

Everyone and No One

All human societies rely on physical matter for survival, yet the way in which people believe how resources should be divided and appropriated varies greatly. This chapter examines the cultural discourses of resource distribution, access, and entitlement in ancient Greece. By reconstructing these cultural truths in Olympianism, a social configuration that rejects the logic of the state or the market, we discover a unique property system that fulfills many desirable social ends that include safeguarding subsistence, augmenting independence, and bolstering service. For the first two related goals, great value is assigned to basic productive resources as well as the subsequent need to distribute them broadly in order to maintain the greatest number of free, self-sustaining producers and workers. With economic autonomy, primary producers are most able to take charge of and bear responsibility for their work. This outcome is in direct contrast to one in which a few individuals lay exclusive claim to a large bulk of resources exceeding what they themselves can use, an arrangement that deprives others of the free access to the means of production. For example, imagine a baron who has inherited the titles to all the land in a village, or a boss of a taxi company who controls vehicle licensing. Such concentrated ownership—whether as a result of patrimony, luck, outright violence, competition, or some conflux thereof—compels primary workers (e.g., farmers or drivers) to submit themselves to overseers, even if the opportunity to be on top of this food chain is in theory equal. Given that these two scenarios—one of broad independence and the other of wide subjugation—are mutually exclusive, Olympianism unequivocally affirms the former, which creates the material conditions for an egalitarian and horizontal society.

In the Olympian model, once the need for broad-scale self-subsistence and autonomy has been met, surplus resources are then deployed to promote public service. This way, the procurement of extra goods—accompanied by prestige—encourages benevolence rather than avarice. Although in this case, absolute equality gives way to material differentiation commensurate with contribution and sacrifice, the securing of economic privilege indebts those in power and authority to the community and urges them to reciprocate in kind with integrity and largesse. The ensuing study presents the Olympian ideals of *kleros*, *temenos*, and the commons, and demonstrates how they generated an ensemble of truths that advanced the twin principles of self-sufficiency and public virtue for individual autonomy and group well-being.

KLEROS AND ECONOMIC INDEPENDENCE

Land was the single most important economic resource in all premodern societies and ancient Greece was no exception. The system of land tenure in ancient Greece was heavily influenced by a discourse that I call *kleros*, which turns self-reliant possession into a basic natural right. The word *kleros* means "allotment" in Greek. The etymological origin of *kleros* is a piece of wood,[69] likely the one being cast to allocate land in lottery-style draws. In the broader social context, *kleros* refers to a viable plot of land sanctified by custom and tradition to be worked and passed down in a household. In our discussion, *kleros* will serve as a broad umbrella term to designate the dispersion of land that hinders ownership concentration and bolsters wide-scale subsistence and independence.[70] In some circumstances, even unequal holdings could be consistent with the values of *kleros*, since variation in acreage can compensate for difference in yield and productivity, or accommodate other redistributive mechanisms (e.g., *temenos* and the commons).[71] In this sense, the aim and design of distribution programs say more than just the absolute size of individual lots. In the following analysis, we will examine the truths that initiated, sustained, and rejuvenated *kleros*, as well as the threats and challenges it confronted from the rise of the market system.

The cultural discourse of *kleros* regards equitable division as the just and proper beginning of every social order. The gods themselves set the prime example for dividing things fairly: during the time of genesis before humans, Zeus splits the universe into three realms and assigns them by lot to himself and his brothers (*Il.* 15.190).[72] In the epic world, when the virtuous Phaiakians settled in Scheria, they first made a wall around the city and built the houses; then they made the temples and allotted the land (*Od.* 6.7–10). The act of propitiating deities first suggests tacit divine approval for the ensuing economic scheme and encases the practice in religious veneer. It is telling that the word *moira*, which like *kleros* denotes a portion or part of given land, also means fate, one of the greatest ineluctable forces in Greek cosmology.[73] This mythical aura helped *kleros* become a force to be reckoned with in the regime of land tenure in ancient Greece.

The origins of older Greek communities like Athens and Sparta, which both go back beyond 1200 BCE, are alluded to primarily in legendary and folk tales.[74] Although such accounts likely contain only a kernel of reality, they place *kleros* at the center of the formation of an ideal society. Athens, according to Thucydides, was founded by the hero Theseus through a process called synoecism, which unified largely independent and autonomous small villages in Attica (2.15). After the amalgamation, the residents, who had governed largely by themselves and settled their own affairs up to this point, continued to cultivate their *own* lands as before (2.15.2). Thucydides' observation supplies the image of a relatively free and powerful peasantry, which could have only resulted from wide entitlements to land. Records on

---

[69] Robert Beekes, *Etymological Dictionary of Greek*, vol. 1 (Leiden: Brill 2010), 715.

[70] Other words like *dasmos*, *anadasmos*, *moira*, and *isomoiria* in the texts—all with the general meaning of a division, sharing, or distribution—also belong to the *kleros* ilk.

[71] For variation in land conditions, see Victor Davis Hanson, *The Other Greeks: The Family Farm and the Agrarian Roots of Western Civilization* (New York: Free Press, 1995), 183.

[72] It is true that this division still occurs within the divine family, but at this early point in Greek myth, the world was rather barren, with few other significant deities—and nearly all of them are related by blood.

[73] Margaret Visser, *The Rituals of Dinner: The Origins, Evolution, Eccentricities, and Meaning of Table Manners* (New York: Penguin Books, 1991), 508.

[74] Jonathan M. Hall, "Approaches to Foundation Accounts," in *Greek Colonisation: An Account of Colonies and Other Settlements Overseas*, vol. 2, edited by Gocha R. Tsetskhladze (Boston: Brill, 2008), 383.

the intervening years become sparse until the sixth century BCE, when Solon, the famous Athenian lawgiver, came into the office of archonship (chief magistrate) to save his home region of Attica from debilitating economic hardship and social conflict. In the famous poetry attributed to him, Solon claimed to have honored his fatherland "founded by the gods" by removing boundary stones likely used for expropriation by the rich[75] and freeing native citizens who had been sold abroad as slaves (*Apologia of His Rule* 4–9).[76] This poetic language advances the conception of a hallowed city that is free of the discord sowed by steep inequality or widespread servitude. This ideal would only materialize when the majority of farmers did not work as tenants, wage labor, bondsmen, or slaves, but rather in their own right with the secure possession of their own farms.[77] Outside of Athens, we know of Hesiod, the only archetype of a peasant, who harped on the challenges and rewards of operating his own estate in Boeotia. In Sparta, the legendary lawgiver Lycurgus is said to have given equal shares of land to all citizens in the eighth century BCE, according to the later author Plutarch (*Lycurgus* 8.1–2). Even if this egalitarian regime was never strictly implemented and showed signs of erosion in the Classical period,[78] this archaizing tale emphasized the key role an equitable and just property regime plays in establishing a stable, harmonious, and enduring polity. Indeed, subsequent generations of Spartans exploited this historical memory when they confronted acute inequality during their own day.[79] Overall, these representations redound to the centrality of *kleros* on the ideological plane of the Olympian moral economy.[80] Particularly valuable for our understanding is an interpretation of human equality and dignity through the enablement of self-sufficiency and rejection of (economic)

---

[75] Given the objection that it would be anachronistic to see those stones as markers of mortgage deals, Lewis reasonably proposes that they were being used to enclose common sacred and public land by the rich. See John Lewis, *Solon the Thinker: Political Thought in Archaic Athens* (London: Duckworth, 2006), 113, contra Harris, who takes the reference to the mortgage stones as a metaphor. See Edward Harris, "A New Solution to the Riddle of the *Seisachtheia*," in *The Development of the* Polis *in Archaic Greece*, ed. Lynette G. Mitchell and P. J. Rhodes (London and New York: Routledge, 1997), 55–60. Overall, I do not support Harris' general theory about this period, as it leaves out the role of economic change. See later note 111.

[76] Willis Barnstone, *Ancient Greek Lyrics*, 4th ed. (Bloomington: Indiana University Press, [1962] 2010), 85.

[77] To the Greeks, all those aforementioned forms belonged to the same continuum of "unfree labor" or "unequal labor," which amounts to being in servitude and slavery, see section titled "Self-directed Labor in Homer."

[78] Hodkinson argued that the idea of Lycurgus distributing equal-sized *kleros* at Sparta was fabricated by later authors like Plutarch and Polybius, who created the false impression of Sparta as a society in which each family retained the same plot of land continuously, contradicting the reality in the Classical period. See Stephen Hodkinson, "Land Tenure and Inheritance in Classical Sparta," *The Classical Quarterly*, New Series 36, no. 2 (1986): 378–406.

[79] See reforms of Agis in Plutarch, *Agis* 6. According to the author, the younger generation wholeheartedly supported the king Agis' attempt to redistribute the land in the third century. For more detailed discussion of Sparta and Plutarch, see later section.

[80] Walter Donlan concluded that "essential common proprietorship... of permanent possession by a lineage of the land that it traditionally worked was in existence generations before Homer." See Walter Donlan, "The Homeric Economy," in *A New Companion to Homer*, ed. Ian Morris and Barry Powell (New York: E. J. Brill, 1997), 649–67.

masters/bosses, with the concrete illustration that a resource distribution program for an entire society is feasible and desirable.

The discourse of *kleros* can also be discerned in the better-documented Greek colonial expansion movement (c. 750–400 BCE). Echoing the archetypical foundation myth, the narratives of establishing new settlements display a certain religious character: the immigrants frequently performed rites and consulted the gods to obtain divine blessing for their ventures.[81] The performance of ritual essentially subjected any newly occupied territory to the sanctified customs and norms of *kleros*. Herodotus, for example, wrote that earlier settlers of Cyrene in Libya invited all Greeks to join them and promised to divide and distribute land among them upon the advice of the Delphic oracle (4.159).[82] A separate decree from the fourth century BCE contains an oath allegedly undertaken by the colonists: "Since Apollo spontaneously told Battus and the Therans to colonise Cyrene…On equal and fair terms are they to sail…kinsmen who later sail to Libya shall be entitled to the citizenship and offices and shall be allotted portions of the land which has no owner" (*Supplementum Epigraphicum Graecum* IX 3.25–34).[83] Although the inscription itself may be a later fabrication rather than a copy of the real oath from the seventh century,[84] it is at least clear that "equal and fair" is being emphasized for land distribution and political power-sharing in the recounted event.[85] In fact, equal and fair is a recurring apothegm in the narration of colonial projects.[86] Thucydides, for example, used it for the Corinthians when they established Epidamnus (1.27.1). The existence of a stock phrase for presumptive fairness and equality indicates the strength of these two values in initial communal organization beyond just the provisioning of land. Overall, it is possible to see the theme of equitable division as a common thread that runs through the immortal gods in the primordial days of the universe, the noble people in Homer, the legendary figures in the tales of early Athens and Sparta, and the brave settlers in the colonial narratives. These stories render the unconditional egalitarian endowment of basic resources as most natural and fair. Later Western philosophies and religions emphasize a humanity born out of sin and guilt, and thus deserving to suffer in order to pay back or to prove worth. Contrarily, in the natural state of Olympianism, humans unconditionally received the seed capital to build a dignified and promising life. This grand gesture of largesse, coming from society itself, supports the logic that when people are given the means to prosper for free at the onset, they are more likely

[81] A. J. Graham, *Colony and Mother City in Ancient Greece* (Oxford: Manchester University Press, 1999), 25–26.

[82] The Greek word for lot here is *anadasmos.*

[83] Alan H. Sommerstein and Andrew J. Bayliss, *Oath and State in Ancient Greece* (Berlin: De Gruyter, 2013), 30.

[84] Scholars have long disagreed on the authenticity of the oath. For more opinions regarding what it purports, see Joseph Roisman, *Ancient Greece from Homer to Alexander* (West Sussex, UK: Wiley-Blackwell, 2011), 63. However, it is certainly safe to claim that the document at least wants to give the appearance of being genuine; see Sommerstein and Bayliss, *Oath and State in Ancient Greece*, 29.

[85] For details about the translation of this oath, see James H. Oliver, "Herodotus 4.153 and SEG IX 3," *Greek, Roman and Byzantine Studies* 7, no. 1 (1996): 26; J. H. Jeffery, "The Pact of the First Settlers at Cyrene," *Historia: Zeitschrift Für Alte Geschichte* [Historia: Journal for Ancient History] 10, no. 2 (1961): 140.

[86] Jeffery, "The Pact of the First Settlers at Cyrene."

reciprocate the goodwill in turn—to their children, neighbors, and fellow compatriots.[87] In this way, goods and resources can engender diligent, caring, and compassionate citizens, who strive for success are also in a position to aid others because they had already benefited from free gifts.

Even during the fifth century, the practice of *kleros* was very much alive—a text attributed to Plutarch mentions Lysias inheriting his father's *kleros* property at an Athenian colony in Thurii.[88] An inscription from the Athenian colonists near Brea in Thrace, which was dated to the 440s, ordained that ten land-distributors (*geōnomoi*), one from each tribe, should distribute the land.[89] In similar narrative language, Plutarch stated that after overthrowing tyranny in Syracuse, Corinth wished to repopulate the city by dividing up the land also on "just and equal terms."[90] Through this power of *kleros*, possessory right to equitable productive instruments becomes not only optimal and desirable, but critical for maintaining a level playing field for an equitable society. This ownership regime, regarded as the state of nature and embodiment of divine justice, left a strong and persistent mark on the political economy of ancient Greece.[91] While in our society, land no longer constitutes the most important means of production for livelihood, autonomy, and surety, there is no reason why we cannot apportion modern-day resources and tools in order to secure for each and every citizen what *kleros* did for the ancient Greeks.

Tradition in Land

In addition to fostering egalitarian beginnings, the discourse of *kleros* engendered rootedness, belonging, and membership through the articulation of enduring ties to family, kinship, and community.[92] Whether it was Achilles' home territory in Phthia, Hector's in Troy, or Odysseus' in Ithaca, each was a sacred and irreplaceable place that furbished the stories and memories that made the heroes who they were. As Walter Donlan observed, "household, both as a social unit and as a subsistence unit, was conceptually inseparable from the land" in Homer.[93] In many extant sources, disrespecting the ancestral land, which was seen almost as an extension of the person, was simply unthinkable—a sentiment shared by many preindustrial and traditional societies.

---

[87] My gratitude goes out to Charles Eisenstein. His book *Sacred Economics: Money, Gift, and Society in the Age of Transition* (Berkeley, CA: Evolver Editions, 2011) has helped me to think about reciprocity along this line.
[88] Plutarch, *Lives of Ten Orators, Lysias* (*Plutarch's Morals, vol. 5.*), trans. William W. Goodwin (n.p., 1878).
[89] Russell Meiggs and David M. Lewis, *A Selection of Greek Historical Inscriptions to the End of the Fifth Century B.C.* (Oxford: Clarendon Press, 1969), 128 (no. 49).
[90] Plutarch, *Timoleon* 23.2.
[91] This claim is made with caveats. The displacement of native populations, such as the Libyan inhabitants of Cyrene, and the exclusion of slaves, women, and other marginal groups from ownership, certainly show the limitations of the Olympian system in practice. However, these prominent cases represent an ideal that needed not to have been adopted by each and every Greek community.
[92] Walter Donlan, *The Aristocratic Ideal*, 289; Peter Walcot, *Greek Peasants, Ancient and Modern: A Comparison of Social and Moral Values* (New York: Barnes & Noble, 1970), 14.
[93] Donlan, *The Aristocratic Ideal*, 306.

The extent to which deep emotional attachment to native soil structured people's sense of the self becomes manifest in the passage whereby Thucydides documented the evacuation of Athenians during the Peloponnesian war in the later fifth century.

> The Athenians thus long lived scattered over Attica in independent cities. Even after the centralization of Theseus, old habit still prevailed; and from the early times down to the present war most Athenians still lived in the country with their families and households, and were consequently not at all inclined to move now, especially as they had just restored their establishments after the Persian invasion. Deep was their trouble and discontent at abandoning their houses and the hereditary temples of the ancient state, and at having to change their habits of life and to bid farewell to what each regarded as his native city. (Thucydides 2.16)[94]

The temples from time immemorial, which the Athenians loathed to leave behind, symbolically stored the personal and family ties to the transcendental gods. In other texts, such shrines are listed together with ancestral tombs of the native land when family background, citizenship, and genealogy—the essentials of a person's identity—are being discussed.[95] This mythological network of the gods, ancestors, territory, and personhood effectively transformed the landscape into a sacred entity that bound people to the soil. This imaginative and poetic truth about land was so persuasive that many cities envisaged their ancestors to have been autochthonous—born from the ground itself. The most well-known examples include the early king Erichthonius of Athens, who was born from the soil, and king Cadmus of Thebes, who planted dragons' teeth in a field from which sprang the race of Spartoi (the ancestors of the Theban nobility). In the *epitaphios* of Lysias, the region of Attica is explicitly invoked as "mother," and in Plato's *Menexenus*, the Athenians are spoken of as the proud children born from the soil. A common epithet treating Earth as a mother-figure divinity—*Ge Kourotrophos*—literally means boy-nurturing.[96] These narratives which depict the natural elements as sacred kept the distant past alive and created a conception of land that contrasts strongly with one of an abstracted commodity that can be bought and sold according to anonymous price fluctuations. Classical scholar Alfred Zimmern nicely summed this up: "Thousands of things have changed since Homer. The love of the Greeks for the land has remained the same."[97]

Anti-commodification

The truth of land being sacred persisted well into the fourth century, even when market exchanges flourished. Several sources from the Classical period confirm an

---

[94] Unless otherwise specified, all passages of Thucydides come from the translation of Richard Crawley in *The Landmark Thucydides*, ed. Robert B. Strassler (New York: Touchstone, 1996).

[95] Aristotle, *Constitution of the Athenians*, 55.3; Aeschines, 2.23; Demosthenes, 57.28.

[96] Robert Parker, *Polytheism and Society at Athens* (Oxford, Oxford University Press, 2005), 426.

[97] Alfred Zimmern, *The Greek Commonwealth: Politics and Economics in Fifth-century Athens*, 5th ed. rev. ed. (London: Oxford University Press, 1952), 230.

oath that was sworn by Athenians when they enrolled in the Ephebic College, a youth camp that prepared future citizens with military and civic training upon turning eighteen.[98] As a part of the solemn ritual, each new generation of Athenian youth promised the following to the sacred deities who also nurtured their fathers and grandfathers:

> I will not bring dishonor on my sacred arms nor will I abandon my comrade wherever I shall be stationed. I will defend the rights of gods and men and will not leave my country smaller, when I die, but greater and better, so far as I am able by myself and with the help of all. I will respect the rulers of the time duly and the existing ordinances duly and all others which may be established in the future. And if anyone seeks to destroy the ordinances I will oppose him so far as I am able by myself and with the help of all. I will honor the cults of my fathers. Witnesses to this shall be the gods Agraulus, Hestia, Enyo, Enyalius, Ares, Athena the Warrior, Zeus, Thallo, Auxo, Hegemone, Her[cu]les, and the boundaries of my native land, wheat, barley, vines, olive-trees, fig-trees... (*Lycurgus* 1.77)[99]

From this Ephebic Oath, it is evident that the myths about the gods and landscape continued to structure the outlook and subjectivity of Athenian citizens. Specifically, the sacredness of territory extends to cover the entire political community sustained on its soil, a corollary that in turn inspires group loyalty and identification. Given the civic significance embodied in the discourse of land, it is not coincidental that tending and defending the ancestral lot was spoken of highly by Greek authors from the Archaic to the Classical periods.[100] For the same reason, parting with family property was considered improper and even depraved. In a court speech dated to 345 BCE, the speaker Aeschines ravaged his political opponent Timarchus by portraying him as a monster who sold his ancestral lot for a windfall.[101] The calculated use of this evidence—no doubt intended to shock and horrify the Athenian judges—demonstrates the cultural force that hampered the commercial sale and purchase of *kleros*, even if it was legally permissible.[102] On the other side of this ethical equation,

---

[98] Sources include a marble stele from Akharnai (formerly Menidhi), and a fourth-century *deme* decree of Acharnae (SEG xxi. 519), and the speech of Lycurgus. See M. M. Austin and Pierre Vidal-Naquet, *Economic and Social History of Ancient Greece: An Introduction* (Berkeley, CA: University of California Press, 1977), 96; J. O. Burtt, *Minor Attic Orators in two volumes, 2* (Cambridge, MA: Harvard University Press; London, William Heinemann Ltd. 1962), 70; Peter J. Rhodes and Robin Osborne, *Greek Historical Inscriptions 404-323 BC* (Oxford: Oxford University Press, 2003), 88.

[99] Burtt, *Minor Attic Orators in two volumes, 2*, 68–69.

[100] Kurt Raaflaub, "Power in the Hands of the People: Foundations of Athenian Democracy," in *Democracy 2500?: Questions and Challenges*, edited by Ian Morris, Kurt A. Raaflaub, and David Castriota (Dubuque, Iowa: Kendall/Hunt Pub. Co., 1998), 45.

[101] Aeschines, *Against Timarchus*, 31.

[102] Most scholars believe that such sales were not common. See John Kenyon Davies, *Wealth and the Power of Wealth in Classical Athens* (New York: Arno Press, 1981), 40; T. W. Gallant, "Agricultural Systems, Land Tenure, and the Reforms of Solon," *The Annual of the British School at Athens* 77 (1982), 113; Zimmern, *The Greek Commonwealth*, 234; Donlan, "The Homeric Economy," 658.

the acquisition of another's *kleros* was met with equal social disapproval.[103] When those cultural notions prevailed, they protected land from becoming an anonymously traded commodity in any significant sense and produced citizens who esteemed autonomy, equality, and solidarity.

Owing to this web of complex discourse, *kleros* upheld a system of equitable land distribution that sustained a large number of self-reliant yeoman farmers. As per Victor Davis Hanson, this unique form of agrarianism laid the foundation of ancient Greek civilization by creating the community of interchangeable equals that became the *polis*.[104] The vast majority of historians, both ancient and modern, agree that anywhere from 65 to 95 percent of most city-states' citizens worked the land.[105] Others would downgrade this number to about half of the total population for Classical Athens,[106] but would still concede that the overwhelming majority of them were small, independent farmers who were neither very poor nor very rich.[107] This political economy, made possible by the fair disposition of productive resources sanctified by *kleros*, effectively maximized the amount of power and independence for the individual producer (the obvious contradiction of slavery will be discussed in a later section). Zimmern pointed out the permissible exceptions of dependency for a citizen: "When a Greek was a tenant, he cultivated the land for the state or for a god or for some brotherhood or association; in other words, he is doing for the landlord what the landlord is unable to do for himself."[108]

In addition to the economic implications, it is also worth exploring the political consequences. First, earth that is inalienable and inviolable begets inhabitants who are also not to be alienated or violated, instilling a deep concern for the welfare and sustainability of the community as a whole. Second, such a benevolent progenitor deserves to be propitiated with the return of favors and offerings, including even the sacrifice of one's life.[109] Given these beliefs, it is not surprising that standard Greek citizenship was predicated on native birth, the possession of land (with the notable exception of Athenian democracy), as well as the performance of military service. Only in the fourth century, a few foreign-born patrons who rendered enormous

---

103 John Kenyon Davies, "Classical Greece: Production," in *The Cambridge Economic History of the Greco-Roman World*, ed. Walter Scheidel, Ian Morris, and Richard P. Saller, 333–61 (Cambridge: Cambridge University Press, 2007), 350.

104 Hanson, *The Other Greeks*, 3.

105 Ibid., 7; Zimmern, *The Greek Commonwealth*, 233f. However, while farming remained important in ancient Greece, the degree varied for different city-states and time periods. Recent scholarship indicates that some Archaic/Classical Greek cities were already shifting away from local subsistence farming and were relying on imported food paid with other income.

106 Paul Millett, "The Economy," in *Classical Greece, 500-323 BC*, ed. Robin Osborne (New York: Oxford University Press, 2000), 26; Edward Harris, "Workshop, Marketplace and Household: The Nature of Technical Specialization in Classical Athens and Its Influence on Economy and Society," in *Money, Labour and Land*, ed. Paul Cartledge, Edward E Cohen, and Lin Foxhall (London: Routledge, 2002), 70; Peter Hampden Acton, *Poiesis: Manufacturing in Classical Athens* (Oxford: Oxford University Press, 2014), 2.

107 For example, Hanson, *The Other Greeks*, 187–88; Millett, "The Economy," 28; Michael Jameson, "Agriculture and Slavery in Classical Athens," *The Classical Journal* 73, no. 2 (December 1977–January 1978), 125.

108 Zimmern, *The Greek Commonwealth*, 234.

109 For example, Aeschylus, *Septem* 10–20, 476; Lysias 2.70; Plato, *Republic* 520b.

economic benefits to Athens were lucky enough to receive Athenian citizenship.[110] These exceptional cases only serve to prove the rule that citizenship in general constituted a bundle of privileges and services to be enjoyed and performed by people who were closely linked to one another, reinforced in this case by the attachment to local soil. It is important to note that with regard to military duty, the willingness to take up arms naturally surged in the face of invaders and aggressors, such as when the Persian army entered Greece. But the love for native soil would dim the enthusiasm for prolonged and costly imperial campaigns like the Peloponnesian War. As the aforementioned passage on the forced flight of the Athenians reveals, overly-ambitious military activities wrought devastation on the traditional way of life.[111] In this way, a citizen raised on the discourse of land is conditioned to carry out selfless sacrifice, collective action, and also homeland defense. By the same token, we can deduce the reverse: someone who "debunks" all this as myth and sells off land as a mere resource is less likely to respect other beings and entities, sacrifice for the long-term communal well-being, or oppose imperialism in favor of defensive peace, especially if military conquest promises booty and slaves.

Ownership Concentration and Debt-bondage

Although buoyed by Olympianism, the set of truths embedded in *kleros* nevertheless suffered over time with the ascent of Oeconomism, the cultural system of the market. We turn to Solonian Athens for an illustration of an early confrontation between these two in the late seventh century. By 594 BCE, when many debt-laden Athenians were sold into slavery abroad, Solon was appointed to the office of archonship. Even though actual historical circumstances are elusive,[112] it is almost certain that the rich dispossessed many small family farmers and turned them into precarious tenants/subordinates and even bondsmen/slaves through the consolidation of land.[113]

---

[110] See Philip Brook Manville, *The Origins of Citizenship in Ancient Athens* (Princeton, NJ: Princeton University Press, 1990), 93ff; Austin and Vidal-Naquet, *Economic and Social History*, 35.

[111] This opposition to a hawkish military attitude can be discerned in the traditional farmer figure that recurs in the plays of Aristophanes, which cannot be referenced here in detail as it is outside of the book's scope.

[112] The poems of Solon are notoriously difficult to use for ascertaining details of actual historical events. The other main sources for the period—*Constitution of the Athenians* and Plutarch are very much from later authors—not to mention that they inevitably reflect a certain mystification of Solon that already began in the Classical period. See Morris, "Hard Surfaces," 31; Vincent J. Rosivach, "Redistribution of Land in Solon, Fragment 34," *The Journal of Hellenic Studies* 112 (1992): 154.

[113] The scholarship on the Solonian agrarian crisis is vast, but here I simply refer to the fact that the wealthy ended up controlling much of the land (Aristotle, *Constitution of the Athenians* 2.2). For this argument, I am aware that Edward Harris denied any change in land tenure. Therefore, to him, there is no debt-bondage but only outright slavery caused by bandits and soldiers who seized people in raids. See Harris "Did Solon Abolish Debt-bondage?" 427–28. However, this theory is tenuous, since there is no reference to this routine "lawlessness" in Athens in the two most important and most contemporary sources—Thucydides and Herodotus. In either case, debt-bondage or slavery would be considered equally servile and thus unacceptable for what constituted a free citizen in the eyes of the Greeks. Furthermore, in another article, Harris suggested that the the *hektemoroi*, people who were subject to a one-sixth payment at the time of Solon, were paying not debt but protection money, in a tradition that goes back to Homer. Therefore, *seisachtheia* (i.e., the shaking-off of burdens) was simply the abolition of this tribute; see Harris, "A New Solution to the Riddle of the *Seisachtheia*," 55–60. If so, it is difficult to explain the sudden explosion of violent conflict and strife, or the breakdown of law and order, before Solon (also evidenced in other

For the most plausible reconstruction, it is logical to assume that some sort of major economic restructuring was taking place before the crisis, given the richness in material remains from the eighth century onward.[114] The upsurge in economic production meant that novel cultivation methods were likely being introduced in the Athenian countryside—considering the significance of agriculture in the overall economy.[115] Amidst this transformation, a surety is that leaving this rapid growth in the hands of the free market would have made the ground fertile for painful upheaval and internal strife (which Thucydides referred to as *stasis*). As one scholar noted, in the case of intensification of farming, greater amounts of seed corn, traction animals, manure, and labor would be required.[116] If those inputs were commodified and acquired exclusively through private capital,[117] rather than being socially supervised for fair distribution, the poor would fall behind due to the differentials in productivity gain, becoming losers in a fierce competition in which they had no say or control. Indeed, sources show a confluence of developments tending in the direction of greater marketization. According to the *Constitution of the Athenians* of Aristotle, the laws of Solon made frequent references to naucraric silver (8.3), presumably a type of money used primarily in overseas trade before standard coins became widely available. As David Schaps argued, the adaptation of money signaled a conceptual and social revolution, one that quickens the process of universal commodification that expedites

---

contemporary sources) if there was no profound socio-economic change, especially if these tribute payments functioned like gift-giving that played up reciprocity and consensus in Homer.

[114] Lin Foxhall, "A View from the Top: Evaluating the Solonian Property Classes," in *The Development of the* Polis *in Archaic Greece*, ed. Lynette G. Mitchell and P. J. Rhodes (London and New York: Routledge, 1997), 66.

[115] The change in cultivation practice could be due to population growth or simply economic incentives. Anthony M. Snodgrass theorized a population explosion in eighth century Athens; see Anthony M. Snodgrass, *Archaic Greece: The Age of Experiment* (London: J. M. Dent, 1980), 20–24. By contrast, Ian Morris argued that evidence of increase in the number of graves resulted from a broadening of the population being buried in an archaeologically visible manner; see Ian Morris, *Burial and Ancient Society: The Rise of the Greek City-State* (Cambridge, UK: Cambridge University Press, 1987), 156. Although Snodgrass seemed to have admitted that his estimates of population were too high, there is still some consensus among scholars about the increase of population in the eighth century. See Mogens Herman Hansen, "A Note on the Growing Tendency to Underestimate the Population of Classical Attica," in *Three Studies in Athenian Demography* Historisk-filosofiske Meddelelser 56 (Copenhagen: Royal Danish Academy of Sciences and Letters, 1988), 9. For those who believe that food production expanded as a result of population increase, see A. French, *The Growth of the Athenian Economy* (New York: Barnes & Noble, 1964), 12; and Bresson, *The Making of the Ancient Greek Economy*, 70. This assumption was disputed by Lin Foxhall, "A View from the Top," 69. However, Foxhall disproved only "extensification," as there were no traces of agricultural expansion into new areas, but not intensification, which could be achieved by using more labor and other inputs on existing plots. Lin Foxhall admitted, "This does not mean there were no changes in farming systems and practices, nor that crops were not grown in different ways at different times by different farmers" (69). Furthermore, economic players, such as big landlords, could actively seek to improve farming methods for profit through export even when they were not pressed by more hungry mouths.

[116] Gallant, "Agricultural Systems," 116. Also see preceding note.

[117] The question of money for ancient Greece, especially regarding the precise date of "invention," degree of circulation, and actual impact, entails a long scholarly debate. Here, it is only important to note the concrete evidence for coinage around this time, which would function as money. This development indicated a true conceptual revolution, in a way very similar to the rise of Oeconomism in the cultural struggle I suggest; see David Schaps, *The Invention of Coinage and the Monetization of Ancient Greece* (Ann Arbor, MI: University of Michigan Press, 2004), 15–17.

all types of market activities, as has been outlined in the introduction.[118] Certain liberalizing policies, such as the freedom to bequeath inheritance outside of the clan, also came into existence at Athens around that time, (Demosthenes 46.14; Plutarch, *Solon* 21.1; *Isaeus* 3.68; 6.9, 28). These developments moved property further away from the influence of communal supervision and collective guidance.[119]

Furthermore, as trade and monetary exchange intensified, the wealthy class at Athens could take up and scale up the export of olive oil and wine through the enlargement of its overseas markets.[120] Such commercial channels not only favored large producers of cash crops but also the importation of cheap foreign grain; both worsened the standing of local small farmers. The profit from foreign markets decreased the aristocrats' dependence on the local community, making it easier for them to ignore the plight of the common people. This series of events prompted one historian to conclude: "The situation was thus set for the passage of land from small independent farmers to wealthy proprietors: it merely remained to circumvent the traditional inalienability of the land."[121] When we put all these pieces together, a picture emerges in which burgeoning market forces precipitated the demise of widespread economic independence as well as reciprocal obligation. The resulting loss of social equilibrium called for heavy-handed state intervention, like the program carried out by Solon. Thankfully, owing to the *kleros* discourse, it was difficult for contemporary Athenians and commentators to ignore the fate of independent small producers, who often bear the brunt of commercial expansion in a growing monetary economy.

The nadir in debt-bondage/enslavement would have brought Athens to its knees, had it not been for a number of corrective measures that upheld the truths of Olympianism.[122] It is believed that in response to the crisis, Solon implemented what

---

[118] See Schaps, *The Invention of Coinage*, 15–17. Gift exchange and commercial trade might be mixed in practice, but their underlying beliefs and assumptions are certainly very different and need to be distinguished.

[119] For a longer discussion of social transfer, see under In Opposition to *Homo Economicus* on page 50.

[120] There is debate on whether oléiculture and viticulture were new to this period or merely got scaled up, which does not affect my argument. See Lin Foxhall, "Technology in Context: Questioning the Transformative Powers of Olive and Vine Cultivation," in *La main-d'oeuvre agricole en Méditerranée archaïque: statuts et dynamiques économiques* [The Agricultural Work Force in the Ancient Mediterranean: Statues and Economic Dynamics], ed. Julien Zurbach (Athènes; Bordeaux: École française d'Athènes; Ausonius Éditions, 2015), 110–53.

[121] Lewis Naphtali, "Solon's Agrarian Legislation," *The American Journal of Philology* 62, no. 2 (1941): 145.

[122] French, *The Growth of the Athenian Economy*, 16. I am aware that recently Edward Harris argued that Solon did not abolish debt-bondage but enslavement for debt. The legal distinction is not relevant for my argument here, since the Greeks would have considered both conditions unacceptable and tantamount to being a slave. In addition, the use of a modern legal definition for Archaic Greece exudes economic universalism. For example, where is it in the text that people actually thought about private property as the absolute power someone has over an object as defined by Roman law? Before all that, did the Greeks have a notion of a relationship between a person and a thing? How do we understand property rights if we cannot be sure that they understood property as such? I have already articulated my objections to the use of social science models in general (see Chapter 1). For a detailed critique of New Institutionalism, which Harris subscribes to, see Donni Wang, "Review of *The Making of the Ancient Greek Economy: Institutions, Markets, and Growth in the City-States* by Alain Bresson," *Bryn Mawr Classical Review* 2016.07.35

the Greeks called *seisachtheia*—the shaking-off of burdens. Later authors including Aristotle and Plutarch attribute to him the cancellation of debts and the forbiddance of debt enslavement/peonage; Plutarch also states that Solon banned the commercial export of local food, aside from olive oil.[123] As a politician, Solon was regarded highly by the ancients, and the measures enacted under his name—whether fully accurate or not—established the precedent of regulating excessive marketization for social cohesion.

Apart from the discussion of historical events, it is also instructive to examine the strong presence of Olympianism in the literature associated with Solon. In his poems, the narrator presents himself as someone who, by being mindful of the gods and attentive to the calls of justice, combats commodity relations that fueled repugnant exploitation and spiraling social disintegration.[124] One of his most famous pieces begins with the call upon the gods to witness the drastic measures he implements in their honor:

> Black Earth, supreme
> excellent mother of the Olympian gods,
> whose expanse was once pocked with mortgage stones,
> which I dug out to free a soil in bondage,
> Into our home Athens, founded by the gods,
> I brought back many sold unlawfully as slaves.[125]

Solon activated Olympian metaphysics through the invocation of the goddess Earth. In this temporal and spatial framework, the struggle for human freedom is succored by supernatural beings who guard the land and confer protection on the inhabitants against wanton enslavement and subjugation. With deep reverence, Solon was determined to follow the laws of the gods despite enormous hardship: "Whatever I said, I have done with the gods, I did not take pointless measures, nor did it please me with the force of tyranny nor to subject my rich fatherland to an equality of shares between good and evil men."[126] Under the gaze of immortals who preside eternally in the "Court of Time" (*en dikē chronou*) (Solon 36.3–5),[127] Solon, remembered by the Athenians as the founder of their democracy, withstood resentment and temptation. In his words, Solon refused to become a tyrant, forfeiting immediate gains and profits for greater causes. At the same time, his political program aimed to solve immediate, outstanding problems here and now. In adopting this approach, rather than being a "middling" poet who turns away from the gods,[128] Solon devoted himself to an

[123] Plutarch, *Solon*. For the discussion on debt enslavement/debt peonage and *seisachtheia*, see note 111.
[124] Gallant, "Agricultural Systems," 124.
[125] *Apologia of His Rule* 4–9 in Barnstone, *Ancient Greek Lyrics*, 85.
[126] Fragment 34, translated by John Lewis, *Solon the Thinker*, 36. The translation of "compel" is tentative, as the Greek is unclear.
[127] Ibid., 52.
[128] Ian Morris called Solon a middling poet, in contrast to "elitist" ones. The former type extols the average citizen who embodies the principle of equality, and the latter puts the nobles above the rest through exclusive relations to the gods, the heroes, and the East. See Morris, "Antithetical Culture." Yet as I will argue for Homer, the concern of the gods extends to all groups across the social spectrum, creating a basis

immanent mortal community that exemplified the gods' teachings on earth. Judged by short-term results, Solon seemed to have accomplished nothing for himself or his beloved city: strife and disorder soon returned to Athens after he decided to go into voluntary exile once the controversial reforms were put into place (Aristotle, *Constitution of the Athenians* 11, 13). Yet Solon's wish to stay true to his convictions and to fight for a more equitable and just society acquired a life of its own, which still inspires us to this day.

In some narrative accounts, the tyrant Peisistratus further leveled the playing field for small cultivators after Solon, by giving them loans for seed corn and tools (Aristotle, *Constitution of the Athenians* 16.2), and possibly even land confiscated from his aristocratic rivals.[129] If we are amenable to this evidence, then it is a further step in braving the onslaught of market-induced disruption that was poised to tear Athens apart. In fact, soon afterwards, the Athenian people overthrew tyranny in 510 BCE and proclaimed equality before the law (*isonomia*). However, Solon's wisdom and Peisistratus' benevolence addressed the one-time symptoms but not the root problem—the gradual retreat of Olympianism and the void it created for the emergent Oeconomism. Nonetheless, at least during this early wave of economic transformation, Athens and other Greek communities outlawed inordinate ownership of land (i.e., an amount above *kleros*), because excessive control of land not only enabled predatory expropriation in the economic sphere but also nullified civic and moral values in the cultural sphere.[130]

With the fair attainment of basic resources being so critical for a stable and prosperous community in the Olympian narrative, attempts to periodically re-invigorate *kleros* not surprisingly resonated with the Greek populaces, particularly during trying times. The Spartan poet Tyrtaeus mentioned the call to redistribute land after the second Messenian war that left his city in turmoil,[131] and Aristotle wrote about the revolt in Thurii in which the poor forced the rich to relinquish surplus land.[132] More generally, the philosophy of Aristotle, in favoring a middling class that owned moderately sized plots and thus was neither too rich or too poor (*Politics* 1295b39), echoes the basic idea of *kleros*. In Plato's utopian society, egalitarian agrarianism also plays a foundational role (*Republic* 8.565a). Both philosophers might very well have been responding to the growing economic disparity during their lifetimes in the fourth century. Moreover, Plutarch notes that after overthrowing the tyrant Dionysus in 356, the people's assembly in Syracuse, under a democratic leadership, voted to dispense all land and property equally to its citizens.[133] Similarly, in Argos the poor got so angry at the rich that they confiscated half of the latter's

---

of a unified culture that generates a convivial outlook through transcendent beliefs. *Contra* Morris, religious and mythical motifs are made to serve popular politics, and elitist and middling inclinations are made to reconcile each other.

[129] Claude Mossé, *The Ancient World at Work* (New York: Norton, 1969), 12.

[130] Aristotle, *Politics* 1319a9.

[131] Cited in Aristotle, *Politics* 1306b36.

[132] Aristotle, *Politics* 1307a.

[133] Plutarch, *Lives of Dion* 37. Also see Alexander Fuks, "Redistribution of Land and Houses in Syracuse in 356 B. C., and Its Ideological Aspects," *The Classical Quarterly* 18, no. 2 (1968): 207–23.

property, almost certainly with the intention of dividing it among the citizenry.[134] These incidents convey how much the ideals of *kleros* informed the political outlook of the ancients, and specifically, how equitable property redistribution precipitated demotic uprisings that were projected as struggles between freedom and tyranny. As Finley pointed out, all revolutionary movements in the ancient world can be defined by the single slogan: "cancel the debts and redistribute the land."[135] Even more astonishingly, these twin demands were sometimes joined by the call to liberate slaves,[136] an abolitionist sentiment rare before modern times.[137] Through these instances, *kleros* gained purchase on the political imagination of the ancient Greeks as well as of their heirs. Embedded in this web of historical connotation and ideological association, resource redistribution becomes a tool for advancing collective well-being and a means of reversing inequality in the political tradition of the West.

Among the various Greek cities, Sparta warrants our special attention. The *polis* stands out for a number of strictly enforced customs: compulsory martial education (*agoge*), common dining (*syssitia*), and the maintenance of an indigenous tributary servile population of *helots*.[138] For the preclassical period, Plutarch, who lived in the second century CE, is a major source for information on Sparta. According to him, Lycurgus, the much venerated lawgiver, divided land into comparable lots (*kleroi*) to equalize wealth (*Lycurgus* 8.1–2). Although Plutarch has been often faulted for being more of a storyteller than a historian,[139] his account nevertheless betokens the conception of a past marked by a strong communitarian ethos in the historical memory of the Greeks. Logically speaking, a wide distribution of land along the lines of *kleros* was the best way to distribute economic surplus to the greatest number of citizens. Such a setup would allow Spartiates (*Spartiatai*, the full citizens) to fulfill the citizenship requirements of contributing to common dining and participating in full-time military training, so they could live up to the city's fearsome military reputation that was proverbial throughout the Archaic and Classical periods.[140]

---

[134] Alexander Fuks, *Social Conflict in Ancient Greece* (Jerusalem: Magness Press, the Hebrew University, 1984), 72.

[135] Finley, *The Ancient Economy* (Berkeley, CA: University of California Press, 1973), 80.

[136] Ibid.

[137] Edward Harris wrote that when Hyperides wished to liberate the slaves in Athens, he was brought to trial for violating the rights of owners. For more on the jarring existence of slavery in ancient Greece, please see the discussion in the next chapter. However, the fact that the enslavement of human beings was regarded as showing respect for private property, both by the Greeks who wanted to try Hyperides and by modern scholars who praise the universality of such rights, illustrates well what can accompany the legal discourse of private property. See Harris, "The Legal Foundations of Economic Growth," 119.

[138] I am aware there is considerable debate on how much *helots* differ from typical slaves with regard to the distinctive features of their ownership, a point that does not affect my argument here. For this discussion, see Paul Cartledge, "Raising Hell? The Helot Mirage—A Personal Review," in *Helots and Their Masters in Laconia and Messenia: Histories, Ideologies, Structures*, ed. Nino Luraghi and Susan E. Alcock, Hellenic Studies Series 4 (Washington, D.C.: Center for Hellenic Studies, 2003). Cartledge held the view that the *helots* were state-owned, a view I am sympathetic to, *contra* the more recent opinions of Ducat, Hodkinson, and Luraghi.

[139] For issues of using Plutarch for factual history, see C. B. R. Pelling, "Plutarch's Adaptation of His Source-material," *Journal of Hellenic Studies*, 100 (1980): 127–40; revised version in C. B. R. Pelling, *Plutarch and History* (London: Classical Press of Wales, 2002), 91–115.

[140] This is basically the argument from 黄洋 Huang Yang, 《古代希腊土地私有制的确立与城邦制度的形成》 [The

Historically speaking, even if completely equitable land ownership failed to materialize substantially and securely in reality,[141] some proxy arrangement would be necessary to sustain the majority of citizen warriors. More importantly, the notions symbolized by *kleros* lived on: in the face of Sparta's terminal decline, the role of the property system automatically became a focal point in the diagnoses from ancient to current times. For instance, both Plutarch and Aristotle believed that a select few individuals accumulated too much land inheritance, and the practice impoverished the city as a whole.[142] We also know that being aggrieved by growing economic inequity, the younger generations blamed unequal land ownership as the culprit for the woeful state of affairs.[143] While the institutional workings behind Sparta's steady decay were undoubtedly far more complex than just a few bad laws or the greed of the rich, Plutarch and Aristotle certainly were not wrong to attribute the shrinking number of citizens in the fourth century to the very visible disparity in property and wealth.[144] In this way, inequality stemming from the concentration of ownership, rather than being explained away as desirable or inevitable, was perceived as a perversion.[145] This line of reasoning speaks to the way *kleros* politicized the role of property ownership for the task of bringing about a stable and cohesive society.

The Convivial Model under Pressure

Although *kleros* was the bedrock of the Olympian moral economy in many ancient Greek cities, its efficacy nevertheless faced grave tests during the fifth and fourth centuries BCE. Commercializing forces and market mechanisms advanced once again after Solon, rationalizing incentives to commodify land at the risk of leaving small, independent cultivators in a state of precarity and insolvency. Underneath all this, the subtle shift of opinions about religion in the fifth century BCE left Olympianism

---

Establishment of Private Property and the Rise of the *Polis* in Ancient Greece] 《复旦学报》 [Fudan Journal of the Humanities and the Social Sciences] 1 (1995): 46–51. Huang asked what sort of alternative arrangement could free all citizens from economic needs, at least during Sparta's height of military glory. I want to stress that there is no need for absolute equality to exist in the size of the land allotted and inherited, since land yield varies and other mechanisms like the commons and *temenos* (which we will soon discuss) increases overall egalitarianism. The bottom line is that a society which truly values equality will flexibly adjust; for example, via the legislation of Solon at Athens. We may just lack a reliable record of those measures for Sparta.

141 Some studies postulate significant inequity already in the Classical period due to sundry forms of permissible land alienation, see Hodkinson, "Land Tenure and Inheritance in Classical Sparta," *The Classical Quarterly*, New Series 36, no. 2 (1986): 381f. Hodkinson claimed that equality in land was not maintained in the fifth century, and goes so far as to say that the equal redistribution of *kleroi* by Lycurgus is entirely fiction. However, there has been pushback recently against the hypercritical rejection of all ancient sources on Sparta; see Timothy Doran, "Review of Die Wirtschaft Spartas by Lukas Thommen," *Bryn Mawr Classical Review* 2015.09.29. For my purposes, the "mirage" of Sparta has become a certain truth that has greatly shaped the notions of justice and equality in the West.

142 Plutarch, *Agis 5*; Aristotle, *Politics* 1270a15–b6.

143 See reforms of Agis in Plutarch, *Agis* 6. According to the author, the younger generation wholeheartedly supported the king Agis' attempt to redistribute the land in the third century.

144 Aristotle, *Politics* 1270a15–b6.

145 Aristotle, *Politics* 1271a15–b6. This point has also been confirmed by Hodkinson, 2000.

vulnerable and prone to be superseded.[146] As a result, the threat of undoing *kleros* loomed because Oeconomism, the culture of the market, was ready to step in and take over.

This dynamism of conflict and corrosion helps to explain the changing nature of real estate in the second, more thorough, wave of marketization that began in the fifth and fourth centuries BCE. Despite partial prohibitions of sale, land was gradually losing its sacred status and becoming more prosaic and commercial; that is, closer to being a pure commodity.[147] This development is reflected in the alienation of property as real security via mortgage contracts in Athens. The scholar John Fine argued that the use of property to secure loans of a commercial nature occurred rather late, beginning at the end of the fifth century BCE.[148] Others, like Edward Harris, favored an earlier dating. In his view, this use of the state's sovereign power to guarantee economic return through enforcing legally binding contracts happened long before 400 BCE[149] Harris touted it as the source of progress when lenders could seize the property of those who defaulted by legal-juridical means.[150] It should be noted, however, that loan sharks—such as those preying on victims who desperately need to ransom their loved ones from pirates (a real danger as illustrated by Demosthenes' *Against Nicostratus* and the experience of Plato)—would be equally entitled to this state mechanism.[151] By contrast, in the traditional model, pooling resources together to lend a helping hand took the form of voluntary offerings between members united

---

[146] Whether traditional religion declined and society became more secular in the fifth century onward has been hotly debated by scholars. It is true that life in the fifth and fourth centuries BCE did not display any dramatic break: the gods continued to be worshipped in the temples, their festivals were occasions for great celebration, the stories about them were recited in front of the population, and irreverence toward them nominally caused Socrates his life. Yet, the order determined by the gods and the heroes no longer automatically interested the learned men who were major culture makers: members of the intelligentsia like Thucydides and Aristotle left out the Homeric gods in their works without apology. When individuals could cast aside components of fundamental belief as a matter of personal choice, ancient Greece had entered into a "secular age," despite the continued outward appearance of ritual and worship. For more about this way of defining the secular age, see Taylor, *A Secular Age*. Also see my section titled Final Thoughts.

[147] Davies, "Classical Greece: Production," 351; Bresson, *The Making of the Ancient Greek Economy*, 154.

[148] John V. A. Fine, *Horoi: Studies in Mortgage, Real Security and Land Tenure in Ancient Athens* (Baltimore: American School of Classical Studies at Athens, 1951), 196; Fine offered two reasons. First, there was a complete absence of reference to mortgage contracts before the Peloponnesian War—an acceptable *argumentium ex silentio* given the abundance of textual and epigraphic evidence on other aspects of the economy. Second, Fine believed that people became a form of security to guarantee loans during the time of Solon precisely because land was encumbered up to that point. Following others, Fine postulated that the poor farmers remained on their land but became renters who were continually threatened with debt bondage by the nobles. Fine's narrative posits that land commodification, if any at all, began only very slowly in the fifth century.

[149] Ibid., 370. The actual argument is complex. The main point of Harris' study is that instead of two forms of hypothecation, which are attested on mortgage stones, they are both essentially the same type. The dual terminology comes from the legal limbo which allowed for a sort of "free-for-all" interpretation of both sellers and buyers. But the general trend toward more clearly defined rules and enforcement mechanisms that assist the alienation of property is clear, according to Harris (Ibid., 380).

[150] Edward Harris, "When Is a Sale Not a Sale? The Riddle of Athenian Terminology for Real Security," in *The Classical Quarterly*, New Series 38.2 (1988): 379ff; Harris, "The Legal Foundation of Economic Growth, 121.

[151] I picked up this great example from David Graeber, who offers many interesting ideas about ancient Greece. See David Graeber, *Debt: The First 5,000 Years* (Brooklyn, NY: Melville House, 2011), 194–95.

by ties of kinship and solidarity. Should anything unexpected happen to the agreed terms, the parties involved would feel obliged to resort to communally guided negotiation and arbitration. The use of force and bureaucratic procedure by the state, expedient means of achieving results, would have no place in a vibrant community of strong cohesion and self-rule. In the historical fifth century, however, the rise of commercial contracts in Athens was matched by economically liberalizing practices at Sparta, as previously discussed. These wide-scale structural manifestations all point to the attenuation of Olympianism amidst the emergence of market operations during the Classical period.

Yet despite the advent of market forces, Olympianism also showed some signs of resilience. The most up-to-date study of land tenure for Athens during the fourth century confirms high degrees of equality, with most of Attica's land remaining in the hands of smallholders.[152] Although plot sizes varied somewhat, the majority held onto their family lots that ensured economic freedom and security. This regime of self-reliant possession allowed most of the citizenry to have no masters other than themselves. This horizontal configuration, not surprisingly, also ensured better wealth distribution.[153] In these ways, the Classical era was increasingly becoming a battleground for contending cultural visions of land: on the one hand, it was a sacred entity that articulated important values, and on the other, a prosaic commodity that obeyed the profit motive.

TEMENOS: PRIVILEGE FROM SERVICE

We have already seen how the concept of *kleros* advanced large-scale independence and autonomy. The epics also mention the award of tracts known as *temenos*, a type of land allocation that promotes service and altruism in the Olympian model.[154]

Indeed, the majority of scholars highlight reciprocity, consensus, and comity in the dealings of *temenos* in Homeric epics.[155] While the texts offer no precise

---

[152] Ian Morris pointed out that the Gini Coefficient estimates of 0.382 and 0.386 for Athens in the fourth century, based on patterns of landholding, are very low for world history; see Morris, "The Athenian Economy Twenty Years After," 362–63.

[153] Geoffrey Kron, "The Distribution of Wealth at Athens in Comparative Perspective," *Zeitschrift für Papyrologie und Epigraphik* [Journal for Papyrology and Epigraphy] 179 (2011):129–38.

[154] There is considerable scholarly discussion on the prized values in the epic poems, which directly affect the interpretation of key terms like *geras* and *time*, the type of honor pursued by Homeric warriors. Different scholars have identified both "competitive" and "cooperative" virtues, although cooperative values are hard to deny (see note 443). However, in a reciprocal structure, no hard opposition between the self and the collectivity needs to exist. In fact, the interests of the individual and the group can be made to coalesce.

[155] There has been much debate on the nature of *temenos*. See M. I. Finley, "Homer and Mycenae: Property and Tenure," *Historia: Zeitschrift für Alte Geschichte* [Historia: Journal for Ancient History] 6, no. 2 (April 1957): 148ff; Walter Donlan, "Homeric τέμενος and the Land Economy of the Dark Age," *Museum Helveticum* 46, no. 3 (1989): 133ff. Donlan believed that *temenos* occupies the best of privately held land, yet even he conceded that some type of compensation to the owner would be required because it was an exercise of community power. Donlan refuted the claim that *temenos* comes from unclaimed land through seizure or expropriation by presenting a very convincing argument through examining the passages as well as the larger social context. Elsewhere, he concluded that "outright seizure and reallocation of another's cultivated land seems inconsistent with the *kleros* system and the general Homeric picture of the leader-

definition, *temenos* is usually a piece of land granted to someone who has demonstrated public virtue. For instance, when Odysseus meets his mother in the underworld, he is delighted to learn that his son "administers *temenos* and partakes of equal feasts" (*Od.* 11.185–6).[156] In this instance, *temenos* belongs to a young noble who is active in community affairs. Furthermore, all three Homeric passages discussing *temenos* depict it as a consensual transfer that enhances public service and communal integration. In the first story of Meleager, his people, the Aitolians, use *temenos* to persuade the great warrior to resume fighting for them.[157] Next, for the hero Bellerophon, *temenos* comes with the investiture of his new chiefly rank, which the hero has earned through performing extraordinary feats.[158] In the case of Aeneas, the promise of *temenos* is an incentive for fighting valiantly in battle.[159] In a famous speech made by Sarpedon, the hero states that the conferral of *temenos*, among other things, obligates and motivates him to fight in the forefront (*Il.* 12.313–4). Importantly, the prerogative of assigning *temenos* sits in the hands of the people or their representatives.[160] In the examples mentioned above, the texts explicitly refer to men of Lycia, the elders of the Aitolians, and men of Troy as the ones who authorize *temenos*. Even when Agamemnon unilaterally gives cities to Achilles as gifts (*Il.* 9.293), the *generalissimo* claims that he does it for the sake of the Greek army. In these representations, *temenos* is a gift from the people, a favor that obliges the ruler to his subjects.[161] Rather than being an economic object to be alienated for individual profit, *temenos* is an item of recognition adjudicated by the group to acknowledge extraordinary contribution.

Given that *temenos* binds privileged individuals to the community, let us consider how this Olympian paradigm might have played out in the real historical context. According to a number of ancient historians, the population of Greece grew quite significantly at the end of the Dark Age (c. 800),[162] creating pressure to convert pasture and frontier land for cultivation. If this was true, then *temenos* would have met

---

people relationship, which is one of amity and interdependence." See Donlan, "The Homeric Economy," 660. Similarly, Tandy asserted that in none of the cases raised by Finley is land "*necessarily* already in use under some third party's usufructory rights." See David Tandy, *Warriors into Traders: The Power of the Market in Early Greece* (Berkeley, CA: University of California Press, 1997), 129.

156 Unless otherwise specified, all passages of the *Odyssey* are taken from the Lattimore edition, *The Odyssey of Homer* (New York: Harper Perennial, 1991).

157 Owing to a previous grudge, Meleager refuses to fight even as enemies approach the gate of his city, putting his people, the Aitolians, in great danger. In response, "the Aitolian elders/ supplicated him, sending their noblest priests of the immortals,/ to come forth and defend them; they offered him a great gift:/ wherever might lie the richest ground in lovely Kalydon,/ there they told him to choose out a piece of land (*temenos*), an entirely good one of fifty acres, the half of it to be vineyard and the half of it unworked ploughland of the plain to be furrowed" (*Il.* 9.574–80).

158 We are told that "the men of Lykia (Lycia) cut out a piece of land, surpassing/ all others, fine ploughland and orchard for him to administer" (*Il.* 6.194–95). Before Bellerophon reaches this stage, the narrator recounts the extraordinary tasks he has accomplished, such as the killing of ravaging monsters in the territory (*Il.* 6.179–90).

159 In this scene, Achilles taunts Aeneas, illuminating the strings that are attached to *temenos*: "Or have the men of Troy promised you a piece of land (*temenos)*, surpassing/ all others, fine ploughland and orchard for you to administer/ if you kill me?" (*Il.* 20.184–86).

160 The elders are seen as community leaders in epics. Elsewhere, they settle disputes (*Il.* 18.503–09).

161 Hans van Wees, *Ships and Silver, Taxes and Tribute* (New York: I.B. Tauris & Co Ltd, 2013), 22.

162 See note 113.

the challenge of expanding food production by motivating and rewarding elites in a way that aligned them with the needs of the population. In this economic paradigm, the surplus food from newly claimed land would easily find its way back to the people, because *temenos* "entailed liberality on a day-to-day basis, as well as a special type…[in times of] drought, flood, blight, or enemy raid."[163] At the same time, by giving back, those notable individuals would be adequately remunerated for their initiative and effort. This circulation ensured a win-win outcome through reciprocal, consensual, and voluntary exchange, the kind facilitated by cultural negotiations rather than market and state institutions. If this convivial program had been fully operative—we simply know very little about this early period—it would offer a stark contrast to the market-oriented response that produced debt-bondage in early sixth-century Athens.

The Sharing of Booty

Even in the *Iliad* and the *Odyssey*, the division of provisions and prizes—although taking place on a distant military campaign and a faraway journey respectively—displays the same principles of *kleros* and *temenos*. Homer shows the disposition of a typical regime to be one that first gives a fair share to each and every member (*Od.* 9.548–51), and then, in some fitting circumstances, an extra honorary portion to the outstanding warrior (*Il.* 7.313–22, 9.334). This scheme protects the well-being of the group without blurring the distinctions of the individual.

These convivial norms are indeed fully operative in the *Iliad*, a poem born out of a conflict over spoils. To briefly recap the plot, in the ninth year of the Trojan War, the Greeks successfully capture Chryse, an ally town of Troy. Agamemnon, the commander-in-chief of the Greek army is given the captive girl Cryseis, and Achilles, the bravest fighter, is given Briseis. Soon Agamemnon is forced to surrender Cryseis, because her father asks Apollo to inflict the Greeks with a plague until his daughter could be ransomed. To compensate for his own loss, Agamemnon seizes Briseis, incurring the wrath of Achilles.

Throughout the story, Achilles consistently defers to the people, upholding their paramount sovereignty in matters of resource allocation: "But what we took from the cities by storm has been distributed;/ it is unbecoming for the people to call back things once given" (*Il.* 1.125–26). Again and again, Achilles stresses that "the Achaeans made a fair distribution" (*Il.* 1.368), i.e., the prizes were given by them (*Il.* 1.392). Through these statements, Achilles insists that the decisions of allocation made by the group together should not be overturned casually, and particularly not in the unilateral fashion that Agamemnon wishes. To Achilles, proper distribution must address collective needs and certify individual merit. Out of this belief, he is willing to recognize Agamemnon's service in surrendering Cryseis by promising him that the Greeks (*Achaeans*)[164] will "triple and quadruple" the amount of compensation after conquering Troy (1.127–29). Interestingly, even his opponent Agamemnon projects

---

[163] Donlan, "Homeric τέμεωος," 142.

[164] N.B. Some authors translate the word as "Achaians," but I will follow the Latin spelling throughout the text for simplicity.

himself as someone mindful of the common cause: "Still I am willing to give her back, if such is the best way. I myself desire that my people be safe, not perish" (1.116–18). Yet Agamemnon pays mere lip service to the soldiers, for he threatens to veto their decision if necessary:

> Either the great-hearted Achaeans shall give me a new prize
> chosen according to my desire to atone for the girl lost,
> or else if they will not give me one I myself shall take her,
> your own prize, or that of Ajax, or that of Odysseus,
> going myself in person; and he whom I visit will be bitter. (1.136–39)

Agamemnon's willful plan to take away another king's gift amounts to a complete negation of the community's role in resource arbitration. The contrast between the views and outlooks of the two sides—albeit about a female captive—places the rubrics of power at the center of economic redistribution. The clash between Agamemnon and Achilles, in fact, brings to the fore two distinctive paradigms of economic decision-making: one invested in the people and the other wielded by a single person. I will argue in Chapter 6 that religio-cultural hermeneutics puts Agamemnon squarely in the wrong. This reading, by extension, censures Agamemnon's capture of the prize for self-aggrandizement, as well as his dismissal of the people's mandate in the matter. Moreover, instead of endorsing the ruler's sole discretion, Homer draws attention to the lack of proper public supervision and intervention in the dispute. Through his narrative focus, we are able to infer that the *people*, as the supreme body, should have intercepted Agamemnon to resolve the crisis (see Chapter 6). These distinctive narrative elements validate the truth that legitimate economic allocation can only stem from collective deliberation.

Charity to the Poor and Redistribution to the Community

If the *Iliad* problematizes the indiscreet use of property for private ends, then the *Odyssey* might, on the surface, read like an endorsement. As we know, the story recounts how Odysseus, the wily hero, reclaims his patrimony from his wife's greedy suitors. Upon close examination, however, the rights and obligations germane to "private property" in the *Odyssey* in fact affirm the duty of charity and sharing.

First, the suitors, who attempt to waste the sustenance of Odysseus' family suffer no paucity themselves, and their desire for more at the expense of others comes off as sheer destructive greed. The text stresses that the aggressive "guests" belong to the upper crust of Ithaca that basks in comfort: in a telling scene, each one brings Penelope a wondrous gift to compete for her hand in marriage (18.290–303). Their enviable affluence prompts Odysseus to wonder, "If they, who have good things in great numbers, would give me dinner" (15.317). Yet despite being blessed by fortune, the renegade nobles exhaust the household of Odysseus out of malice, knowing well this would reduce his son Telemachus into a pauper. Additionally, Eumaeus, the loyal servant-friend of Odysseus, points out that the suitors never dedicate any offerings to the gods (*Od.* 14.93–95), leveling the charge of impiety on top of those of greed and cruelty. These descriptions function to elicit a strong condemnation of the suitors from the audience.

The narrative of the poem further alludes to the potential for active public intervention, especially when the powerful prey on the powerless, as the suitors do when they threaten the wife and young son in Odysseus' absence. Telemachus, in fact, goes to the assembly and chides the people for their cowardly silence. Interestingly, when the aristocrat begs the masses to interfere, it is the people who fall short of their duty to take action. In a similar vein, when Odysseus returns to investigate the trouble that has buffeted his household, he asks Telemachus, "Do the people/ hate you throughout the place, swayed by some impulse given/ from the gods?" (*Od.* 16.95–97). The rhetorical question implies that if Telemachus was loved and cared for by the people, they ought to have stopped the transgression. In these deliberations, the community is portrayed as the source of moral sanction and collective guardianship against envy and greed that threaten rightfully possessed goods.

By contrast, the members of Odysseus' household, although already besieged and imperiled, nonetheless provision the poor and the needy in obedience to the gods' teachings (*Od.* 14.57–58). The juxtaposition of the suitors, who covet another's possessions while living in abundance, and the protagonists like Penelope (*Od.* 17.550; 21.339), Telemachus (*Od.* 16.79), and Eumaeus (*Od.* 14.520f), who attend to the less fortunate while living in scarcity, highlights the morality of the *Odyssey*. In general, the epics give the impression that the custody of material surplus obliges constant giving back, as opposed to the occasional trickle down.

As consistent with Olympianism, the gods abet, enforce, and sustain "progressive" truths that aid the downtrodden. Whether shielding community-sanctioned *kleros* (for the purposes of subsistence, security, and independence) or insisting on charitable redistribution, the deities forcefully insert the concerns for others, particularly the easily overlooked, into the formulation. Accordingly, the suitors cannot simply deplete Odysseus' livelihood as they please, because the gods watch over Odysseus, who prays and sacrifices to them (e.g., *Od.* 12.334–37). Similarly, Telemachus cannot brush aside the pleas of the beggars and strangers who supplicate him, because they can also call upon the gods. The first scenario indicates the duty of the community to protect the vulnerable against predators, and the second mandates the transfer of surplus resources to the destitute, in both cases the arc of justice bends toward the underprivileged.

The Cattle of Helios

Leaving the affairs of Odysseus' household, we move to Thrinacia, the island of the sun god. The episode here further illustrates the truth about the convivial rules and norms that govern access to goods and resources in the Olympian system. On Thrinacia, when Odysseus' companions steal the cattle without consulting Helios, they wrong the rightful proprietor. The crime is especially noteworthy, because the cattle are "seed" or source cattle—much like the goose that lays the golden eggs. As a result, Zeus comes down harshly on Odysseus' men for an act so sacrilegious

(12.404–19).[165] It turns out that whenever the Greeks eat food they have plundered—instead of hunted or received as a gift—they meet disaster. This pattern occurs not only on Thrinacia, but also among the Cicones (9.44–61), and in Polyphemus' cave (9.231–306). Likewise, when Hercules kills his guest Iphitos for the latter's mares, the narrator does not hesitate to call the son of Zeus "guilty of monstrous actions" and "without shame for the watchful gods" (21.26, 28). Overall, the epics consistently problematize nonconsensual and violent means of material acquisition that deviate from convivial principles.

By contrast, when Odysseus and his son Telemachus plea for help as suppliants during moments of hardship and distress, they receive ample assistance and generous gifts (e.g., with Nestor, Menelaus, and the Phaeacians). This delightful expenditure is referred to as "gift exchange" by scholars, and it takes place frequently among affable persons in the epics. In these encounters, the hosts gladly transfer valuable resources, including precious luxury items,[166] to forge relationships of goodwill and mutual trust. In nearly every instance, gift-giving substantiates great nobility and wins unequivocal approval.

THE COMMONS

Equity, redistribution, and reciprocity govern not only the use of land (via *kleros* and *temenos*) and goods (via gifting and charity), but also primary resources that offer ready utilization in their natural state. In terms of agricultural production, clearly demarcated lots are optimal because well-defined individual ownership promotes self-responsibility and long-term investment. But natural resources like water, forests, and grazing land exist as "pools"—they cannot be easily divided and need to be preserved against depletion. In the Olympian narratives, we can identify the concept of "the commons,"[167] which meets the dual goals of subsistence and conservation, and is anything but a "tragedy."[168]

---

[165] Peter Rose noted the "fact that Odysseus' starving companions cannot adhere to the full ritual proprieties in sacrificing the cattle of the sun—they cannot sprinkle grain between their horns because they have no grain—suggests the dimensions of their criminality in sacrificing them at all." See Peter W. Rose, *Sons of the Gods, Children of Earth: Ideology and Literary Form in Ancient Greece* (Ithaca, NY: Cornell University Press, 1992), 49. Also see Homer's condemnation (*Od.* 1.6–9).

[166] The property regime of Olympianism is very nuanced because it applies different rules to different types of goods. We will discuss extensively productive resources like land and shared goods like water. Similarly, there are other goods like jewels and tripods that do not fit those categories but work according to the gift exchange model.

[167] It is useful to provide a definition of "the tragedy of the commons" in modern parlance as a reference, although our discussion will focus on its meaning in the Greek context. According to Martin Golding, "briefly, a commons is a resource which all have a liberty-right to use, from which no one has normative power to exclude others." In addition, for open-access resources, "anyone may come in and take out units of the resource, but no person or set of persons may sell or manage the resources." For commons property, "selling or managing is collective." Martin P. Golding and William A. Edmundson, *The Blackwell Guide to the Philosophy of Law and Legal Theory* (Malden, MA: Blackwell Pub., 2005), 148.

[168] The "tragedy of the commons" is a phrase used by economists to refer to a situation which assumes that when people have equal and unlimited access to natural resources, they will exploit it without limit. The solution according to those economists is to introduce private property laws that will incentivize people to preserve resources for profit. I will demonstrate the fallacy of this assumption in the ensuing sections.

The literary sources of ancient Greece provide ample examples illustrating the notion of the commons—resources to which free access is maintained for all. For instance, on the arduous journey back home, Homeric heroes and companions freely rest on beaches, draw water from rivers, hunt in the forest, and sail across the ocean, as they are fully entitled to these resources for basic needs (*Od.* 9.155, 9.169, 12.6, 12.330–32). Gustave Glotz noted that when Homer enumerated individual possessions, he did not include pasture land, which provides optimal use when shared rather than partitioned.[169] In addition, we know that the swineherd Eumaeus raised pigs in the forested edges (*Od.* 24.150), and Hesiod mentioned eating the meat of a cow presumably fed in the woods (*WD* 591). Both of them took for granted that the animals roam freely in open space. At least in Homer, it seems that land not under cultivation could be used by any community member for grazing, gathering, hunting, and wood-cutting.[170] For later periods, French asserted that in early Attica, free grazing land on the hillsides was common.[171] Some later sources also mention *epinomia*, the right to access common land that belongs to the city-state, either without cost or for a small fee.[172] In Plato's idealized world, fields and the waters are available for whoever wish to hunt and fish for noble reasons like beautifying physique (Plato, *Laws*, 824a). These descriptions and statements reveal the truth about the ideal of a commons regime, which maintains the availability of resources for apposite usage.

Proper Use of the Commons

A passage that alludes to man's proper relationship with nature in the *Odyssey* well illustrates the conceptual roots of the commons. When Odysseus captures a stag to feed his hungry companions, the hero proclaims that it belongs to the higher beings: "[S]ome god, because I was all alone, took pity upon me,/ and sent a great stag with towering antlers right in my very/ path" (10.157–59). The scene echoes an earlier adventure on the island of Cyclopes, where the hero also receives animals from the daughters of Zeus (9.154–60); in both episodes, the animal is a divine gift. Now let us look closely at how Odysseus conceptualizes the suitable use of natural resources received from the divine in this episode. After establishing the celestial origin of the stag, Odysseus describes how he carefully subdues the creature and carries it back with his very own hands (10.165–72). Upon hearing this marvelous story, his men proceed to enjoy the prey in a communal high feast (10.180–84).

As philosophical allegory, this text enumerates the reasons why Odysseus was permitted to appropriate a resource from the commons: the fulfillment of life-sustaining need and the expenditure of labor.[173] In this narrative, Odysseus is not

---

169 Gustave Glotz, *Ancient Greece at Work: An Economic History of Greece from the Homeric Period to the Roman Conquest* (Hildesheim: George Olms, [1926] 1987), 35.

170 Donlan, "The Homeric Economy," 658.

171 French, *The Growth of the Athenian Economy*, 10.

172 Bresson, *The Making of the Ancient Greek Economy*, 139. Bresson rightly discussed the exclusion of nonnatives, which is attributable to Polisism.

173 The principle of the commons is similar to how *kleros* worked. Donlan stipulated that "once a piece of land was put into cultivation, the labor invested in it conferred permanent title." See Donlan, "Homeric

hunting for amusement or profit, but for the alleviation of dire hunger. In addition, he himself captures and transports the animal, as well as ensures its maximum consumption. In this case, subsistence, labor, redistribution, and group well-being constitute the legitimate grounds on which the hero rightfully taps into the commons.

Against Human Ownership

The Olympian view of the commons values subsistence, charity, and redistribution; it gainsays the type of profit-based private ownership that lends itself to subjugation, rent-extraction, and exclusivity. The practice of the commons arises from a deep-seated conviction that man *cannot* dominate and exploit the physical world as he pleases, for the realm of nature belongs to the immortals who either directly embody it or exercise full jurisdiction over it. Greek mythology, for example, identifies Poseidon with the sea, Zeus with the sky, and Demeter with the earth, as well as other deities with the woods, rivers, and caves. By imagining nature to be full of higher living beings, Olympianism injects voice into an entity that cannot "speak" for itself. This imagination demands mindfulness and care in man's interaction with the environment. With the gods residing everywhere, it becomes unthinkable that humans—let alone any specific individual, household, or nation—can "own" or abuse a resource by exercising absolute power over it. The only fitting task for mortals is to steward these sacred gifts with reverence and gratitude.

The custom of offering coveted land to the gods, a well-attested practice in Classical Greece, reflects the notion of the commons and its origin in "divine ownership." In Athens, for example, sacred land dedicated to heroes and gods was treated like public land; that is, it was managed under the ownership of various local corporate entities.[174] The same term *temenos*, which is connected to public service in Homer as discussed earlier, referred to properties nominally set aside for deities, including public landmarks like the Acropolis and the Pythian race-course. In some cases, even individual trees on private estates were designated as "public" and "sacred," so the owners of the property were obligated to look after them for the city or the sanctuary.[175] According to Burford, this custom generated the consequence of reminding everyone that "all of the land belongs in the last resort not to individuals but to the community and the gods."[176] Those in possession of the estates were then expected to benefit the community and the gods as much as themselves. This sacredized public ownership effectively delivers the collective goals of conservation and sustainability.

By contrast, a "tragedy of the commons" occurs when the pursuit of individual profit puts aside communal considerations. In this scenario, the desire for endless

---

τέμεωος," 133.

[174] For example, *demes*, *phratries*, or the *polis*. See Nikolaos Papazarkadas, *Sacred and Public Land in Ancient Athens* (Oxford: Oxford University Press, 2011). Also see Léopold Migeotte, *The Economy of the Greek Cities: From the Archaic Period to the Early Roman Empire*, trans. Janet Lloyd (Berkeley, CA: University of California, 2009), 47.

[175] See Demosthenes' *Against Macartatus*; Alison Burford, *Land and Labor in the Greek World* (Baltimore, MD: John Hopkins University Press, 1993), 24.

[176] Ibid., 22.

accumulation driven by market calculations will exhaust the commons, resulting in a loss for all. In early modern England, social changes attenuated the duties and responsibilities that were part and parcel of the feudal framework; this moral vacuum then artificially necessitated laws of private property, which disproportionately benefited the capital class. With a phrase that is most telling, private property under English common law allowed "ownership of the land [to reach] from the heavens to the underworld."[177] By contrast, Athens instituted public ownership over the mines,[178] mandated property exchange if a wealthy individual was guilty of not making enough public contribution (*antidosis*),[179] limited the amount of agricultural produce citizens could extract from their holdings,[180] and placed regulations on specific arboricultural practices.[181] As seen from these examples, the Greek city-state acted as proprietor-in-chief on behalf of the gods by placing the greater interest of the polity over the private rights of the individual. This ideology, if mindfully introduced into every aspect of daily life, can avert the so-called "tragedy of the commons" without requiring the state to implement "private property" with the monopoly use of violence. Most importantly, there is nothing inherently different that prevents a commons regime from being implemented today[182]—the shift involves changing from an individualist mindset to a communitarian one.

Despite the strength of Olympianism, we can catch a glimpse of the growing cultural contestation surrounding the commons in the later fourth century in Demosthenes' *Against Macartatus*. In this speech, the defendant has been accused of removing an olive tree sacred to Athena, in violation of the city's decrees. Elsewhere in Greece, similar regulations could be found. For example, in Attica and Delos, it was forbidden to remove wood from Apollo's sanctuary and to dump manure into a spring sacred to the nymphs respectively; both imposed fines as penalty.[183] The underlying notion that these offerings of nature were divine and thus inviolable provides the conceptual basis for public ownership and communal guidance. Such truths helped protect resources from greed and negligence, and supervised their apposite use for long-term well-being. But in Demosthenes' *Against Macartatus*, nothing is said about the supremacy of the gods and the vulnerability of mortals who depend on them. Instead, the litigant treats olive trees as mere objects that either bring profit or incur sanction on the basis of cost and benefit analysis. By now, we have a society that is well versed in the utilitarian rationale of the market and the disciplinary

177 Bresson, *The Making of the Ancient Greek Economy*, 231.

178 Lycurgus prosecuted someone named Diphilus for having mined illegally; see Plutarch, *Vitae* 843; Plutarch, *Morals [Ten Orators]* 843d–3. State ownership of the mines can also be gathered in Demosthenes' *Against Pantaenetus* and *Against Phaenippus*. Other evidence includes passages cited from Herodotus and Xenophon, found in my later section entitled "City Finance and Public Ownership."

179 See Demosthenes, *Against Phaenippus*.

180 We know a great deal about the regulation against cutting down olive trees; see Lysias 7; *Constitution of the Athenians* 60.2; Dem. 43.7 (*Against Macartatus*), discussed next.

181 Plutarch, Solon 23.6. Solon allegedly forbade the planting of trees and building of walls and structures within a certain distance from another man's property.

182 It is not even accurate to say we need one today, for there is already a movement, see http://commonstransition.org/author/commons-transition.

183 David Cohen, *Theft in Athenian Law (Munchener Beitrage zur Papyrusforschung und antiken Rechtsgeschichten)* (Munich: Beck, 1983), 99.

power of state sovereignty. In this new era, through the shallow calculations of the market and the coercive mechanisms of the state, entities risk becoming prosaic and insignificant and thus dispensable and violable. Even in this specific speech of Demosthenes, remnants of old beliefs cross paths with new modes of thinking, leaving fifth- and fourth-century Greece embroiled in an intense cultural struggle.

City Finance and Public Ownership

In addition to physical spaces and objects, the discourse of the commons left a strong imprint on the financial dealings of Athenian democracy. Religious contributions—in the forms of donations, dedications, liturgies, and rents—constituted a major channel of revenue for temples, and this income was then lent out to cities or individuals through public administration.[184] In several inscriptions, a *prytanis*, a member of the executive council at Athens, presided over the treasurers of Athena (Inscriptiones Graecae I^2 3, 4). In correspondence to public administration, the allocation of resources was largely dictated by group needs, particularly during times of military exigencies (Inscriptiones Graecae I^3 363, 369). For example, when the fate of Athens hung in the balance during the Peloponnesian War, Pericles asked the people to take heart in the ultimate financial safeguard provided by the treasures of the gods, including even the gold ornaments on Athena's statue (Thucydides 2.13.5). One scholar believes that no interest was charged when this emergency money was later returned.[185] Through this circulation, economic surplus transferred to the temples in the name of the gods was parlayed into publicly managed resources for the polity.[186]

Moreover, most fiscal expenditures at Athens were redistributive and equalizing in nature—an illustration that even a monetized economy could, to some degree, advance convivial goals. The programs underwritten by the city included religious festivals, jury pay, public buildings, food subsidies, assistance to groups with special needs, etc.,[187] all with the aim to enhance citizen welfare. Particularly with regard to public festivals, no cost was spared on occasions that glorified the gods. For example, the famous festival of the Great Panathenaia, held every four years to commemorate Athena's victory over the giants, slaughtered numerous animals and spent unstintingly on prizes.[188] Other instances include the offering of 118 cows to Theseus and 105 animals to Zeus Soter in the fourth century.[189] The distribution of meat from those occasions could have taken place as often as once a week, which greatly supplemented the primarily vegetarian diet of the Greeks.[190] The Theoric Fund (*theorikon*), taken from regular allocations and surplus revenue, subsidized the poor

[184] Migeotte, *The Economy of the Greek Cities*, 48.
[185] Jennifer Larson, *Understanding Greek Religion* (London and New York: Routledge, 2016), 358.
[186] van Wees, *Ships and Silver*, 40; Davies, "Classical Greece: Production," 358.
[187] Austin and Vidal-Naquet, *Economic and Social History*, 119–20.
[188] Nancy Evans, *Civic Rites: Democracy and Religion in Ancient Athens* (Berkeley, CA: University of California Press, 2010), 54; David M. Pritchard, *Public Spending and Democracy in Classical Athens* (Austin: University of Texas Press, 2015), 28.
[189] Rhodes and Osborne, *Greek Historical Inscriptions*, 403.
[190] Ibid.

so they could also attend communal events.[191] By mid-fifth century BCE, Athens also paid for 6,000 jurymen, 700 magistrates, and 500 councilors to broaden political participation and civic engagement.[192] Other state initiatives brought relief to widows, disabled soldiers, and orphans, as well as food to the hungry and the impoverished. The makeup of the budget points to the truth that the wellness of the citizenry, particularly the needy and the poor, is synonymous with the health of the polity itself. In this light, it is not mere coincidence that the ancient sources always use the Athenians (*hoi Athēnaioi*) to designate the city, rather than by the name Athens.[193] In a speech by the Athenian general Nikias, he reminded his soldiers that they "make the city, not walls or ships without men in them."[194] Given the lack of separation between the citizenry and the polity, it is not surprising that one scholar remarked, "Virtually everyone held that the substantive, material interests of the city came before the freedom of any individual."[195] In this convivial body, the beneficiaries of the public funds were not lucky recipients of charity, but rather rightful stakeholders in the common pool of wealth, which was "owned by everyone and also no one." In this way, the discourse of the commons thoroughly percolated into the administration of public finance at democratic Athens.

Furthermore, especially with regard to natural resources, the Olympian notion of nature as commons boosted the legitimation of public ownership. Several of the silver mines in southern Attica were named after the gods: including *Aphrodisiakon*, *Apolloniakon*, and *Athenaikon*,[196] and this conception of divine origin was essential for activating the commons. In the account of Herodotus, the mines of the gods are indeed spoken of as a common treasury (7.144.1). In addition, scholars also inferred public ownership for two major quarries at Athens based on the lack of reference to the cost of stone in public building accounts.[197] The Athenians were not alone in acknowledging precious resources as gifts from the gods that warranted collective ownership. Herodotus related another example:

> The Siphnians at the time were at the height of their prosperity. They were the wealthiest among the islanders, as there were mines of gold and silver in their country, and of so rich a yield, that from a tithe of the ores the Siphnians furnished out a treasury at Delphi which was on a par with the grandest there. Every year they would divide out among themselves the yields of the mines. (3.57.2)

[191] For details, see Mogens Herman Hansen, "The Theoric Fund and the *graphe paranomon* against Apollodorus," *Greek and Byzantine Studies* XVII, no. 3 (1976): 235–46.

[192] van Wees, *Ships and Silver*, 63.

[193] Philip Brook Manville, *The Origins of Citizenship in Ancient Athens*, 6.

[194] Thucydides 7.77.7.

[195] Robert W. Wallace, "Personal Freedom in Greek Democracies, Republican Rome, and Modern Liberal States," *A Companion to Greek and Roman Political Thought*, ed. Ryan K. Balot (Chichester, UK: Wiley-Blackwell, 2009), 173.

[196] Jon D. Mikalson, *Ancient Greek Religion*, 2nd ed. (Chichester, UK: Wiley-Blackwell, 2010), 156.

[197] Acton, *Poiesis*, 206.

That the Siphnians dedicated a portion of their wealth to the Delphic Oracle can be seen as an expression of gratitude for the material matter that they did not create in the first place: indeed, since gold and silver had perfected themselves underground for centuries without any human involvement, their existence could only be credited to the higher beings. It would then only be fitting to distribute such a divine gift among the citizens. In a third example from Herodotus (4.46), the Thasians also applied the money from their mines toward better ships and strong walls, demonstrating once again a collective ethos with regard to the appropriation of key resources.

The famous Laurion mines at Athens offer the best illustration of the public orientation in resource management, since the proceeds first went to the citizens, and then to common defense, but never to private coffers. Specifically after the first Persian invasion, rather than splitting the income as before, the Athenians agreed to build a fleet with the silver in wise anticipation of future conflict with the Persians. With this Athenian navy, the Greeks routed the Persians—a historical event often touted as a symbol of the triumph of freedom over tyranny.[198] This memorable episode in Western historiography forges the solid nexus between common ownership on the one hand, and democracy and liberty on the other. Under the influence of those truths, the establishment of public ownership over natural assets becomes just and laudatory. The fourth-century author Xenophon considered it a great disadvantage when only private individuals, but not the polity, could profit from the mines.[199] He proposed that the city should also acquire ownership of the natural resource to benefit the *polis* and its inhabitants.[200] Given this historical context, the use of naturally existing wealth (i.e., objects that do not require extensive human labor) for the collective good is indeed ideal and optimal to the Greeks who subscribed to Olympianism. In the Olympian dispensation, the "resource curse"—the modern paradox in which countries endowed with abundant resources end up with less democracy, more inequality, and worse development outcomes—would not occur. The effective implementation of Olympian values in the Greek case confirms that social outcomes do not depend so much on physical conditions—a materialist interpretation anyway—but cultural guidance. When Olympianism prevails in political discourse and policy in the form of equitable ownership and public stewardship, the discovery of natural resources can be a true blessing in the way it was intended by the gods.

In Opposition to *Homo Economicus*

The practices of *kleros*, *temenos*, gifting, and the commons facilitated autonomy, service, reciprocity, and redistribution. These ideals differ sharply from those of either private ownership that rewards endless accumulation or state ownership managed by a central bureaucracy.

To categorically differentiate this Greek model from the market system, we must first refute the identification of private property with the early centuries of Greek

[198] For example, Aeschylus, *Persians* 240.
[199] Xenophon, *Ways and Means* 4.1–17.
[200] Ibid.

history. Finley's article "Homer and Mycenae: Property and Tenure" was largely responsible for popularizing this view. The essay begins by debunking the earlier suppositions of both feudal-style conditional tenure and community-held, *ager publicus* systems in Homer.[201] The conclusion that land was not controlled by a centralized, hierarchical state has rightly been accepted,[202] but the subsequent capitulation to "private ownership" must be firmly resisted.[203] The cases adduced by Finley, although unequivocally showing the free disposition of land between individuals without a higher authority (be it an overlord or a central government) operate on a bundle of truths vastly differently from those in the market system.

Upon closer examination, we discover that the actors in Homer studied by Finley transferred land to assist newcomers or to deepen existing social ties. In other words, they complied with the core values of the Olympian dispensation, which subjected material exchange to the needs of collective flourishing. The first example is Adrastos, who gave Diomedes' father the hand of his daughter along with wheat-bearing fields when the latter wandered to Argos (*Il.* 14.119–25). The second one is Alcinous, who pledged an *oikos* (household) and other possessions to Odysseus should the hero marry his daughter. The third instance concerns Odysseus, who promised a *kleros* to his swineherd Eumaeus (*Od.* 14.61–64). In addition, we can suppose that in the *Iliad*, Peleus had endowed Phoenix—an erstwhile fugitive who had become family—with some land for financial security. It is largely in gratitude of this extraordinary kinship that Phoenix later raised and educated Achilles to be the best of Greek warriors. In these stories, the parties seek to achieve mutual satisfaction rather than unilateral advantage, and property changes hands through voluntary agreement, rather than legally-binding contracts. The results of such decisions are better termed as social transfers rather than commercial alienation. Social transfers that deliver convivial goals must be distinguished from enforced transactions that maximize individual gain—with the difference being that in historical reality, individual chiefs oversaw social transfer in the Archaic world, whereas later the city acted as proprietor-in-chief.

In the ideal Olympian model, the convivial actors, unlike *homo economicus*, strive to align themselves with the interest of the multiple others to whom they are inextricably connected. Using land as an example again, by first asserting the divine origin of all properties, the community could then, on this basis, redistribute, assign, or confiscate allotments as needed.[204] At the same time, the design of *kleros* as a whole functioned with a view toward the prosperity, wellness, and independence of the individual. As a result, each member ought to uphold and reinforce *kleros* by taking responsibility for his own subsistence and by respecting others' claims to their respective shares. The faith in convivial convergence dispels the imagination of an isolated, threatened *homo economicus* who constantly lives in a state of hostility and

[201] Finley, *Economy and Society in Ancient Greece*, ed. Brent D Shaw and Richard P. Saller (London: Chatto & Windus, 1981), 218.
[202] See Donlan, *The Aristocratic Ideal*, 306.
[203] Finley, *Economy and Society in Ancient Greece*, 217. Finley was himself aware that applying terms like "private" and "ownership" to archaic societies is controversial.
[204] Davies, "Classical Greece: Production," 350.

rivalry. Intrinsic to the Olympian paradigm is the preference for interacting with worthy peers, rather than to tread on underlings and serfs. Mutual codependence, instead of cut throat competition, produces a society in which the individual does not fear the exigencies and wishes of the collective, nor does the collective begrudge the success and flourishing of the individual. By examining the Greek terminology pertinent to land possession, Burford characterized the property regime as neither centrally controlled nor market-based. "None of these or any other terms indicate absolute private ownership…this is not to say, however, that private property rights in the Greek world actually went unrecognized and unprotected, but they had come into being and always existed within the context of the community."[205]

In summary, we have identified several distinctive Olympian discourses that shaped the administration of property. The Olympian legacy includes *kleros*, which upheld egalitarian land distribution and economic independence; the commons, which ensured access to and the sustainability of natural resources; and *temenos* and gift-giving, which encourages benevolence, service, and reciprocity.

LITURGICAL GIVING AND THE COMMODIFICATION OF KNOWLEDGE

Public contribution from capable individuals was praiseworthy and vital during high Olympianism, and this continued to be the case in the *polis* of the Classical era.[206] In many Greek cities, the wealthy class either volunteered or was appointed each year to fund and supervise essential communal functions. At democratic Athens, these duties included the sponsorship of artistic performances (*chorēgia*), athletic schools and competitions (*gymnasiarchy*), the citizen-operated navy (*trierarchy*), and banquets (*hestiasis*), among others. The citizens who contributed generously could expect to enhance their reputation among their compatriots.[207] This liturgical culture, which hews to the truth that honor comes from public giving and shame from private hoarding, helped to secure the material base for the Athenian way of life.

This spirit of voluntary giving, which took the form of liturgy and munificence in the Classical period, dwindled toward the fourth century, when the overall economy became more monetized and commercialized. A speech given by Demosthenes accused the rich of being more concerned with themselves than their city:[208]

> If any of you knows by chance the sort of house that Themistocles, or Miltiades or one of the great names of that time had, he can see that it is no more impressive than that of the common people, whereas the public buildings and constructions are so grand and of such quality… But nowadays

[205] Burford, *Land and Labor*, 15–16.

[206] The Greek term liturgy (*lēitourgia*) combines the word "public" and "work." The etymology underlines the duty of successful individuals to use their resources and time toward the greater good.

[207] C. M. Carmichael, "Public Munificence for Private Benefit: Liturgies in Classical Athens," *Economic Inquiry* 35 (1997): 262.

[208] Scholars have noted that though speakers and orators of the Athenian democracy come from the wealthy upper class, they must win over the lower classes who vote on the basis of their speeches. In this sense, the view of the rich expressed by Demosthenes could very well reflect the thinking of the masses. See David M. Pritchard, *Sport, Democracy and War* (Cambridge: Cambridge University Press, 2013), 10f.

> all professional politicians are so wealthy that they have built themselves private houses which are more impressive than many public buildings.[209]

Demosthenes was not the only one who reminisced about or projected back to the old days when the well-to-do put the city before themselves. Even in the fourth century, the author Xenophon exalted the same ideals of aristocratic behavior in the *Cyropaideia*, an educational text that resonated with an array of common political and philosophical themes.[210] The central character Cyrus, a Persian prince, emulates the best of the Greeks by dressing frugally, pouring libations to his relatives and ancestors, preferring public praise over wealth, and spending money on friends. The evocation of those conventions underscores the continued strength of Olympianism in asserting the truth about the public orientation in excellence and heroism even toward the Hellenistic era.

Although traditional aristocratic values held on, the pursuit of self-aggrandizement was on the rise in the fourth century, as indicated by the lawsuits charging the rich with liturgical avoidance or wealth concealment.[211] Those court speeches—even bearing in mind certain measures of rhetorical exaggeration—reflected the enervation of reciprocal obligation and civic solidarity. To fully understand this shift, we must discuss the variable of knowledge in the overall three-way cultural contestation.

The scholar John Davies noted that public giving began to lose its appeal from the fourth century onward.[212] He theorized that the privileged class began to reckon that rhetorical, financial, and administrative expertise yielded more concrete economic and political advantage than conscientious deeds that earned merely gratitude and favor (*charis*) from the people.[213] Davies interpreted this new trend as positive for democracy, because technical skills lack inheritability.[214] Yet the rise of the professional class suggests a more complex story.[215] As Davies himself admitted, only those who were at least moderately wealthy could afford the necessary

---

209 Demosthenes, *Against Aristocrates* 206–09, cited in Austin and Vidal-Naquet, *Economic and Social History*, 351.

210 For the diverse but predominantly educational nature of this text, see Houliang Lu, *Xenophon's Theory of Moral Education* (New Castle upon Tyne: Cambridge Scholars Publishing, 2015).

211 Davies considered these practices as forms of the use of negative power by the rich, see Davies, *Wealth and the Power of Wealth*, 89.

212 Ibid., 114ff.

213 Ibid., 92, 114.

214 Ibid., 126.

215 It is true that in an era when rhetoricians and speech writers dominated politics, public opinion still mattered to the degree that the populace could influence what it desired to hear. See Josiah Ober, *Mass and Elite in Democratic Athens: Rhetoric, Ideology, and the Power of the People* (Princeton, NJ: Princeton University Press, 1989). But the positions of those who can formulate speeches or hire such services versus those who can only respond to it passively are not equal, not to mention the possible manipulated use of rhetorics. The disparity and disconnect are unfitting for a direct democracy like Athens. More importantly, the transmission of new skills as a private good is troublesome, for it excludes the public from participating in making and supervising their use. The Athenian people could not know who paid how much to hire whom for what purpose; each piece of this information matters for evaluating the meaning of political/public speech.

education.[216] In this light, the promise of a "meritocratic" regime could never be fulfilled when the very basis of acquiring merit rested on skills and knowledge that were being monetized and commodified. Indeed, despite opening the door to a few gifted individuals from the lower classes,[217] the rich more or less monopolized the new forms of arcane knowledge that allowed them to dominate the political stage.[218] In this process, wealth played a key role: many politicians of this period made their money from owning industrial slaves and built their careers by mastering oratory; both resulted from amassing disproportionate economic and cultural capital, respectively.[219] The expedient path of converting money into power bypassed the need to accumulate *charis* in the community—the political currency in the earlier days of high Olympianism.[220]

This new political economy of knowledge in essence pronounced the inferiority of action vis-à-vis technique. This devaluation sent reverberations throughout the political system and is key to the debate of whether or not the tenor of Athenian democracy changed between the fifth and fourth centuries (or more specifically, between the Persian Wars in the 490s and the death of Pericles in 429 BCE). Contemporaries like Thucydides and the author of the *Constitution of the Athenians* claimed that politics was beginning to work differently, but their reasoning that noble, aristocratic leaders like Pericles died out and were replaced by devious ones like Alcibiades and Cleon, is devoid of structural analysis. It is true that Pericles came from a typical aristocratic family of wealth and distinction, but he won admiration because of his enduring political vision for Athens. We can and should fault his imperialism, but Pericles dedicated himself to the primacy of Athenian selflessly until the day of his death, in spite of grave and fluctuating circumstances. Someone like Alcibiades, on the other hand, also came from an aristocratic background, but was defined by shrewd and capricious political maneuvers. This charming student of Socrates famously changed alliances many times at Athens, before defecting altogether to Sparta and then Persia. His preference for strategies that brought instant gratification over those that serve deep-seated conviction and commitment is indeed extraordinary. Based on this example, even if aristocrats like Alcibiades were forced to fashion themselves as leaders who put the people above their own private dealings[221]—a recurring image in the court speeches indeed—it would still be difficult for the masses to know the truth when paid experts manipulated crucial information and knowledge. W. Robert Connor described the ramifications of the new "technological revolution":

---

[216] Davies, *Wealth and the Power of Wealth*, 127.
[217] Ibid., 117.
[218] Manville, *The Origins of Citizenship in Ancient Athens*, 17; Robert Connor, *The New Politicians of Fifth-century Athens* (Indianapolis and Cambridge: Hackett Publishing Company, 1992.), 153; Schaps, *The Invention of Coinage*, 136.
[219] Davies, *Wealth and the Power of Wealth*, 41ff; Connor, *The New Politicians*, 153.
[220] Schaps, *The Invention of Coinage*, 136.
[221] For those who believe that democracy continued to function as before, in the sense that the opinions of the people still exerted great influence, see M. I. Finley, "Athenian Demagogues," *Past and Present*, no. 21 (1962): 3–24; M. I. Finley, *Democracy Ancient and Modern* (New Jersey: Rutgers University Press, 1973, rev. ed. 1996), 38-75; and Ober, *Mass and Elite in Democratic Athens*.

> In the old pattern proven reliability was exceedingly important; time and military experience would test it and eventually create the backing of confidence which a politician needed. His deeds in battle or his long apprenticeship in the art of government would show that he was worthy of trust. Under the new pattern a good speaker could rout his opponents with a clever argument, emotional appeals, or additional information.[222]

Here, we see the devastating impact of knowledge commodification even in an overarching democratic framework. A day would come when substance and representation would no longer be distinguishable, creating confusion for the process via which meaningful human action achieves its end.

In the authentic Olympian model, being in the company of peers and under the gaze of the gods ensured that all actions and speech constantly disclosed identity. In other words, real life was thoroughly politicized in the Olympian dispensation. Indeed, according to Niall Livingstone, at democratic Athens, civic education—the art of performing meaningful deeds—was "pervasive and immersive, woven into the daily practice of citizen life itself."[223] Yet as the forces of the market and the state advanced, they constantly sought to obscure and narrow the scope of the Olympian "identity politics," which was intended to be holistic and all-encompassing. First, altruistic deeds like liturgy and sacrifice shed their intention and utility to become low-performing "investments." Furthermore, when the state responded by mandating financial contributions via law, it chipped away the agonistic glory that could only be obtained by deeds performed out of volition.[224] At the same time, the new currency of purchasable knowledge facilitated exclusion and manipulation. The Socrates in Aristophanes' *Clouds*, for example, is an unscrupulous sophist who flaunts the ability to reverse right and wrong and make worse arguments better for career purposes. Although being grossly unfair to the real historical figure, this caricature must have resonated with the Athenian audience, whose city witnessed an influx of such newfangled teachers. In this light, Aristophanes and some of the juries at Socrates' trial could be justified to feel that these trendy educators who glorified dazzling skills and capabilities at the price of justice and virtue were "corrupting the youth" and "introducing false gods." This conservative attitude might have stemmed from the intuition that through the marketization of knowledge, skillful words in selective performative moments would begin to matter more than what a person actually did with his precious mortal life. In fact, the concerned critics of Athenian democracy charged the politicians after Pericles not with incompetence, but dishonesty.[225] The feeling of distrust should be squarely attributed to the novel regime of technical

222 Connor, *The New Politicians*, 149–50.

223 Niall Livingstone, *Athens: The City as University* (London: Routledge, 2016), vii.

224 Dimitris J. Kyrtatas, "Domination and Exploitation," in *Money, Labour and Land*, ed. Paul Cartledge, Edward E. Cohen, and Lin Foxhall (London and New York: Routledge, 2002), 147. According to Kyrtatas, elites in the later centuries "were not happy to contribute part of their wealth for the benefit of the poor, *unless* this was done on a voluntary basis."

225 Schaps, *The Invention of Coinage*, 137.

know-how, which enabled a culture in which outward appearance and bureaucratic competence counted more than morally grounded authentic action.

As with everything else we examined so far, the market was not the only way to advance and spread knowledge. In the days of high Olympianism, community-based oral poetry was the medium that conveyed common discourse, engaging many in the process of its creation, dissemination, and preservation.[226] This form of "low-tech," vernacular communication,[227] combined with populist religious teaching and participatory story-telling, was more democratic in that it lowered the threshold for the masses. Indeed, much of the great literature that we cherish from ancient Greece was intimately connected to oral culture, and scholars note the critical function of informal speech in the service of democratic politics.[228] At the same time, the dispersal of knowledge along horizontal and populist lines can be seen in the legends that credit important inventions to noble-minded benefactors. In these tales, divine and extraordinary figures share their "secrets" unreservedly to benefit humanity.[229] This mode of transmission was respectful of the truth that we ultimately owe everything, including intangible cultural and artistic goods, to the divine. Eumaeus opines that a good singer learns his songs from the gods (*Od.* 17.518–19). On another occasion, upon hearing the wonderful Demodocus, Odysseus intimates that the singer must have been taught by the Muses or Apollo (*Od.* 8.488). The narrators in the *Iliad*, the *Odyssey*, and the Hesiodic poems all pay tribute to the Muses from the onset, and there is reason to assume that these invocations express genuine belief.[230] This particular Olympian treatment of knowledge is diametrically opposed to the approach of the market, which privatizes intellectual and cultural property through copy rights. The former case is characterized by inclusion, horizontality, and a low common denominator; the latter is marked by narrow reach, superfluous technicality, and difficult access.

Even if new types of skills like writing, rhetoric, and accounting became necessary for Athens at some point, they should be taught to everyone, with costs

[226] It is true that at one point in Homer, Telemachus tells his mother to leave the poetry performance that was taking place in the grand hall (*Od.* 21.350), illustrating the exclusion of women from cultural production. Nevertheless, oral culture that prevailed in ancient Greece was still relatively participatory and collective. Surely not everyone played equal roles, but there were lower barriers for the masses to partake in oral culture. For the involvement of the audience in oral composition, see Ian Morris, "The Use and Abuse of Homer," *Classical Antiquity* 5, no. 1 (April 1986): 89.

[227] See David Elmer, *The Poetics of Consent: Collective Decision Making and the Iliad* (Baltimore, MD: Johns Hopkins University Press, 2013), 11f. Elmer hypothesized that the epics were a result of a "long-term collective decision-making procedure" that involved audiences and performers.

[228] Josiah Ober, in a series of books, discussed the role of knowledge in Athenian democracy. See Ober, *Mass and Elite in Democratic Athens*; Josiah Ober, *Athenian Legacies: Essays on the Politics of Going on Together* (Princeton: Princeton University Press, 2005); Ober, *Democracy and Knowledge*. With this general understanding, I would like to highlight the contribution of informal knowledge that is neither institutionalized nor expert-controlled.

[229] For example, the god Aristaios is supposed to have invented many labors and pastimes of the countryside, such as bee-keeping, olive-growing, and the preparation of wool. See Robin Hard, *The Routledge Handbook of Greek Mythology* (London and New York: Routledge, 2004), 153. At one point, Athena endowed the Rhodians with useful skills like weaving, spinning, and statue-making. See Hard, *The Routledge Handbook of Greek Mythology*, 180.

[230] For more evidence, see Tandy, *Warriors into Traders*, 169.

defrayed by the state. The intellectual class should always be alarmed by the neutralization and technocratization of education and its unmooring from democratic virtues. Indeed, as one scholar intimates, "thinking must be for the city; the love of wisdom cannot be a private activity but must be subordinate to the city's good."[231] With the Olympian model, human intelligence at its most powerful can be harnessed to further the discovery of meaningful identity and relationships in a convivial framework, rather than be instrumentalized for the pursuit of abstracted utility at the price of collective well-being. In this way, knowledge emanating in a nonhierarchical and inclusive fashion facilitates mass empowerment and participation, both of which boost democracy.

At the close of this chapter, let us review the ways in which property and knowledge functioned on the basis of Olympianism. We first examined *kleros*, the foundation of a land tenure system that maximized independence and security of small farmers. Second, we explored *temenos*, the granting of surplus land with the goal of encouraging service. Next, we outlined the paradigms of gifting and the commons, as well as how they guided the management of natural resources and public finance. In addition to the creation of physical objects, we have discussed how cultural and intellectual goods could be created and disseminated in the convivial model to support inclusion, participation, and access. These features of the Olympian model were buttressed by a greater truth about human nature: a *self* that is deeply embedded in interdependent, reciprocal, and horizontal relationships. In this and other aspects, the political economy of Olympianism evinces striking differences with the market system. Overall, Olympianism successfully offers a set of solutions for economic independence, social inclusion, and political solidarity—the key ingredients of a democratic society.

---

[231] Timothy Burns, "The Problematic Character of Periclean Athens," in *On Civic Republicanism: Ancient Lessons for Global Politics*, ed. Geoffery Kellow and Neven Leddy (Toronto: University of Toronto Press, 2016), 19.

CHAPTER 3

In Praise of *Homo Faber*

In the previous chapter, we examined the ideals of property in the Olympian dispensation. Yet access to raw material is only one part of political economy. In this chapter, we will explore labor—productive activities undertaken by humans—and how it was shaped by the cultural truths of Olympianism. As we shall see, the effort devoted to improving and transforming the material world was considered most worthy by the Greeks. In this study, this truth of man as someone who transforms the natural world is named *homo faber* (Latin for "Man the Maker").[232] A survey of earlier literary sources and evidence from democratic Athens confirm the cultural emphasis on creativity, mastery, and control, as well as horizontality in economic production. This constellation enabled the success of *homo faber* and was responsible for the high-quality craftsmanship, widespread small-scale production, and horizontally coordinated manufacturing that characterized the economy of Classical Athens.

To begin expounding on the concept of *homo faber*, we must first challenge the common misconception that the ancient Greeks lived off the backs of slaves. While scholars no longer endorse this position, it nevertheless has taken on a life of its own in the popular domain.[233] Pejorative attitudes toward the working masses at Athens originate from antiquity itself in texts attributed to Plato, Aristotle, and in part, Xenophon.[234] These authors reasoned that it was impossible for manual workers to master statecraft.[235] In doing so, they favored a traditional aristocratic oligarchy over an inclusive, class-blind democracy. In a similar manner, nineteenth-century scholars who feared popular government also propagated the myth that democratic Athens was a city of idle mobs.[236] To some of them, the basis of ancient Greek civilization fit the bill of the "consumer city,"[237] a term employed by Max Weber for an urban center that siphons off surplus from the hinterlands to sustain its material needs. These views, which continue to influence the popular image of ancient Greece, stem from commentators who either disapproved of democracy or lived much later in time, or both.

---

[232] The term comes from Hannah Arendt in her discussion of Greek democracy. See Hannah Arendt, *The Human Condition*, 2nd ed. (Chicago: University of Chicago Press, 1998).

[233] The exaggerated role of slave labor has already been emphasized by others. In particular, see A. H. M. Jones, "The Economic Basis of the Athenian Democracy," *Past and Present*, no. 1 (1952); Ellen Meiksins Wood, *Peasant-Citizen and Slave: The Foundations of Athenian Democracy*, corrected paperback ed. (London: Verso, 1989).

[234] Xenophon's portrayal of the corselet maker Pistias, for example, is less negative (Xenophon, *Memorabilia* 3.10.9).

[235] For example, Aristotle, *Politics* 1278a; Plato, *Laws* 8.846d; Xenophon, *Oeconomicus* 4.2–3.

[236] Wood, *Peasant-Citizen and Slave*, 10–28; 15; Catharina Lis and Hugo Soly, *Worthy Efforts: Attitudes to Work and Workers in Pre-Industrial Europe* (Leiden: Brill, 2012), 15.

[237] Finley, *The Ancient Economy*, 191–95.

In truth, the association with idleness and parasitism in ancient Greece elides a number of cultural truths to the contrary.[238] For example, the heroic figures in Homer are full of enthusiasm and pride when performing a variety of diligent tasks and physical labor. Their self-motivation—not to be confused with the compliance induced by overbearing lords and natural severities—earned them admiration and praise from the narrator. In terms of actual economics, Classical Athens did not function as a city of pure deficit consumption either. Owing to a set of truths embodied by *homo faber*, the Athenian *demokratia* cultivated a vibrant work environment in which numerous small-scale yeoman farmers and independent artisans, craftsmen, and workshop-owners thrived.[239] Such a large percentage of free citizenry—in the sense of not having masters either politically or economically—is arguably without any earlier precedent or modern parallel. Against this positive picture, slavery will be discussed under extractionism at the end of this chapter.

THE FARMER AS *HOMO FABER*

Let us begin with Homer, who commends the production of *homo faber* by introducing Odysseus' father Laertes literally amidst the fruit of his labor.

> The others went from the city, and presently
> came to the country place of Laertes, handsomely
> cultivated. Laertes himself had reclaimed it,
> after he spent much labor upon it. (24.205–07)

The poet used "handsomely" to describe Laertes' garden and stressed that the king "himself" brought it back to life. For Laertes, the effort put into the garden is also a defiant gesture against the evil suitors who are laying waste to his household and forcing him into exile. His son, Odysseus, who has been gone for many years and has yet to reveal himself to his father, praises the labors right away: "Old sir, there is in you no lack of expertness in tending/ your orchard; everything is well cared for, and there is never/ a plant, neither fig tree nor yet grapevine nor olive/ nor pear tree nor leek bed uncared for in your garden" (24.244–47). With this heartfelt praise, Odysseus declares Laertes to be royal, despite the latter's squalid clothing (24.250–53). In this scene, manual labor graces the elderly king with virtue and nobility.

Another positive portrayal of agricultural work can be found in the famous passage on the shield for Achilles in the *Iliad*.

> He [Hephaestus] made upon it a soft field, the pride of the tilled land,
> wide and triple-ploughed, with many ploughmen upon it
> who wheeled their teams at the turn and drove them in either direction.
> And as these making their turn would reach the end-strip of the field
> a man would come up to them at this point and hand them a flagon

---

[238] The complexity is duly noted in Lis and Soly, *Worthy Efforts*, 17.

[239] Davies, "Classical Greece: Production," 354; Bresson, *The Making of the Ancient Greek Economy*, 188.

> of honey-sweet wine, and they would turn again to the furrows
> in their haste to come again to the end-strip of the deep field.
> The earth darkened behind them and looked like earth that has
> been ploughed though it was gold. (18.541–49)

In this description, a harmonious and prosperous community basks in the joy of collaborative labor with intermittent periods of rest and play; this kind of "pleasant" toil turns the field into "gold." The language alludes to the possibility of a fully-fledged convivial relationship between human and nature. In this ideal existence, the physical environment would be regarded not as a set of brutalizing forces to be subdued and conquered, but as an assembly of kind entities to be honored and thanked. This poetic imagination proposes a model in which collective, joyful, and harmonious work pleases both mortals and the gods/nature.

The third example that features a favorable conception of labor performed by *homo faber* can be found in the exchange between Eurymachos and Odysseus in Book 18 of the *Odyssey*. Here, the most offensive of Penelope's suitors—ignorant that the king himself stands before him—accuses Odysseus of laziness and gluttony. To this intolerable affront, the wily and wise hero answers:

> Eurymachos, I wish there could be a working contest
> between us, in the spring season when the days are lengthening
> out in the meadow, with myself holding a well-curved sickle,
> and you one like it, so to test our endurance for labor,
> without food, from dawn till dark, with plenty of grass for our mowing.
> Or if it were oxen to be driven, those of the best sort,
> large ones and ruddy, both well fed with grass, of an equal
> age and carrying power, and their strength is not contemptible,
> and there were four acres to plough, with the glebe giving to the plowshare.
> There you would see if I could carve a continuous furrow. (*Od.* 18.366–75)

With these remarks, the king of Ithaca reveals a thorough knowledge of farming from firsthand experience. In this speech, the ability to work in the field—rather than inviting contempt or stigmatization as would be the case in more stratified and class-based societies—signifies instead strength and virtue.

The love for farming by the princes is matched by that for weaving by the princesses. Helen, Andromache, and Penelope, the queenly figures in the *Iliad* and *Odyssey*, accrue their feminine virtue through weaving, both with their own hands and by overseeing their handmaidens. Moreover, the goddesses Circe and Calypso are weaving and Arete spinning her own wool when we first encounter them in the *Odyssey* (10.226–27, 5.62, 6.52–53). In nearly all cases, high status women are entirely comfortable with manual work as well as its association.

Besides farming and weaving, aristocrats also carry out a variety of other jobs that contribute to autonomy and self-sufficiency. Odysseus, for instance, shows he is a capable ploughman, mason, roof-maker, woodsman, carpenter, cabinet-maker, and ivory-worker. He builds his own house and his famous bed—about the latter he proudly declares, "I myself, no other man, made [this]" (*Od.* 23.189). As a true *homo faber*, Odysseus builds a raft with the ease of a skilled carpenter (*Od.* 5.249–51) and a resting place out of leaves on his route home (*Od.* 5.482–84); most significantly, he devises the famous wooden horse that wins the Trojan war for the Greeks. His equally crafty wife continuously weaves and then unweaves the famous shroud to fool the suitors. Even in the idyllic, semi-utopian land of Scheria in the *Odyssey*, self-reliance is a normal part of quotidian life for the nobles. Queen Arete devotes the whole day to the spindle beside the hearth (6.52), her daughter Nausicaa drives the wagon and washes laundry (6.85–98), and her brothers unload the wagon (7.7). As positive moral examples, these heroic characters carry out physical tasks without warranting any special remark by the narrator.

In addition to Homer, Greek myths of early origins also testify to the ranks of working heroes. We find Anchises tending the flocks, Apollo being a shepherd, and other princes taking up animal husbandry. Furthermore, the famous Jason of the Argonauts is known for his passion for tilling the land: he was found ploughing in the fields when summoned by his evil uncle.[240] The intimacy with land and animals is indicative of the extent to which it was taken for granted for heroes to lead a productive life, just like ordinary people.

Besides direct descriptions, the Homeric narrator also employs a number of work-centered metaphors. Comparisons are made, for example, between falling corpses and trees felled by builders (*Il.* 16.482–84), the war over Patroclus' corpses and the tanning process (*Il.* 17.389–93), and festival dancing and a potter's wheel (*Il.* 18.599–601). These usages suggest that the Homeric audience—many assumed to be of princely background—was familiar with manual jobs. Through this array of depictions, motifs, and analogies, epic and myth furbish a conception of the hero who is also an outstanding *homo faber.*

Self-directed Labor in Homer

Central to *homo faber* is the control of one's own livelihood, which translates into not working under another.[241] To enjoy true independence, one must avoid the interference of an overseer, whether this occurs in slavery (chattel, serfdom, or helotage), debt-bondage, or wage employment.[242] For the ancient Greeks, all those aforementioned forms belong to the same continuum of "unfree labor" or "unequal labor,"[243] which cannot be reconciled with the notion of a freeman who is masterless

[240] Hard, *The Routledge Handbook of Greek Mythology*, 381.
[241] For more discussion of this notion in ancient Greece, see Edward Cohen, "An Unprofitable Masculinity," in *Money, Labour, and Land*, ed. Paul Cartledge, Edward E. Cohen, and Lin Foxhall (London: Routledge, 2002), 101. I repeat the point because it is crucial for the overall argument.
[242] There is debate on whether a laborer (*thes*) actually receives wages (*misthos*) or only maintenance in Homer. The passage in *Od.* 18.357–61 seems to suggest payment in the form of grain, clothes, and shoes. In any case, the difference would not change our definition of a *thes* as someone who works for the benefit of another.
[243] Dimitris J. Kyrtatas, "Domination and Exploitation," 143–44. Kyrtatas confirmed that the subdistinctions are only important to modern scholars.

and servant to none.[244] Finley rightly reminded us that "Greek writers regularly used *doulos* (a slave) and *douleuó* (being a slave) for any form of economic subjection, whether strictly that of a chattel slave or not."[245] Among the orators and philosophers of later times, Aristotle defined freedom as not living under the command of another (*Rhetoric* 1367a32). To his contemporary Isocrates, hired employment was indeed a hallmark of servitude (14.48). Based on these remarks, slavery to the Greeks is any compromise of complete economic freedom in its fullest form—regardless of the form or extent.

Many Greek sources evince repulsion and disgust toward laboring for another. The epics, for instance, which served as a benchmark for cultural values and mores, contain narratives brimming with feelings of humiliation and degradation for unfree labor. In the *Odyssey*, Achilles says that he would rather be working on earth as a *thes*, a hired laborer, than be king over all the dead in the underworld (*Od.* 11.488–91). The juxtaposition pits the pitiful hireling who lacks his own means of livelihood against miserable death, with the latter being only slightly better off. When the god Hercules describes his experience of performing prescribed labor in atonement for a crime, horror and repugnance overtakes him. As Hercules recalls, "I had an endless/ spell of misery. I was made bondman to one who was far worse/ than I, and he loaded many difficult labors on me" (*Od.* 11.621–22). To both heroes, working under someone else is insufferable. Their grievances, as Finley pointed out, concerned not the type of work *per se*, but the conditions or status under which it was carried out.[246]

Based on Hercules' lament, we can extrapolate two reasons why unfree/unequal labor was objectionable. First, social disparity, such as the one between Hercules and his master, diminished the interest and well-being of the weaker party. In the case of Hercules, his master indeed treats him brutally, showing not the slightest regard for the hero who toils. The outburst of abuse and sadism in unbalanced relationships repeats in the story of Poseidon and Apollo; the two gods who offended Zeus were made "servants" to the proud mortal Laomedon as a punishment. After performing hard labor, their heartless employer refuses them the promised remuneration and even threatens them with bodily harm (*Il.* 21.441–55). Such breaches of basic decency and fairness in the form of reneging on wages and resorting to violence could very well reflect real, common employment conditions for the disempowered.[247] As Glotz intimated, in an unequal relationship forged by material interest, "the contract that binds [the workers] does not bind their employer. For there is no right against might."[248] This insight, captured vividly in the tales, affirms the truth that no one

[244] The chorus in Aeschylus' *The Persians* tells the king's mother what being an Athenian citizen is like in those terms (241–43).

[245] Finley, *Economy and Society in Ancient Greece*, 156. Scholars dispute the precise meanings of *thetes*, *pelates*, and *hektemor* and their differences with slaves, the Lakedaimonian *helots*, and the Thessalian *penestai*, but Finley's overall point is still valid.

[246] This point has been well established. See Finley, *Economy and Society in Ancient Greece*, 99; Edward Cohen, *Athenian Prostitution: The Business of Sex* (New York: Oxford University Press, 2015), 43.

[247] In a parallel to the modern world, Robert Dahl questioned the conferral of dictatorial rights to private ownership over the fate of employees. See Erik Olin Wright, *Envisioning Real Utopias* (London: Verso, 2010), 51n15.

[248] Glotz, *Ancient Greece at Work*, 33.

should willingly surrender his or her independence and choose to work at someone else's discretion; doing so could be a result of coercion. This is the reason why, when Eurymachos offers to "hire" Odysseus, Homer expects his audience to feel outraged (*Od.* 18.357–64). With this culturally ingrained sensitivity to the rubrics of power, it is not surprising that the Greeks saw master-slave polarity in the relationship between employers and wage-earners.[249]

The second problem of unequal labor exchange is that the overseer may not deserve or have earned his authority properly. Indeed, in addition to enduring exploitation and oppression, Hercules complains he must also obey someone inferior: his master Eurystheus is not only a mere mortal, but a malicious and cowardly one.[250] Similarly, Apollo and Poseidon must also obey the aforementioned Laomedon, who wantonly orders them "what to do, and how to do it" (*Il.* 23.445). The command exercised by the employer or master in these two parables does not rest on any proof of excellence, benevolence, or popularity that are critical for good leadership. By placing evil mortals in charge of divine immortals, these narratives highlight the outrage of a perverse hierarchy. Objecting to unequal conditions and false authority, the cultural aversion to any form of economic subordination, including wage employment, speaks volumes about the core values of Olympianism.

Compulsion: The Source of Shame

The fervent pursuit of autonomy and independence leads to heightened awareness of deprivation, poverty, and fear—the best accomplices for creating an involuntary and vulnerable work force. Odysseus openly decries the shameful urges brought about by the belly, a fitting metaphor for the overwhelming power of biological distress (*Od.* 17.286–89). In a later period, a speaker named Euxitheus told his Athenian audience: "Poverty forces the free to do many slavish and base things" (Demosthenes, *Against Eubulides* 45). It is not just material scarcity alone that aids economic subjugation, but also physical intimidation. The *Odyssey* relates the suffering of the singer Phemius, who is being forced to perform for the suitors. The narrator says that they "made him" (1.154) and that "he had been singing among the suitors/ under compulsion" (22.331–32). Although here the text does not go into more detail, it nevertheless unequivocally condemns the use of force. In this passage, the performance of unwilling labor, either through direct coercion or out of economic necessity, is treated as disturbing and unsettling. By contrast, the desire for work to be volitional, meaningful, and enjoyable is essential for realizing the *homo faber* ideal. Overall, in the scheme of the Olympian political economy, inequitable distribution of resources leads to coerced labor, which in turn constrains identity formation as well as producing disparity and degradation. These culturally inflected truths put pressure on society to minimize compulsion and domination, and to maximize access, abundance, and security. Only under the latter material conditions are individuals free to cultivate public deeds and speeches that a healthy democracy feeds on.

---

[249] Kyrtatas, "Domination and Exploitation," 145.

[250] Hard, *The Routledge Handbook of Greek Mythology*, 245.

The Proud Self-standing Hesiod

Hesiod, the rare literary figure of a farmer and shepherd in the ensemble of elite personas, embodies the essence of *homo faber*. On the one hand, Hesiod bitterly complains of the endless toil (*kamatos*) he undergoes, because men in his day no longer reap generous bounty from the earth, as did the previous generations in the Golden Age. Yet, on the other hand, Hesiod bravely struggles against fate by being in charge of his own destiny: he essays to outdo his neighbors in a fair contest of honest work that endears man to the gods (*WD* 303–13). Here, it is not the whip of an overlord but the desire to better his own lot that pushes him to surmount difficulties and to apply himself diligently. In this *homo faber* narrative, dignity and pride, rather than coercion or avarice, motivate labor. Likewise, Herodotus says that when Athenians were oppressed by (political) masters, they were cowards, but when they were freed, they were eager to pursue their own goals (5.78). Although Herodotus discusses this in the context of war, we could easily apply it to economic behavior as well—the enthusiasm of working for oneself is never the same as for someone else. With *kleros* and the commons dispersing and protecting the instruments of production along egalitarian principles (see last chapter), figures such as Hesiod could discover meaning and satisfaction in their daily labor, even when facing difficulties.

The Skilled Worker as *Homo Faber*

In this section, we consider further how those who were no longer living off the land, i.e., working in non-agricultural professions, could achieve security and status on par with their farming peers. Both in the epic world as well as in the later more urbanized and specialized economy at Athens, a set of culturally informed notions that emphasized access to means of production, artistry and creativity, direct and horizontal modes of exchange, and apposite levels of technology and scale made it possible for *homo faber* to succeed.

Access to the Means of Production

Even though farming and pasturing were the mainstay in the Homeric economy, enough surplus was produced to also support specialized workers (*dēmiourgoi*). Four types of them are identified in the *Odyssey*: soothsayers, doctors, singers, and *tektónes*. The last category, often translated as "carpenters," includes all those who work with wood, metal, leather, or clay. Without specifying the rules of ownership directly, the epics give the impression that the necessary tools were always in the personal possession of the craftsman. When describing the smith-god Hephaestus, for example, Homer tells us that "he set the bellows away from the fire, and/ gathered and put away/ all the tools with which he worked in a silver/ strongbox" (*Il.* 18.412–13). A parallel passage also shows mortals possessing the means of production: "The smith came, holding/ in his hands the tools for forging bronze, his handicraft's symbols,/ the anvil and the sledgehammer and the well-wrought pincers/ with which he used to work the gold" (*Od.* 3.433–35). Moreover, singers, healers, and seers could carry out their work with few or no additional tools. They performed the services of art, medicine, and divination by employing their intrinsic physical and intellectual faculties. With wieldy tools and techniques that augment human puissance, Homer's professionals could practice their art with freedom and mastery.

Beholden to no one else for equipment or technology, the *homo faber* figure of the Homeric epics oversees both the conception and execution of his labor. The mythic figure of Daidalos, the legendary craftsman in Greek mythology, represents this ideal. Daidalos was taught by his father Metion and his grandfather Eupalamos, whose names respectively mean "forethought" and "skillful-handed." This personification underlines the import of both mind and body in work. Daidalos, for example, invents a wooden bull to satisfy queen Pasiphae's desire for Poseidon's bull. It is also he who builds the bovial apparatus and the labyrinth himself.[251] In the *Iliad*, Hephaestus both designs and forges the famous shield for Achilles (*Il.* 18.463–617). Exhibiting great control, the craftsmen and artists in Homer conceive and execute their own work to realize their ideas and visions.

It is not by chance that the same word, *techne*, is used for both art and craft in the ancient Greek language, underscoring the fundamental overlap of these two domains. As Zimmern remarked, "All men who knew the joy of creation, whether with hand or brain, were ranked as poets or artificers."[252] In the passage that details the forging of Achilles' shield, we witness the artist-workman Hephaestus carrying out his craft as a part of a highly creative endeavor. Homer carefully described the elaborate decorations wrought by the god on the shield, which convey not only the natural order of the cosmos, but also the cultural ideals of society. To this Hephaestus, the divine creator of splendid objects, Homer assigned a number of positive adjectives: renowned/glorious/famous (*Od.* 8.286, 287, 8.345, 8.349, 8.357, 24.75); inventive/subtle (*Od.* 8.297; *Il.* 1.607, 18.393, 18.462, 18.590, 18.613); knowledgeable (*Il.* 21.355); and glorious (*Il.* 21.379). Through these descriptions, the production of material goods approximates the making of fine art, and the producer, far from being an anonymous purveyor of labor to be incentivized or exploited, exhibits the greatness of someone who is special and extraordinary.

In addition, the craftsman approaches the epic hero in obtaining undying fame (*kleos*) through doing excellent and meaningful work. In the aforementioned example with Helen, weaving is the means through which she achieves a female version of *kleos*. By weaving her unique experience of the Trojan War into a piece of cloth, Helen ensures that her own story will not be forgotten. In the same vein, the epics preserve the names of the following individual craftsmen: Epeios, the constructor of machines; Phereclos, the boat-builder in Troy; Icmalios, the cabinet-maker in Ithaca; Laerces, the goldsmith at Pylos; Tychios, maker of shields at Hyle; and Polybus, maker of balls at Scheria.[253] The listing of names in Homer corresponds to the fact that ancient Greek craftsmen and artists left behind their signatures on pots as well as epigraphic dedications. One of the inscriptions from a Chiot sculptor in the sixth century BCE reads: "Far-shooting Apollo, receive this beautiful statue, one of the

[251] Hard, *The Routledge Handbook of Greek Mythology*, 336.
[252] Zimmern, *The Greek Commonwealth*, 260.
[253] Glotz, *Ancient Greece at Work*, 28.

works accomplished by Archermos in his wisdom." Another one from a painter in Cyrene in the second century CE states: "In case you, wayfarer, know by hearsay of Loukios Euthykles the figure painter—I who made the palace at Cyrene glorious among the nations for my surpassing *techne*—I who brought forth as a great benefice to my paternal city the likenesses of the divinities—here at that place where I figured prominently among the members of the Council do I lie."[254] In both texts, the artists eloquently professed to the audience the pride for their creation. Moreover, the second dedication pairs technical excellence with political achievement, underlining the affinity of the two in a culture that prized the fashioning of identity through both creative work and political action. By assimilating the productive work of *homo faber* to the immortal deeds of the hero, the truth that man establishes his unique personhood and wins glory from others even in material dealings becomes tenable in Olympian culture.

In Service of the Public

The discourse of *homo faber* applies not only to the making of material products but also the creation of cultural goods: both endeavors transform the environment into an artificial world that is full of meaning for humans. In Olympianism, mortals receive creative inspiration and artistic talent from the gods. This truth obliges artists and creative workers to use their god-sent gifts for the good of society. For example, the singer Demodokos is "prized among the people," a description that highlights his role in the community (*Od.* 8.472). Elsewhere, when the singer Phemius pleads for his life with the vengeful Odysseus, he plays up his public function: "I sing to the gods and to human people, and I am/ taught by myself, but the god has inspired in me the song-ways/ of every kind" (22.347–48). In moments when artists speak truth to power without constraint or censorship, they bring honor to the gods. By contrast, men commit hubris when they seek to appropriate art for their own corrupt agenda. In the *Odyssey* (3.265–71), we are told that the villainous Aegisthus took a bard to a deserted island and left him there to be the prey and spoil of birds, presumably because the bard failed to comply in some way. Likewise, the suitors defile Phemius' role as the voice of the community by forcing him to sing against his will. In both instances, Aegisthus and the suitors commit hubris and meet a terrible end. We are reminded by Homer that "[f]or with all peoples upon the earth singers are entitled/ to be cherished and to their share of respect, since the Muse has taught them/ her own way, and since she loves all the company of singers" (*Od.* 8.471–73). In this web of truths, artists as cultural producers achieve semidivine stature as integral members of the polity; they create art for reasons of divine inspiration or social solidarity, rather than political expediency or economic profitability.

---

[254] Burford, *Craftsmen in Greek and Roman Society* (Ithaca, NY: Cornell University Press, 1972), 208.

Horizontal and Equal Exchange

In the Olympian dispensation, direct, peer-to-peer, horizontal, and personalized mode of interaction is preferred because it favors consensual agreement and mutual satisfaction. When exchange occurs in this framework, the fulfillment of needs and wants typically comes before the pursuit of advantage. Deducing in part from the etymology of *dēmiourgos* (public worker), George Thomson speculated that at least in the early pre-*polis* period, craftsmen worked for the community and were paid in kind.[255] At that time, most households would have simply summoned the craftsman directly to their place of residence.[256] In the *Odyssey*, for example, Nestor tells his sons, "[A]nd yet another go tell the worker in gold Laerkes/ to come, so that he can cover the cow's horns with gold" (3.425–26). The one exception is the blacksmith, whose forge was not easily transportable; yet it was an open place where a peasant would be able to go, beggars could stay warm at night, and neighbors could exchange gossip (*WD* 493). An example of such intimate "transaction" occurs in the aforementioned scene of Achilles' shield. The hero's mother Thetis comes to Hephaestus and relates to him the tragic events that have befallen her son.

> Therefore now I come to your knees; so might you be willing
> to give me for my short-lived son a shield and a helmet
> and two beautiful greaves fitted with clasps for the ankles
> and a corselet. What he had was lost with his steadfast companion
> when the Trojans killed him. Now my son lies on the ground, heart
> sorrowing. (*Il.* 18.457–60)

To this sorrowful plea, Hephaestus replies,

> Do not fear. Let not these things be a thought in your mind.
> And I wish that I could hide him away from death and its sorrow
> at the time when his hard fate comes upon him, as surely
> as there shall be fine armor for him, such as another
> man out of many men shall wonder at, when he looks on it. (*Il.* 18.463–67)

Teeming with pathos, this dialogue exemplifies the solidarity and goodwill in a peer-to-peer, horizontal, voluntary interchange, the kind that fosters empathy and trust. The texts indeed present both parties as authentic and sincere, and capable of negotiating their interests without resorting to anonymous market pricing mechanisms or needing bureaucratic supervision.

The subsequent creation of the shield owes itself to the extra-economic factors: the marvelous object was born not out of Hephaestus' acquisitive desire for gain nor fear of destitution, but his genuine wish to succor the goddess who has rescued him in the past (*Il.* 5 394–405). In this memorable illustration, the one who wishes to give

[255] George Derwent Thomson, *Studies in Ancient Greek Society* (London: Lawrence & Wishart, 1954), 355.
[256] Glotz, *Ancient Greece at Work*, 42.

and the one who desires to receive achieve mutual satisfaction through thoughtful communication and dialogue. Their voluntary and trustful association nullifies the need for immediate prestation and demonstrates the superiority of convivial exchange.

To conclude this section, we have examined the paradigm of *homo faber* in the Olympian model. To fulfill this role as the creative maker, man must possess the necessary resources and instruments, wield control over production and conception, and experience joy and pride in the process of modifying the world according to his own ideas. At the same time, the Olympian *homo faber* associates and interacts freely with the community to forge consensual and mutually beneficial relationships reposed in trust and solidarity. In this tradition, man becomes *homo significans*, a being that articulates social and cultural understanding via material activities.[257]

CRAFTSMEN IN CLASSICAL ATHENS

After rendering the discourse of Olympianism in poetic sources, we now turn to its manifestation in the economic life of Classical Athens. There is evidence indicating that Olympianism, Polisim, or the market all indeed operated on the ground during the fifth and fourth centuries. Although in much retreat by this time, the Olympian tradition continued to elevate craftsmen in Athenian society. More than anything else, at the apogee of Athenian democracy, those who earned a living from physical labor were acquainted with Olympianism. For example, the religious offerings of a potter's stele on the Athenian acropolis as well as a statue made by Antenor from the potter Nearchos have survived. A potter named Aischines offered "one-tenth of his works" to the goddess Athena, and others like Andokides and Mnesiades made similar dedications.[258] Additional inscriptions dedicated to Athena, including ones from miners, have also been found.[259] At the Hephaisteion, a temple located in the "Potters Quarter" of the city, workers regularly paid homage to Hephaestus and Athena the Ergane ("Workeress"),[260] and both deities were celebrated at the annual festival of Chalkeia (the festival of bronze-workers).[261] From 540 onward, paintings on Attic vases also depict gods as working craftsmen—an iconography that highlights both the growing social prestige of artisans and the centrality of artisanal production.[262] Sometime before 428 BCE, the association of shipmasters (*naukleroi*) at Piraeus left an inscription recording the funds for the upkeep a temple (c. 418–17 BCE).[263] These

[257] In this light, Mossé was wrong to maintain that "there is really no difference between the artisan who sells his own products and the workman who hires out his services. Both work to satisfy the needs of others, not their own." See Mossé, *Ancient World at Work*, 28. Under the right social and economic conditions, the artisan can "sell" to the community without being dominated by a single individual, whereas the worker who takes orders from the boss becomes subordinate.

[258] Burford, *Craftsmen in Greek and Roman Society*, 170.

[259] Davies, "Classical Greece: Production," 338. IG II^2 2940; 4598; 4633.

[260] Mikalson, *Ancient Greek Religion*, 155.

[261] Ibid.

[262] Juliusz Ziomecki, *Les représentations d'artisans sur les vases attiques* [The Representations of Artists on Ancient Vases] (Wroclaw: Zaklad Narodowy im. Ossolinskich, 1975), 135–46, cited in Josef Ehmer and Catharina Lis, *The Idea of Work in Europe from Antiquity to Modern Times* (Farnham: Ashgate Publishing Limited, 2009), 52.

[263] H. Michell, *The Economics of Ancient Greece*, 2nd ed. (New York: Barnes and Noble, 1957), 141.

cases suggest that owing to the continued strength of Greek religion, the Athenian laboring class was privy to the cultural narratives of Olympianism even in the Classical period.

In the milieu of Olympianism, citizen workers and sole proprietors of Athenian democracy gained easy access to the means of production, thanks to the fact that most jobs did not require large capital or elaborate equipment.[264] Anvil, hammer, tongs, and a furnace, simple objects used by the smith in Homer, still functioned sufficiently in the Classical period.[265] Pictorial illustrations show that in the shoemakers' shops, the lasts and implements, pincers, awls, and a knife typically hung on the wall.[266] In addition, it was customary for clients to provide raw material, reducing upfront costs and increasing work flexibility.[267] Sculptors often carried portable tools and raw materials for the convenience of executing their craft wherever they travelled.[268] These manifestations point to the emphasis on people in the design of the production process: by privileging wieldy, compliant tools that conform to human skills and capacity, the control and aptitude of workers are being amplified, not the might of machines, technology, or capital (or computer algorithm and robotic automation in our time).

With the valorization of independence and mastery, it is no coincidence that Classical Athens accommodated small businesses in terms of cost. One scholar, for instance, concluded that with the exceptions of bakeries, smithies, and fulling plants, nearly all other workshops were easy to set up. Even the pottery kilns, which were relatively expensive to build, were still within the reach of moderate means. As a result, anyone could start a pottery at home with unit costs comparable to those of a staffed workshop.[269] Since what counted was the workers, rather than infrastructure, a backroom or courtyard of the craftsman's home sufficed for most jobs.[270] When a workshop had to move, the owner only needed to bring his workmen along.[271] Thanks to this combination of low technology and capital,[272] and flexible entry and exit,[273] even the large enterprises using slaves did not enjoy decisive advantages *vis-à-vis* the small units. In these ways, an enterprise was fully operable and viable for the average Athenian, who was bulwarked against the competition from big capital. This unique economic environment, which exalted the truths about *homo faber*, protected independent production and empowered small independent businesses.

---

[264] Glotz, *Ancient Greece at Work*, 268; Zimmern, *The Greek Commonwealth*, 266; Bresson, *The Making of the Ancient Greek Economy*, 189.

[265] Acton, *Poiesis*, 127.

[266] Michell, *Economics of Ancient Greece*, 172.

[267] Glotz, *Ancient Greece at Work*, 42, 270–71; Zimmern, *The Greek Commonwealth*, 266.

[268] Philostratos, Life of Apollonius of Tyana 5.20.

[269] Acton, *Poiesis*, 99.

[270] Helmuth Schneider, "Technology," in *The Cambridge Economic History of the Greco-Roman World*, edited by Ian Morris, Walter Scheidel, and Richard P. Saller (Cambridge: Cambridge University Press, 2007), 169.

[271] Burford, *Craftsmen in Greek and Roman Society*, 78.

[272] From this view, the belief that the technology of the Greeks was "primitive" is reductive. The Greeks did not develop elaborate technology for massive production because such technology would diminish the power of the workers.

[273] This is the general point in the latest work of Acton (2014). See Action, *Poiesis*, 40, passim.

We can assume that those who labored for themselves had every incentive to make conditions pleasant to the extent possible. In Homer, singing is common when women are in the midst of weaving, washing, or other female tasks.[274] We also know instances in which music was played when several men worked together or performed monotonous tasks in the workshops.[275] Boeotian terracotta figures from the sixth century depict several women kneading bread while another plays the flute.[276] Additionally, over sixty religious holidays punctuated the Athenian calendar, setting aside days when everyone in the community paused labor for communal celebration.[277] Even in the highly urbanized manufacturing city, the pace of a small workshop was still leisurely enough to permit extensive civic interaction; Socrates allegedly conversed with a shoemaker named Simon in his shop at the market.[278] The cynic philosopher Diogenes named thirty-three Socratic dialogues as "leather cutters' talk,"[279] suggesting the regularity of those occurrences. Lysias' speech *Against Pancleon* features a barbershop near the agora where Athenians from the *deme* of Dekeleia (a municipal unit in Athens) regularly gathered (*Lysias* 23.2–3). These integrative and fraternizing encounters were by no means accidental, but a result of the constant confluence of diverse occupations in quotidian life.[280] True to the *homo faber* model, the citizen-producer, cherished by the gods and the democratic city, led a work life replete with convivial engagement. Zimmern went as far as to say that for the Greeks what was menial was not doing work with hands, but carrying out monotonous activity without joy.[281]

The Division of Labor in Classical Athens

Given the ideals formulated by the *homo faber* discourse, we should consider how the quality of working life withstood the pressure placed on the division, relegation, and organization of tasks. In the Archaic period, the division of labor was modest because the craftsman or the artist would dabble in a variety of pertinent undertakings to broaden skills. For example, Theodorus of Samos was a famous maker of jewelry and the inventor of statue-casting (Herodotus 1.51, 3.41; Pausanias 8.14.5.s.8). Rhoecus, who pioneered the art of casting statues together with Theodorus (Pausanias

---

274 Andromache Karanika, *Voices at Work: Women, Performance, and Labor in Ancient Greece* (Baltimore, MD: John Hopkins University Press, 2014), 2.

275 Glotz, *Ancient Greece at Work*, 279.

276 *Female workers making bread and a flute player sets the work pace*, boeotian terracotta figurine, 525–475 BC, from Thebes. Louvre Museum (Photo: Marie-Lan Nguyen. Wikimedia Commons). It is also possible to see music being used to regiment the pace of production, although we shall never really know. For this possibility, see Victor Ehrenberg, *The People of Aristophanes, A Sociology of Old Attic Comedy* (Oxford: B. Blackwell, 1951). However, if this were the case, it is much more likely to happen with slaves, embodying a profit-driven pursuit defined by highly unequal relations that contradict the core of Olympianism. For a full discussion, see the following section at the end of this chapter.

277 Glotz, *Ancient Greece at Work*, 283; Michell, *The Economics of Ancient Greece*, 131.

278 Zimmern, *The Greek Commonwealth*, 271.

279 Action, *Poiesis*, 167.

280 Robert Sobak, "Sokrates among the Shoemakers," *Hesperia: The Journal of the American School of Classical Studies at Athens* 84, no. 4 (2015): 669–712.

281 Zimmern, *The Greek Commonwealth*, 272.

8.14.5.s.8), was also an architect and ship builder (Herodotus 3.60). In the fifth century, Pythagoras of Samos and Micon of Athens excelled in both painting and sculpture (Pliny, *Natural History* 34.59, 33.13.s.56, 35.6.s.25; Pausanias 6.6.1)—two forms of art that complemented one another. On the basis of signatures, scholars have attributed works of both pottery and painting to Euphronios, an important figure in the transition of artistic style from the late Archaic to early Classical period.[282] In these examples, the possession of a wide set of skills and the lack of strict specialization helped the craftsman to become more versatile and well rounded.

Urbanization and population growth in the Classical period has prompted scholars to deduce more specialization and division of labor in the historical fifth and fourth centuries.[283] With the confirmation of roughly 170 occupations at Athens, Edward Harris believed that increased division of labor was undeniable.[284] But even so, Harris was careful to stress its "horizontal" quality.[285] By this, Harris referred to the kind of specialization that allowed workers to master a single product or a line of production, in contrast to vertical integration, which forces workers into simplified, low-skill jobs.[286] Despite high output and technical innovation, the pottery industry at Athens, with the richest surviving material evidence, fits Harris' observation. A recent study on the pottery industry confirmed a shift in the division of labor, but it did not diminish the centrality of worker skills. According to the findings, potter-painters, ones who made pots as well as painted them, were first common in the early sixth century.[287] For example, the well-known master Execias left signatures indicating that he was responsible for both making and decorating the vases, and Nicosthenes almost certainly painted over 80 percent of the vases he produced as well.[288] They both oversaw the two most important stages of production. In their days, the majority of pottery workshops, although small in size, completed most of the steps in-house rather than outsourcing them.[289] The shift to red-figure technique around the 520s called for more skillful independent painters, such as the itinerant Psiax, who travelled from workshop to workshop to grace vases with exquisite drawing.[290] In this case, technological progress guided by the *homo faber* model did not necessitate the

[282] Dietrich von Bothmer, "The Subject Matter of Euphronios," in *Euphronios, Peintre: Actes De La Journée D'étude Organisée Par L'Ecole Du Louvre Et Le Département Des Antiquités Grecques, Étrusques Et Romaines Du Musée Du Louvre, 10 Octobre 1990* [Euphronios Painter: Proceedings of the Workshop Organized by L'Ecole Du Louvre and the Department of Greek and Etruscan and Roman Antiquities], ed. Euphronios and Martine Denoyelle (Paris: Documentation française, 1992), 13.

[283] However, Burford was skeptical of this view. She argued that the paucity of references to specialized jobs in earlier sources does not necessarily mean their absence or insignificance, but this opinion is the minority view. See Burford, *Craftsmen in Greek and Roman Society*, 98–99. To Burford, writers of the Classical era like Hesiod, Homer, Thucydides, and Aristophanes simply referenced economic and industrial conditions less than later authors did. In addition, she believed that some of the high-sounding technical terms and professional titles could have been invented for the conceit of the worker.

[284] Harris, "Workshop, Marketplace and Household," 68–69.

[285] Ibid., 70.

[286] Ibid.

[287] Philip Sapirstein, "Demographics and Productivity in the Ancient Athenian Pottery Industry," in *Athenian Potters and Painters III*, ed. John Oakley (Oxford and Philadelphia: Oxbow Books, 2014), 181.

[288] Ibid.

[289] Acton, *Poiesis*, 75.

[290] Ibid.

introduction of monotonous and rudimentary chores that made workers dispensable, as in the Industrial Revolution. On the contrary, it afforded them more artistic creativity, individual expression and leverage power. The display of both broad and niche skills in the interest of the worker is also evident in the records for public building projects. Although the account on the construction of the Erechtheum at Athens lists clearly defined titles—mason, sculptor, wax modeler, carpenter, and painter—the divisions break down upon close examination. For instance, there are records of a wax modeler working as a sculptor, another modeler working as a woodcarver, and stonemasons working as laborers.[291] Similarly, in the building of the Delian sanctuary during the third century, we discover instances of woodworkers carrying out other tasks, such as brick construction and stone masonry.[292] This flexible division of labor, whether along generalist or specialized lines, does not deviate from the central goal of augmenting the talent, knowledge, and power of *homo faber*. Overall, even intensified division of labor, when assuming a horizontal quality, accommodated technological progress and economic demands without sacrificing the worker.

The cultural emphasis on, first, self-reliance and household autonomy,[293] and, second, quality and artistry, also contributed to the well-roundedness and versatility of the craftsman. Because the Greeks strove to be capable and effective amateurs in a range of basic tasks, specialists competed on the basis of artistry and creativity, not low prices and mass production. The textile industry, for example, developed to supplement, but not to replace, domestic weaving and spinning.[294] Well-crafted weights discovered at Olynthus suggest that textile manufacturers there produced refined and luxury items for export.[295] This type of high-value market rewarded the independent *homo faber* for creating quality products, rather than the large enterprise owner for exploiting deskilled laborers.

In addition to investigating actual practice, it is useful to examine the ancient theory on the division of labor, and how it might offer contrast to the modern version from Adam Smith. A passage from Xenophon, which comments on the superior quality of different dishes prepared in the kitchen of the Persian king Cyrus (*Cyropadia* 8.2.5), has often been adduced as proof for the appreciation of divisions of labor in antiquity.[296] However, let us not forget that Xenophon is describing the affairs in the Persian royal court, where subjugated servants and slaves sweat away for the pleasure of the king. Similarly, the division of labor in Plato's *Republic*, also cited by some scholars as proof for the omnipresence of market principles,[297] takes place in an imaginary state that forces lower-class citizens to toil for the philosopher kings. In

[291] Burford, *Craftsmen in Greek and Roman Society*, 100.
[292] Ibid., 99–100.
[293] Walcot, *Greek Peasants*, 32–33. Walcot provides a number of examples in the epics where lay people fill in the role of specialists when necessary.
[294] Bresson, *The Making of the Ancient Greek Economy*, 191; Glotz, *Ancient Greece at Work*, 264–66.
[295] Acton, *Poiesis*, 156–57.
[296] So far, no convincing argument has been made against Finley's opinion that Xenophon is concerned with the excellence of quality, not the increase in productivity. See M. I. Finley, "Aristotle and Economic Analysis," *Past and Present*, no. 47 (1970): 4.
[297] Bresson, *The Making of the Ancient Greek Economy*, 108.

both scenarios, the social contexts for specialization come at the sacrifice of primary producers—much like in the days of the Industrial Revolution—and assault the Olympian truths of equality and autonomy, the pillars of democratic politics.[298] Consequently, these passages are problematic as evidence that ancient Greeks endorsed the type of division of labor touted by modern economists as the marvelous engine of growth.

This love for excellent workmanship, which was closely linked to the dignity and mastery of the worker and a free citizenry, permeated all facets of the economy and impressed many a modern commentator. Jean-Pierre Vernant, for example, concluded that even grueling tasks at the gold mines undertaken by slaves were assigned according to strength and skills.[299] Adding to this assessment, Finley compared the aesthetic quality of the work in the Athenian mines with that of the famous temples and public buildings.[300] Similarly, the scholar Mossé maintained that the techniques of metallurgy and stonework employed by the Greek laborers were closer to those of an artist. Indeed, when examining the commonest object from ancient Greece, we encounter the truth about the overwhelming moral and economic advantages of an outstanding working force that enjoys creativity, artistry, and mastery.

For gruesome but necessary work, the Greek solution was to distribute labor equitably so as to eliminate an underclass within the citizen body that would "specialize" in undesirable jobs (see the end of this chapter for slavery). Several times, Greek cities proscribed the entire populace for urgent public projects by appealing to their civic spirit. This was how whole populations, including women and children, built walls at Athens in 479 BCE and at Argos in 417 BCE (Thucydides 1.90, 5.82.6), and a causeway at Chalcis (Diodorus Siculus 13.47). Burford also speculated that nonfinancial reasons motivated those to build the Parthenon, the chief monument of Athenian democracy. She intimated that for many casual workers, patriotism, piety, or simply the desire to be part of something extraordinary was the driving factor, while the pay was merely an extra.[301] These examples highlight that noble values can incentivize *homo faber*; at the same time, they also help reject lowly, degrading jobs that contribute to social inequality and economic stratification.

The Agora and Democratic Culture

The agora—the center of all public life, especially before the assembly was moved to the Pnyx—provided open access to all. This erstwhile communal meeting place later became also a public market without ever shedding its character as a site of the commons.[302] Zeus Agoraios was the guardian of justice in agoras throughout ancient

[298] We can see from these examples that division of labor is not simply a technical term, but a discourse with hidden power relations. It is imperative that we become aware of the implications, for it boosts the free market system that affects society at this very moment.

[299] Arendt, *The Human Condition*, 47n38.

[300] Finley, *Economy and Society in Ancient Greece*, 177–78.

[301] See Burford, "The Builders of the Parthenon," in *Greece & Rome, Second Series* 10 (Supplement: Parthenos and Parthenon, 1963), 34.

[302] Mikalson, *Ancient Greek Religion*, 155. Schaps stressed that in earlier times (i.e., Homer), the agora functioned as a place for gathering and assembly, thus the verb ἀγορεύω, and only later did the commercial

Greece. Under the aegis of the deity, officials appointed by the city prevented fraud, standardized weights and measures, and carried out quality control to ensure fair dealings.[303] Since Greeks did not think much of those who bought low and sold high at the expense of both producers and customers, retailers were subject to taxes and price regulations to curb profiteering in the agora.[304] By minimizing economic intermediaries, this public space fostered horizontal, consensual, and balanced exchange in proper convivial style. For a modest entrance fee to offset the cost of maintenance,[305] small consumers, vendors, and traders all benefitted from access to this essential infrastructure, which was administrated in a fair, transparent, and unbureaucratic fashion.

Not only could producers/laborers and customers/patrons engage directly at the agora, thus making it easy to bypass middlemen,[306] but shops and workshops always remained open to visitors and idlers.[307] As mentioned above, Socrates spent much time dallying in such venues, conversing with his fellow citizens in trade and crafts. A client of Lysias remarked that "each of you makes a habit of hanging around a certain place—one goes to the perfume shop, another to the barbers, and yet another to the cobbler's" (*Lysias* 24.20). From this evidence, we can picture the liveliness of the small Athenian shop due to the constant visitation of curious and friendly bystanders who provide welcome "distractions."[308] The free intermingling of autonomous, independent economic actors as beloved peers no doubt created extensive horizontal and congenial ties, which in turn enhanced a civil society that fortified the world's first democracy.[309]

But these civic and convivial functions of the agora had to contend with the growing market mentality that put profit before civic *philia* (friendship among citizens). On the one hand, the tradition of the agora as a site of direct, horizontal interaction persevered; on the other hand, evidence from the fourth century onward portrays the marketplace as a locus of deceit and ruin.[310] Market transactions shift the attention toward pricing and calculation, and away from reputation acquired within the traditional network of reciprocity and kinship. As a result, the attempt to maximize profit—even via dishonest means as long as there was no law against it—made sense.[311] If these truths shaped the larger culture, then when men entered the agora, their minds naturally turned only to cost and profit margin and nothing else.[312] For a democratic community like Athens, the greed unleashed by *homo economicus* necessitated the interference of the state to protect the love and solidarity among its

aspect win out. See Schaps, *The Invention of Coinage*, 111–12.

[303] Bresson, *The Making of the Ancient Greek Economy*, 240–43.

[304] Ibid., 255.

[305] See Bresson, *The Making of the Ancient Greek Economy*, 238.

[306] Polanyi, "On the Comparative Treatment," 334; Zimmern, *The Greek Commonwealth*, 267. Also see Bresson, *The Making of the Ancient Greek Economy*, 188.

[307] Zimmern, *The Greek Commonwealth*, 268; Glotz, *Ancient Greece at Work*, 280.

[308] L. R. Lind, "Economic Man in Ancient Athens," *The Classical Journal* 35, no. 1 (October 1939): 33.

[309] See Ober, *Mass and Elite in Democratic Athens*.

[310] Harris, "Workshop, Marketplace and Household," 76–77.

[311] Bresson, *The Making of the Ancient Greek Economy*, 235.

[312] This account is based on the speech of Diogenes in *Stob*. 3.1.9; Harris, "Workshop, Marketplace and Household," 77.

citizenry. It is no coincidence that the number of state officials regulating the market began to increase in the late fourth and the third centuries, when the market mentality was on the rise.[313] The mixed truths of the agora—as a sacred space for all citizens to communicate, gather, and assist one another on the one hand, and as an expedite commercial center that revolved around profit and utitlity on the other—once again speaks to the dynamics of cultural contestation.

Itinerancy of the Worker

In the Homeric epics, specialized workers enjoy unrestricted freedom to travel from village to village in search of suitable employment—an unquestioned right of *homo faber.* In fact, no restrictions and regulations on the movement of laborers can be found in ancient Greece.[314] A key passage in the *Odyssey* plainly underscores this absence of barrier. Eumaeus retorts to Antinous, who scolds him for bringing the mendicant Odysseus into the house:

> Antinous, though you are noble, this was not well spoken.
> For who goes visiting elsewhere so as to call in another
> stranger, unless he is one who works for the people, either
> a prophet, or a healer of sickness, or a skilled workman,
> or inspired singer, one who can give delight by his singing?
> These are the men who *all over the endless earth* are invited.
> (*Od.* 17.381–86, emphasis mine).

While this remark sufficiently establishes the value of itinerant specialists, some scholars believe they were treated less equally in their host communities.[315] If true, such discrimination would invalidate the mode of symmetric horizontal exchange suggested for *homo faber*. Yet, as Finley pointed out, Eumaeus also includes heralds and bards in this category.[316] By grouping itinerant craftsmen with highly honored

---

[313] Robert Garland, *The Piraeus: From the Fifth to the First Century B.C.*, (London: Duckworth, 1987), 77–78. Garland informed us that the *agoranomoi* ensured that no fraudulent goods were sold (*Constitution of the Athenians* 51.1); the *metronomoi* checked the accuracy of all weights and measures (*Constitution of the Athenians* 51.2); the *sitophulakes*, whose decemviral ranks swelled to thirty-five in the 320s, ensured fair prices in corn (a label that referred to all essential grains including barley-meal, barley, wheat, and bread). In the 320s, their numbers increased from five to fifteen for Piraeus and five to twenty for the Asty (*Constitution of the Athenians* 51.3).

[314] Harris, "Introduction," in *The Ancient Greek Economy: Markets, Households and City-states*, ed. Edward Harris, David Lewis, and Mark Woolmer (New York: Cambridge, 2016), 17.

[315] Kentarô Murakawa, "Demiurgos," in *Historia: Zeitschrift für Alte Geschichte* [Historia: Journal for Ancient History] 6, no. 4 (October 1957): 396.

[316] It is indeed perhaps more than a coincidence that *demiurgos* later became a designation for magistrates or artisans. See W. G. Runciman, "Origins of States: The Case of Archaic Greece," in *Comparative Studies in Society and History* 24, no. 3 (July 1982): 359. He also discussed parallels to other societies in which heralds and goldsmiths are highly valued. In *Il.* 7.273–82, for example, the heralds transcend their usual role as messengers who dispatch the latest tidings as ordered. Rather, they work and speak for Zeus and command respect from princely warriors in a way that reflects the general ecumenism of Olympianism. In other passages, the herald Talthybius is referred to as god-like (*Il.* 4.192) and described as having a god's voice (*Il.* 19.250).

bards and heralds, and stressing that they "work for the people," Eumaeus provides the rationale to also cherish the former.[317] The openness toward "outsiders" is displayed in the exemplary behavior of characters in the epics: Achilles loves Phoenix and Patroclus, adopted kin from foreign lands, and Eumaeus welcomes Odysseus in disguise as a stranger. The decoupling of birth origin and social acceptance in these instances provides the basis for conceptualizing a fluid, nonterritorial citizenship defined by mutual dependence, empathy, and compassion.

As the swineherd Eumaeus explains, communities "all over the endless earth" welcome those who possess skills and talent, no doubt in recognition of their contribution. The gratitude for foreigners with useful skills, special talents, or simply the willingness to work hard is consistent with Olympian culture. The progressiveness is pronounced, since the majority of itinerants in early Greece were not privileged aristocrats who could readily tap into the connections of an overseas network. Although Eumaeus announces, "But nobody would ask in a beggar, one who would feed on himself" (*Od.* 17.387), his hospitality toward Odysseus, the destitute foreigner, belies this remark. Eumaeus' behavior in reality illustrates the possibility—albeit not fully developed here—of a global kinship/citizenship based on suffering, vulnerability, and mortality shared by the common lot of all humans.

Extant historical narratives contain accounts of craftsmen entering and leaving communities in search of work with unhindered liberty.[318] According to Thucydides, the famous Corinthian shipwright Ameinocles built four ships for Samos and then settled there (1.3). Phidias and Ictinus, the chief architects of the Parthenon, came to Athens after contracting assignments in the Peloponnese.[319] More generally, records on public building projects indicate many resident aliens (*metic*) were employed in Athens, and that local citizens and *metics* from all over Greece won contracts on equal terms.[320] Such evidence corroborates the flourishing of a "regional common market of labor and expertise,"[321] which spawned a race to the top for workers.[322]

Scale and Decentralization

Insisting on fending for himself, *homo faber* is naturally unwilling to work under the direction of another. This refusal to be hired continued as a prominent cultural feature even in the increasingly commercialized economy of the fifth and fourth centuries. De

[317] See Runciman, "Origins of States," 359.
[318] Harris, "Introduction," 17–18.
[319] Burford, "The Builders of the Parthenon," 25.
[320] Davies, "Classical Greece: Production," 353.
[321] This should not lead to any generalization about recruitment practice and the makeup of workers in ancient Greece in general. The historical situation most likely varied from place to place and project to project; see Christophe Feyel, *Les artisans dans les sanctuaires grecs aux époques classique et hellénistique à travers la documentation financière en Grèce* [The Artists in the Greek Sanctuaries in the Classical and Hellenistic Periods in the Financial Documents of Greece] (Athènes: Ecole française d'Athènes, 2006), 367–68. Nonetheless, I argue what happened at Athens was not random, but sustained by the cultural system of Olympianism.
[322] Ibid.; see Richard H. Randall, "The Erechtheum Workmen," *American Journal of Archaeology* 57, no. 3 (July 1953): 203.

Ste. Croix correctly noted that wage labor (hired) was scarce.[323] Finley declared that the vast majority of free men in ancient Greece were engaged in productive labor through tilling their own land or working as craftsmen and shopkeepers.[324] With this strong emphasis on economic independence, a large number of sole proprietors who produced on a small scale flourished in Greek communities.[325] In fact, self-employed craftsmen dominated a variety of trades, including construction, stone masonry, carpentry, smithing, leather work, cobblery, weaving, midwifery, sheep shearing, and oarsmanship.[326] The lack of scale or vertical integration was evident in Athenian manufacturing, with the exception of some large enterprises that used slaves.[327] The making of pottery, the most renowned sector at Athens, met the high demand in volume and quality with a decentralized, fragmented, but highly effective industry. The production at Ceramicus, a pottery district in Athens, was not concentrated in big factories, but interspersed among a multitude of small and medium enterprises.[328] The potter, in the style of an industrial cottager, typically worked at his own place with a large degree of control and flexibility.[329] As a class of goods, Attic ceramics, buoyed by small-scale production, outperformed its Corinthian rival in craftsmanship and artistry.[330] In this specific illustration, the *homo faber* model that put workers at the center did not lose out in economic performance and competitiveness.

Even for large scale public projects, a system that supported small orders, frequent and advance payments, and flexible quantity accommodated small contractors.[331] Because workers in construction needed no more than the basic outfit they already possessed, most stonemasons and sculptors were self-employed.[332] In the building of the great temple Erechtheum, for example, different groups of stonemasons fluted the six columns, but each worked as an independent unit (IG I^2).[333] In the mines at Laurium, which belonged to the Athenian state as a commons, individual prospectors could opt to operate underground on their own for a modest

---

[323] G. E. M. De Ste. Croix, *The Class Struggle in the Ancient Greek World: From the Archaic Age to the Arab Conquests* (Ithaca, NY: Cornell University Press, 1981), 179.

[324] Finley, *Economy and Society in Ancient Greece*, 97. This point has been followed by Edward Cohen, *Athenian Prostitution*, 43. This notion that dependent labor was scarce was contested by Morris Silver in "Slaves versus Free Hired Workers in Ancient Greece," *Historia: Zeitschrift Für Alte Geschichte* [Historia: Journal for Ancient History] 55, no. 3 (2006): 257–63. However, the debate is ultimately about degree, not the validity of this cultural norm—the extent to which wage labor could also exist is being accounted for by Oeconomism in my model.

[325] Burford, *Craftsmen in Greek and Roman Society*, 79. The largest enterprise is found in Lysias, which employed 120 workers.

[326] E. Welskopf, "Free Labour in the City of Athens," in *Non-slave Labour in the Greco-Roman World*, ed. Peter Garnsey (Cambridge: Cambridge Philological Society, 1980), 23–25.

[327] Austin and Vidal-Naquet, *Economic and Social History*, 102; Michell, *The Economics of Ancient Greece*, 130f. In addition, the tanning industry enjoyed better-than-average margins with large establishments. The unpleasantness of the work and the restriction are probably reasons for the uniqueness of the tanning industry. See Acton, *Poiesis*, 164.

[328] Glotz, *Ancient Greece at Work*, 140–41.

[329] French, *The Growth of the Athenian Economy*, 124.

[330] The decline of Corinthian pottery is attributed to inferior quality. See Acton, *Poiesis*, 75.

[331] Michell, *The Economics of Ancient Greece*, 130. Michell notes the exception of Callicrates and Ictinus, who apparently contracted together to build the entire Parthenon.

[332] Zimmern, *The Greek Commonwealth*, 261.

[333] Burford, *Craftsmen of Greek and Roman Society*, 79.

fee.[334] In fact, an extant court speech mentions someone buying the rights to mining properties with a loan of merely twenty *minai* (Demosthenes 40.52). Another speech features a litigant who made his fortune by toiling in the mines himself (Demosthenes 42.20). Even the huge size of the Athenian fleet, which in the fifth century included merchant ships and over 300 navy vessels, offered no advantage to big conglomerates. Builders from fifty-nine different yards contracted for the 183 ships that are on record.[335] In all these large-scale undertakings, Athenian citizens eager for work did not lose out to those with more capital, and the collective outcome of their spontaneous and horizontally coordinated efforts also did not fall short.

The success of small producers in this economy was reinforced by direct democracy, which dispersed and distributed decisions about economics. The people's assembly had much say in financial matters; it deliberated and voted on the outlay of public projects as well as appointed and evaluated their superintendents and treasurers.[336] With extensive democratic oversight, even large-scale economic ventures could be administered in a decentralized and participatory manner that did not require a professional management class.

What are we to make of the fundamental cultural truth of *homo faber*, which gave rise to the series of economic outcomes we witness in Classical Athens? Considering the avoidance of regular salaried employment by free male citizens, Edward Cohen called it unprofitable and blamed it on the harmful cultural conception of masculinity (*andreia*).[337] By contrast, he extolled the entrepreneurial spirit of women, *metics* (foreign residents), and slaves, who submitted themselves to the labor market for economic opportunities and business expertise outside of family and kinship.[338] Cohen was correct to denounce a notion of citizenship configured on gender and nativism, but this was the doing of a territorially defined *polis* that betrayed the ecumenical and convivial platform of Olympianism. Let us not lose sight of the key point: the unwillingness to be bound to a master and the insistence on self-directed labor made possible wide-scale egalitarian and horizontal relationships, the foundation of a democratic order. The deep and lasting wounds of missing respect and love experienced by noncitizen groups—made institutional through exclusive native male citizenship—could not be healed by the pursuit of wealth. The appropriate Olympian redress would be to rehabilitate women, slaves, and *metics* into the polity as beloved kin, empowered *homo faber,* and equal citizens, rather than implicate them in rapacious market competition that pits individuals against one another.

All in all, the small scale of production, the lack of entry barriers, the easy access to capital and technology, and the focus on quality were deliberate results of the Olympian political economy. These interlinked phenomena thwarted the extent to which labor commodification could proceed, while safeguarding the status of workers. In terms of concrete outcomes, studies show that the average wage of a craftsman in Classical Athens was six times higher than the level of surviving merely

[334] Acton, *Poiesis*, 118.
[335] Glotz, *Ancient Greece at Work*, 268.
[336] Michell, *The Economics of Ancient Greece*, 200.
[337] See Cohen, "Unprofitable Masculinity."
[338] Ibid., 102–05.

hand-to-mouth; and half of Athens' population lived decently compared to the average in Holland and better than the average in Britain in the eighteenth century.[339] Equally important, scholars also believe that Athenian democracy was far more egalitarian than nineteenth-century England,[340] a society where cruelty and inequality were often glossed over in celebration of rapid "technological innovation and economic development."

Interestingly, the exchange between dignified, equal members who relate to each other on the basis of love and trust would also eliminate the need for organized labor or government regulation.[341] When rooted in dense social bonds, employment was much more likely to be stable and secure, *mutatis mutandis*, than in an anonymous market prone to cycles of bust and boom.[342] In Classical Athens, state interference in industrial relations was minimal.[343] Citizen workers could find protection by going to the democratic institutions that upheld equality and justice.[344] Occasional disputes and conflicts were adjudicated by market superintendents or taken directly to the people's court.[345] Unions in our modern sense of the term did not exist, and religious and social associations were formed to strengthen and coordinate the cohesiveness of a trade.[346] In general, autonomous and empowered workers did not need hierarchical representatives or bureaucratic intervention for security and protection.

Likely due to the same principle of self-governance, it was not taken for granted that authorities from the top could demand regular tribute from direct producers. Whereas the unfree peasants in Egypt, Mesopotamia, and later Hellenistic kingdoms surrendered a share of their crops to replenish the private purses of the monarchs, the citizens of Greek city-states only consented to taxation—often modest and infrequent—that served some communal purpose.[347] At Athens in the early sixth century, the tyrant Peisistratus foisted a one-tenth tax (Aristotle, *Constitution of the Athenians* 16.4), and his sons declared a one-twentieth tax (Thucydides 6.54.5). According to both Thucydides and Aristotle, the tax was abolished after the Peisistratids were overthrown and democracy was established. Moreover, in an episode from Aristotle, the tyrant learned from a peasant farmer that his tithe was tantamount to pains and aches, laying bare the assault inflicted on primary producers by taxation. Both the narrative chronology and moral parable create the strong

---

[339] Peter Acton, "Industry Structure and Income Opportunities for Households in Classical Athens," in *The Ancient Greek Economy: Markets, Households and City-states* (New York: Cambridge University Press, 2016), 149.

[340] Geoffrey Kron, "Classical Greek Trade in Comparative Perspective," in *The Ancient Greek Economy: Markets, Households and City-states* (New York: Cambridge University Press, 2016), 363.

[341] Michell remarked on the absence of trade unions. See Mitchell, *Economics of Ancient Greece*, 142–43.

[342] The passage of Xenophon, *Ways and Means* 4.6 mentions craftsmen going out of business, but this occurs precisely due to price fluctuations that result from the cycles of bust and boom created by large markets that did not prioritize job security and social needs. The time when Xenophon was writing was also a time of more market penetration in Greek societies, according to my argument.

[343] Glotz, *Ancient Greece at Work*, 276; Lind, "Economic Man in Ancient Athens," 33; Michell, *Economics of Ancient Greece*, 142–44.

[344] Zimmern, *The Greek Commonwealth*, 269.

[345] Michell, *Economics of Ancient Greece*, 143; Zimmern, *The Greek Commonwealth*, 269.

[346] Ibid., 269f.

[347] Bresson, *The Making of the Ancient Greek Economy*, 106; Signe Isager and Jens Erik Sydsgaard, *Ancient Greek Agriculture* (London: Routledge, 1992), 143.

association—rightly expounded by Finley—between direct taxes and tyranny.[348] Along similar lines, the *eisphora*, a property tax at Athens, was levied for a long time only on occasions of military emergency, because it was seen as an extraordinary measure.[349] Outside of Athens, when the state of Thasos was overflowing with income from the mines, it exempted first and foremost its farmers (Herodotus 6.46). In these examples, it is possible to deduce the correlation between the valorization of primary production and the emphasis on economic autonomy and political self-rule. In turn, the loathing for state intrusion impeded the rise of an extensive tax-extracting apparatus and its concomitant centralized bureaucracy. It is telling that in stark contrast to modern states, the Greek cities did not impose income, council or value-added taxes, which amounted to great savings to the working poor.[350] As a result, for much of Greek history, even the lowest-ranking citizen farmer or producer did not automatically owe something to "the state."[351] Ellen Meiksins Wood was right to marvel at ancient Greece for the presence of a large peasantry that was free from rent, tribute, or *corvée* (forced labor)—forms of surplus extraction regularly imposed in other societies.[352] In this way, the first principle of honoring workers turns the discourse of taxation around—instead of asking how the sovereign can tax effectively, the question becomes why it is entitled to any revenue at all, and if it does, whether there is consent, accountability, and public benefit.

The cultural ethic of *homo faber* also continued to encourage amenability and tolerance toward "foreign" workers as in the epics, despite the conflicting agendas from Polisism and Oeconomism in the Classical era. Previously, Solon and Cleisthenes granted citizenship to immigrant craftsmen and artisans—a policy that reflects an appreciation in consonance with the principles of interdependence and mutual thriving.[353] Classical Athens as a territorial state, however, denied citizenship to all outsiders in a dramatic pivot to Polisism, even as the city benefited heavily from foreign personnel and goods. Although state power instituted this grotesque division,[354] the democratic polity, under the aegis of Olympianism, still afforded noncitizens broad economic rights and opportunities, in stark contrast to its rival Sparta. The anonymous author of the *Constitution of Athens* stated: "For this reason we have set up equality between slaves and free men, and between *metics* (resident aliens) and citizens. The city needs *metics* in view of the many different trades and the fleet. Accordingly, then, we have reasonably set up a similar equality also for the

[348] Finley, *The Ancient Economy*, 90. We do know that in 375/4 BCE, Athens imposed a 8.33 percent tax on the islands of Imbros, Lemnos, and Skyros, its colonies; see Ronald Stroud, "The Athenian Grain-Tax Law of 374/3 B. C.," *Hesperia Supplements* 29 (1998): iii–140. In addition, Sparta and Crete seem to have imposed regular taxes on agriculture, but these two cities were oligarchies that employed noncitizens to farm the land; see Isager and Sydsgaard, *Ancient Greek Agriculture*, 138–39.

[349] Finley, *The Ancient Economy*, 175.

[350] Harris, "Introduction," 20; Isager and Sydsgaard, *Ancient Greek Agriculture*, 142.

[351] Wood, *Peasant-Citizen and Slave*, 56ff.

[352] Ibid., 56.

[353] Michell, *The Economics of Ancient Greece*, 148, fn 2. The source of this law is Plutarch, *Solon*, 24, which has been generally accepted at face value.

[354] For example, Michell notes that according to Plutarch's *Pericles*, 5000 *metics* who falsely claimed grain assistance reserved for citizens were sold into slavery. Michell, *The Economics of Ancient Greece*, 147.

metics."[355] Owing to this frank acknowledgement, financially savvy and lucky foreigners could enjoy economic success and social equality, so much so that Edward Cohen has argued that Athens was a cosmopolitan nation rather than a small, inward-looking city.[356] This juxtaposition of informal equality and official exclusion is best seen through the struggle between the Olympian tradition that strove to uphold universal convivial principles socially and the program of the *polis* that sought to discriminate against out-groups institutionally.

Nevertheless, while the city stripped slaves and foreigners of equal status, it could not sever their ties to the gods. Religious life at Athens was open to noncitizenship groups so they could join festivals, rituals, rites, and other public activities.[357] A law against hubris, a word denoting religious sacrilege against the gods, threatened anyone who committed outrage against a slave with death, even though Athenian jurisprudence backed slavery.[358] Still, those who lost their liberty could flee to refuge at the Theseum or the altar of the Eumenides on the Acropolis, sanctuaries that protected them from life-threatening danger.[359] Particularly at temples—the earthly homes of the divine—immortal beings that are far wiser and greater than humans held the divisive lines demarcated by the state and the logic forwarded market in temporary abeyance.

Given its emphasis on fairness and equality, the Olympian legacy likely improved the overall economic experience of noncitizens in Classical Athens as well. Slaves worked alongside citizens in agriculture, commerce, manufacturing, and domestic work rather than in exclusively servile sectors, with the exception of mining.[360] Moreover, an inscription on the construction of the Erechtheum on the Acropolis (408–407 BCE) shows that craftsmen, despite being assigned different tasks, worked together and earned the same wages.[361] Owing in part to this milieu, Olympianism reduced the vulnerability of slaves and migrant workers who were denied citizenship. In this way, the ecumenical and convivial discourses of Olympianism injected a strong progressive streak into a society that was otherwise adumbrated by harsh societal exclusions.[362]

---

355 Xenophon, *Constitution of Athens* 1.12. *Xenophon in Seven Volumes*, 7, trans. E. C. Marchant and G. W. Bowersock (Cambridge: Harvard University Press, Rev. ed. 1925; London: William Heinemann, Ltd., 1984).

356 See Edward Cohen, *The Athenian Nation* (Princeton, NJ: Princeton University Press, 2000).

357 For the participation of women in religion, see Barry S. Strauss, "Genealogy, Ideology, and Society in Democratic Athens," in *Democracy 2500? Questions and Challenges*, ed. Ian Morris, Kurt A. Raaflaub, and David Castriota (Dubuque, Iowa: Kendall/Hunt Pub. Co., 1998), 148; for the protection given to noncitizen groups, see Josiah Ober, "Chapter Five: Quasi Rights: Participatory Citizenship and Negative Liberties," in *Athenian Legacies: Essays on the Politics of Going on Together* (Princeton: Princeton University Press, 2005), 92–127.

358 Demosthenes, *Against Midias*, 47; Aeschines, *Against Timarchus*, 16,7; Michell, *The Economics of Ancient Greece*, 157. For the protection given to noncitizen groups, see Ober, "Quasi Rights," 92–127.

359 Michell, *The Economics of Ancient Greece*, 158; for the shrine of Theseus serving as a sanctuary for runaway slaves, see Josiah Ober, "Conditions for Athenian Democracy," in *The Making and Unmaking of Democracy: Lessons from History and World Politics*, ed. Theodore K. Rabb and Ezra N. Suleiman (New York: Routledge, 2013), 10.

360 Austin and Vidal-Naquet, *Economic and Social History*, 102.

361 Ibid., 106; see Michell, *The Economics of Ancient Greece*, 131, 164.

362 Strauss, "Genealogy, Ideology, and Society," 151.

Yet, as the truths of Olympianism tottered in the fifth and fourth centuries, the dialectics of sacred work that celebrated the gods, community, kinship, and democratic politics began to lose ground. In its place, the market funneled the sinuous impulse into a utilitarian mindset that normalized iniquitous employment relations to the detriment of free labor. The increased presence of regular paid employment in critical areas of life—found in professions like education (e.g., sophists), the creative arts (e.g., paid poets), military (e.g., mercenaries), and other areas—signaled new ways of thinking and "doing business." As a result, many of the phenomena we have examined, even from the very same source, provide conflicting readings and interpretations that demonstrate the appeal of both Olympianism and the market. Through this specific lens of labor, Athens was, more than ever, caught in conflicting trajectories and divergent paths.

Commodification of Money

Besides resources and labor, the Olympian cultural system also directed the surplus wealth in the form of money, with important ramifications for the economy as a whole. In Athens, groups of citizens who subscribed to a common fund administrated a type of lending very similar to modern-day microfinancing.[363] These loans, which were interpersonal and collective rather than anonymous and unilateral in nature, are called *eranoi.* [364] The terminology underscores its horizontal and reciprocal tendencies: *eranoi* designate community potlucks in the earlier non-monetized Homeric world, and societies of monetary mutual assistance later. A high percentage of loans at Athens, *eranos* or otherwise, did not charge interest.[365] Athenians also borrowed for noncommercial purposes, such as ransoming a captive, financing a liturgy, paying for a dowry or a funeral, and purchasing a necessary good.[366] These noncommercial transfers strengthened the bonds between citizens in a civic community that prized friendship (*philia*) and solidarity.[367] In a similar manner, a citizen discovering himself short of equipment or funds necessary for joining the military would typically turn to his fellows rather than the state or a bank.[368] These gifts and loans, when forgoing witnesses and securities, charging zero or little interest, and preferring third-party arbitration over formal contractual safeguards, relied on

---

[363] Paul Millett, *Lending and Borrowing in Ancient Athens* (Cambridge, UK: Cambridge University Press, 1991), 153–54. The analogy to microfinancing is mine.

[364] For the associational nature of *eranos*, see Cohen, *Athenian Economy and Society*, 209.

[365] Gabriel Herman claimed *eranoi* loans are interest-free; see *Morality and Behaviour in Democratic Athens: A Social History* (Cambridge: Cambridge University Press, 2006), 390. Cf. Edward Cohen argued against it largely based on evidence of silence; yet even he noted that a number of regular bank loans did not carry interest; see Cohen, *Athenian Economy and Society*, 210. My point here is not to debate the classification of different type of loans, but to illustrate the fact that many of them did not charge interest at Athens.

[366] Schaps, *The Invention of Coinage*, 245.

[367] Cf. Cohen, *Athenian Economy and Society*, 211. Cohen highlighted the commercial dimension of lending practices. However, even in the example of Apollodoros, friendship was highly emphasized along with other considerations.

[368] Lysias 16.14, 31.15 in van Wees, "The City at War," in *Classical Greece, 500-323 BC*, ed. Robin Osborne (New York: Oxford University Press, 2000), 106.

trust and goodwill.[369] In the peer-to-peer, mutually assisting, solidarity-fostering model of finance, citizens could produce a safety net and credit service among themselves without private, for-profit banks backed by a coercive legal apparatus.

The Olympian model of savings for solidarity and mutual aid, however, was challenged by the other two competing cultures, just as in other areas. According to Edward Cohen, the credit structure in the fourth century was highly composite and hybridized. Profit calculations, lawsuits, and the demand for collateral began to accompany *eranoi* and other credit operations.[370] Moreover, large-scale commercial loans, which charged exorbitant rates with the help of legal enforcement, began to appear.[371] In this Oeconomical model, surplus money circulated among wealthy private individuals and a handful of entrepreneurs for speculative, high-risk, high-return ventures, dwarfing the horizontal informal credit network in which citizens assisted one another.[372]

In addition, Edward Harris observed a gradual but definitive shift toward the activation of market responses and state enforcement with regard to mortgage security in the fifth century. Before then, individuals relied on the trustworthiness of the debtor and the strength of the communal intervention as true sureties. By the fourth century, the creditor could simply resort to jural force to guarantee monetary payoff.[373] From this development, we see the market and the state suppressing the Olympian truth of weaving together a strong community through the fabric of love and trust. The most potent illustration of this conflict comes from Demosthenes' *Against Nicostratus*. The speaker Apollodorus, upon learning that pirates have kidnapped Nicostratus, a neighbor he loved and cared for like a brother and compatriot, pitched in money to pay for ransom. Apollodorus explained in detail his friendship with Nicostratus, as was typical among citizens, and he was so moved by the latter's misfortune that he gave away every penny he had at hand (53.4–7). However, the money lender who released the funds soon demanded the full balance in a month, or else the owed amount would double. Although the big twist is that Nicostratus made up lies in order to cheat Apollodorus, the existence of cold, calculating, anonymous entrepreneurs that took advantage of people on a rainy day must have been commonplace for the story to be believable. We are told that being short of cash, Apollodorus mortgaged off his property—a promise now under legal contractual obligation—to save Nicostratus (53.12). Apollodorus' lamentable fate reflects not so much the naiveté and futility of a traditional culture but how much it could be ravaged by the warping incentive to pursue wealth by any and all means.

While Olympianism and Oeconomism contended over whether the use of surplus money should be for human well-being or monetary profit, those endorsing Polisism also advocated its agenda of preserving *philia* (friendship) among native male citizens. Most profit-based, contractual credit and banking operations in Athens were

[369] Julie Vélissaropoulos-Karakostas, "Merchants, Prostitutes and the 'New Poor,'" in *Money, Labour and Land*, ed. Paul Cartledge, Edward E. Cohen, and Lin Foxhall (London and New York: Routledge, 2002), 132.
[370] Cohen, *Athenian Economy and Society*, 209.
[371] Ibid., 211–14.
[372] Bresson, *The Making of the Ancient Greek Economy*, 280–81.
[373] Harris, "When Is a Sale Not a Sale?" 381.

relegated to noncitizens, for the reason that "impersonal and potentially exploitative relationship[s]" did not befit the community of equals as the *polis*.[374] Given this reasoning, it is not surprising that foreigners, slaves, *metics*, and women, having been excluded from the polity, were more likely to "prosper" in international maritime usury in the fourth century. Once again, through the lens of cultural contestation, we can understand the tension between safeguarding democracy by constraining entrepreneurial activities and pursuing gain at the cost of sacrificing civic *philia*. In other words, on the one hand, Polisism fought to protect social cohesion by offloading unseemly, exploitative tasks to outsiders, i.e., women, *metics*, and slaves. On the other hand, market forces sought to transform bonds of reciprocal obligation and mutual aid into anonymous economic exchange.

Countervailing Trends in Extractionism

Finally, we must confront the complex and troubling relationship between the Olympian convivial model and the historical forces of slavery,[375] military aggression,[376] and rentierism, which all crossed paths on the actual historical stage of ancient Greece.[377] At their core, enslavement, conquest, and enclosure hold in common the expropriation of someone else's labor and resources. These various forms of violence, which in essence diminish and devalue honest work, coincided with the rise of the market after the Archaic period. Herodotus, writing in the fifth century, supported this hypothesis. In his ethnographic account of the Egyptians, Herodotus wondered if it was in imitation of them that the Greeks had recently become contemptuous of manual craft (2.166–7). Michell also concluded that prejudice against manual labor among the Greeks was of comparatively late origin.[378] He argued that the shift in attitude came about due to the Persian war (c. 490 BCE), an event that made the Greeks valorize martial prowess above all.[379] In fact, state-sponsored militarism was critical to Greek states for extracting economic surplus both at home and abroad. Sparta exemplified the first model by becoming a collective agent of terror in order to seize the fruit of labor from the *helots*. The Spartan poet Tyrtaeus described them in the following way: "Just like asses worn out by heavy burdens, bringing to their masters out of grievous necessity half of all the produce that the land brings forth."[380] After the Persian war, we also begin to observe a kindred trend at Athens, where the tributes from subjugated allies and domestic chattel slaves "supplemented" the economic output of the citizens. This indelible mark of economic

---

[374] Millett, *Lending and Borrowing*, 220.

[375] Other Greek historians prefer to consider the practice of slavery as "rent-seeking," although the general meaning of economic appropriation is the same. For example, Ober, *Democracy and Knowledge*, 24.

[376] For example, tributes imposed on other Greek city-states by the Athenian empire.

[377] Famous figures like Nikias, who owned over a thousand slaves in the mines; Apollodorus, the son of Paison who inherited estates, and Demosthenes, who owned two factories from his father, were all able to live a comfortable rentier existence. See S. C. Humphreys, *Anthropology and the Greeks* (Oxon: Routledge, [1978] 2004), 153–54.

[378] Michell, *The Economics of Ancient Greece*, 11.

[379] Ibid.

[380] Bresson, *The Making of the Ancient Greek Economy*, 105.

extractionism in Classical Greece, boosted by the legal apparatus of exclusive native citizenship and a foreign policy of realpolitik, must be distinguished from the older Olympian form of warfare impelled by the quest for identity and recognition (see Chapter 5).

The booty pillaged from military conquest greatly debased self-labor: why bother to produce with one's own hands when the sword easily hauls in so much more? This simple truth did not escape the ancients themselves. Hybrias of Crete allegedly sang while pointing to his spear and shield, "With these I reap, with these I harvest the sweet wine of the grape, and I make my serfs call me lord."[381] Along a similar line, a passage in pseudo-Aristotelian *Oeconomicus* (1353a25–b5) juxtaposes the violence of extraction and expropriation with the justness of subsistence farming: "Agriculture is the best because it is just, for it is not at the expense of other men, whether willingly as in trade (*kapēleia*) or wage-earning (*mistharnikai*) or unwillingly as in war."[382] However, by circumventing self-sufficiency, the parasitic overlord or expropriator forfeits the chance to shape his identity through productive activities. Furthermore, practitioners of extractionism do not truly escape toil: they must master ever greater means of coercion in order to secure compliance.

By not heeding the imperative of self-producing, Sparta and Athens followed similarly degenerative courses. According to Thucydides, the Athenians, who had so valiantly resisted the Persians for freedom, glowed with lust upon hearing the proposal to conquer Sicily by force, knowing very well that the plan's success would capture land, slaves, and riches for Athenian utilization. Their subsequent expedition was an utter disaster that crippled its military might for decades. The Spartans, known throughout Greece for their piety, discipline, and bravery, could not face up to the task of growing their own food. As a result, they busied themselves with physical training in order to terrify the *helots* into permanent submission, preferring to abuse and mistreat, rather than respect and honor, those who lived amidst them. Yet even full militarization did not prevent Sparta's worst nightmare from being realized: after the defeat at Leuctra in 371 BCE, the *helots* in Messenia were emancipated with the help of a foreign army. Once the unthinkable took place, Sparta lost its economic bloodline and never recovered as a major power on the Greek stage. The extractionist policies of these two famous Greek city-states—in a dramatic departure from the autonomy, equality, and reciprocity mandated by *homo faber*—brought utter ruin.

Indeed, without the deeply secularized "rational" argument of "might makes right," the modes of state-sponsored extractionism deployed by Athens and Sparta were difficult to justify in traditional Greek thinking. Thucydides noted that the more clairvoyant Athenians were not impervious to the fear that their imperial wars had incurred the wrath of the gods (Thucydides 2.54). But Pericles responded that although the Athenian empire had slid into despotism, it was dangerous to abort it (Thucydides 2.63.2). The Spartans, in their proverbial laconism, left no words apologizing for the brutal treatment of the indigenous population. The *helots* and other dependents, deeming their fate neither just or fixed, never gave up on the fight

[381] Athenaeus 15.695f–696a; skolion 909, translated in Glotz, *Ancient Greece at Work*, 84.
[382] Quoted in Millett, *Lending and Borrowing in Ancient Athens*, 165.

for freedom, and their struggle always found ready support in the rest of the Greek world,[383] including Athens itself.

It is important to stress that institutionalized surplus extraction was facilitated by Polisism, which defined at birth who was to be cherished and loved and who was to be exploited and abused. The systematic exclusion of out-groups, which bolstered external and internal imperialist projects, deeply violated the ecumenical and convivial truths of Olympianism. This great tension between Olympianism and Polisism can be seen in the spending priorities of Classical Athens: religious celebration and war were the top two items in the budget.[384] The choice reflects how much Athens in the Classical period was torn: it vacillated between the twin goals of bringing the community together through song, dance, and contest (including those in the larger Greek world), and of exalting only its own citizens through discriminating and brutalizing others.

Slavery

The emergence of slavery, the most hideous and blatant form of extractionism, clearly undermined the integrity and coherence of truths that laid at the heart of the Olympian political economy. Even so, a simple identification of Greek civilization with slavery misses important nuances and struggles.[385] In fact, a number of Olympian narratives implicitly undermine the rationale for the enslavement of men by depicting far more desirable alternatives. The poet Hesiod, for instance, characterized the Golden Age as a time of abundant surplus provided by nature (*WD* 116–19). His utopia presents conviviality in the truest form: humans bring honor to the gods and Earth and receive bountifully in return. Such a society would eliminate the need for *anyone* to perform painful and crushing labor. We see this holistic anti-toil ideal again among the Cyclopes in the *Odyssey*: "[They], putting all their trust in the immortal/ gods, neither plow with their hands nor plant anything,/ but all grows from them without seed planting, without cultivation,/ wheat and barley and also the grapevines, which yield for them/ wine of strength, and it is Zeus' rain that waters it for them" (9.108–11). Similarly, great rapport with the gods earns the Phaeacians ample food and water (*Od.* 7.112–32). This labor-free state also graces the Hyperboreans, who, according to Pindar, being free of toil, old age, or illness, devote themselves to singing, dancing, and feasts (Pindar, *Pythia* 10). Unfortunately, how this blessed existence will return, those authors do not explain—a silence we ought to pursue. It is certain, however, that the answer does not come from the subjugation of weaker groups through economic coercion, political domination, or military aggression. More specifically, the lost paradise Hesiod longed for cannot be built on the backs of forced and exploited laborers, be they hirelings, chattel slaves, or *helots*. The mere transfer of undesirable

---

383 Bresson, *The Making of the Ancient Greek Economy*, 106.

384 Although recent scholarship shows that annual spending on war far outstripped the total combined from religion and politics, the high, "inelastic" cost of warfare does not signify the same proportion in significance. See Pritchard, *Public Spending and Democracy*.

385 Interestingly, this idea works well for Marxist historiography, which places the slave mode of production at the beginning of human society's unilinear trajectory toward modern industrialization.

work—instead of its elimination through better methods and organization—would compel people just like Hesiod to work for the benefit of another.[386] In fact, *Works and Days* repeatedly thematizes the injustice of obtaining livelihood and wealth without work (29, 41, 302–06, 319–25, 498–501). So long as men do not live in perfect conviviality with nature, the self-standing *homo faber* represents the second best solution, one that Hesiod embraces.

When someone like Hesiod urges his audience to use a slave or two to ease the weight of the plow (*WD* 406), the contradiction is glaring, because Hesiod himself owed much of his independence and freedom to the convivial and ecumenical tenets of Olympianism. As an independent farmer, Hesiod understood the dignity of self-employment and the humiliation of subordination. Consequently, he should have thrown in his lot with the slaves, who belonged to the lowest end of the same continuum of unfree labor. Hesiod indeed had the solution to his intermittent need for extra hands: he mentioned the possibility of going to his neighbors for reciprocal aid (*WD* 345–46). Yet his distrust of friends, kin, and women (*WD* 345, 370–75), a sign of convivial failure, prevented him from seeking their assistance and rendered compliant slave labor more attractive. In fact, what made Hesiod less "aristocratic" was not his burning desire to work and succeed, but the lack of friends and allies. Such an extensive kinship network based on love and trust was far more valuable than a good harvest.[387]

In any case, the exploitation of slave labor, however convenient in the short run, ultimately undercuts someone like Hesiod, because the rich could amass more dependent labor, be it hireling or slave. As one scholar observed, "[S]mall-scale craftsmen could hold their own against slaves, but in cases where gangs of slaves could be employed the free laborer was at a very serious disadvantage and could not successfully compete."[388] Especially in a monied society, the endowed class could simply command a larger pool of dependents for greater profit. Even if this decisive edge may not necessarily hurt the lifestyle or pay of small producers right away,[389] it can be converted into undue power and influence in politics to undermine general social equality. To see this big picture, Hesiod needed to transcend his own immediate interest, an achievable feat if he permitted himself to be guided by the truths of the gods.

When market forces began to accelerate in the Classical era, two different types of slavery existed in Athens and the larger Greek world. Like Hesiod, the majority of small producers owned a slave or two to enhance their role as *homo faber* and citizen—that is, to do *more* in politics, warfare, and economic self-production, not less.[390] A small group of elites with disproportionate ownership in land,

[386] Hesiod's own use of slaves will be discussed in the next paragraph.

[387] The value of the international network for Greek elites was immense. See Raaflaub, "Power in the Hands of the People," 57.

[388] Michell, *The Economics of Ancient Greece*, 165.

[389] There is considerable debate on whether there was fierce competition between slaves and the poor especially in terms of wages, see Austin and Vidal-Naquet, *Economic and Social History*, 106. The discussion here focuses more on the relative wealth of the rich through slave labor.

[390] According to de Ste. Croix, well-to-do Greek shop owners possessed twenty to fifty slaves, which contrasted greatly with Roman senators who owned hundreds. See de Ste. Croix, *Class Struggle*, 116. Wood

manufacturing, or mining, however, used slaves to avoid work altogether.[391] The exploitation of slave labor put the parasitic proprietors well ahead of the self-supporting citizens, a dynamic which in turn eroded the egalitarian basis of democracy. Examples of this extractive class include Lysias, whose shield factory employed 120 slaves; Demosthenes, whose two factories were operated by thirty-two or thirty-three slaves; and other known individuals whose tanneries hired gangs of slaves.[392] While some of these business owners could well have been exemplary citizens, their privileged position nevertheless came from the expropriation of someone else's labor. Such anti-convivial economic power—as opposed to the surplus accumulated through years of hard work or community service—undermined the proper order of Olympianism.[393] Furthermore, the exemption from everyday work gave this class the leisure to engage in high-end intellectual pursuits like oratory and philosophy, which propelled them further ahead in society. The wedge between the citizens who earned their livelihood from self-reliant production and those who profited from exploiting underlings laid the seed for economic and social disparity.[394] Glotz concurred, for he intoned: "Slavery lay like a load on the condition of the craftsmen and laborers. It tended to create ever greater inequality in the distribution of wealth, to make the situation of the middle class more precarious, and to change wealth to opulence and poverty to destitution."[395]

In historical terms, the growth and institutionalization of slavery affected all parts of Greek society and worsened the station of self-employed workers.[396] We have

---

also noted that "there were no slave plantations, huge estates worked by slave gangs living in barracks, like the Roman latifundia." See Ellen Wood, *Democracy Against Capitalism: Renewing Historical Materialism* (Cambridge, UK: Cambridge University Press, 1995), 184. Hanson also commented on this: "Nor under such a system would there be a few despots on top to siphon off the work of thousands as was typical in the East." See Hanson, *The Other Greeks*, 70. The great exception is of course Sparta, which had to become fully militarized in order keep the food-growing servile population under its rein. Throughout its history, Sparta lived in constant fear of domestic revolt—the price it paid for not securing its own economic autonomy.

[391] Finley discussed "absentee urban-dwellers who left the management and operation of their estates either to tenants or to slavers and slave bailiffs." See Finley, *Economy and Society in Ancient Greece*, 188. Also see Michael H. Jameson, "On Paul Cartledge, 'The Political Economy of Greek Slavery,'" in *Money, Labour and Land*, ed. Paul Cartledge, Edward E. Cohen, and Lin Foxhall (London: Routledge, 2002), 168.

[392] Acton, *Poiesis*, 163.

[393] Among authors like Aristophanes and Thucydides, scholars have observed a distaste for Cleon, a caricature figure for the new class of so-called demogogues whose fortunes largely derived from slave workshops.

[394] Wood saw the issue of labor playing into the larger contestation of the state as an instrument of private appropriation or, conversely, a protection against exploitation. See Wood, *Democracy against Capitalism*, 30ff.

[395] Glotz, *Ancient Greece at Work*, 86.

[396] Cf. Walter Scheidel, "The Hireling and the Slave: A Transatlantic Perspective" in *Money, Labour and Land*, ed. Paul Cartledge, Edward E. Cohen, and Lin Foxhall (London: Routledge, 2002). Scheidel documented the same correlation between slave labor and the contempt for service and manual jobs in the antebellum American South. He argued that slavery, a perverse and iniquitous phenomenon, gave dependent labor undue bad reputation. However, we must be careful to distinguish between manual work and dependent (unfree) labor. One could perform independent manual work as a craftsman or skilled dependent labor as a paid/enslaved poet. The Olympian culture rejects the conditions of the latter but praises the former, while the Greek aristocratic writers of the later age were contemptuous of the former. Democracy, in preserving the convivial heritage, as I argue, accommodated free workers; only the turn

already noted that in Homer, the independent craftsman or farmer who executes his own work finds himself among the ranks of the gods and legendary figures. In the Archaic Age, respect for the divine *homo faber* was sufficient for Solon to urge Athenians to learn arts and crafts. It was also around that time in ancient Greece, unlike in the neighboring monarchies, that craftsmen began to leave their signatures on pottery and their own images on bronze pieces and vase paintings.[397] Yet, the scholar Murakawa stated that "from the fifth century B.C., when Greek industry began to rely on slavery, craftsmen were given such names as *cheirotechnês* or *banausos*, both of which, especially the latter, expressed more or less contempt for manual work."[398] The growth of slave labor led to the separation of intellectual conception and physical execution, and delegated the second component to those at the bottom of the social ladder. For example, the same inscription on the frieze and columns of the Erechtheum from the year 408/7 that we had mentioned earlier indicates that more citizens, in relation to *metics* and slaves, took on trade and managerial jobs, despite being paid the same.[399] In this case, job hierarchy interestingly blended with equal pay, and stratification was mixed with equality. This specific example reinforces the bifurcating nature of labor in ancient Greece in the Classical period. It incongruently moved between the two poles: the model of the divine *homo faber* sustained by relationships of independence, horizontal exchange, and equality, and the other of debasement as a result of extraction, domination, and exploitation.

Market Corrosion

The Olympian model of honest, hard work contended not only with violent forms of extractionism, but also the legalized market activities of rent-seeking in the Classical era. To affirm once again the kingly status of productive work in ancient Greece, we turn to Hesiod's discussion of strife. Citing potters, craftsmen, and singers as examples of the quintessential *homo faber* of his time, Hesiod openly embraced competition in self-directed, fulfilling, and creative economic production, for it was ordained by the gods (*WD* 398). Hesiod also included beggars in this group: although they do not produce, they beseech others openly, rather than seize stealthily. However, allowing corrupt deeds—such as bribery, manipulation, cheating, and intimidation—to compete with honest work opens the floodgate to corruption and degeneration. This type of deleterious strife was exemplified by Hesiod's brother Perses. Perses and Hesiod were enmeshed in a quarrel over the family patrimony. Hesiod condemned his depraved brother for contemplating crooked legal intervention and urges him to put himself to hard work instead. The rhetoric once again confirms the centrality of self-directed productive labor in the Olympian dispensation.

Even if we treat the scheming of Perses as a problem of political malfeasance, the market still pays rent, profit, and interest—remunerations that come not from

toward Polisism fueled slavery.

[397] Acton, *Poiesis*, 7; Mossé, *The Ancient World at Work*, 92.

[398] Murakawa, "Demiurgos," 407; Mossé, *Ancient World at Work*, 25.

[399] Austin and Vidal-Naquet, *Economic and Social History*, 277; Randall, "Erechtheum Workmen," 203.

productive activities, but ownership of enclosed resources or exploited labor. Whether in nature or consequence, self-directed work and socially extractive ownership are not comparable. Yet by monetizing them through abstract arithmetic, they become undifferentiated except in numeration only. Nicias, a fifth-century Athenian, earned an income of one *obol* a day for the 1,000 slaves he owned, without needing to move a finger himself.[400] Pasion, a banker in the fourth century who was later granted citizenship because of his "economic contribution," made high-interest loans, then invested the profits in land and slaves, which brought him further income.[401] His story as the token successful entrepreneur demonstrates how money could beget more money even in antiquity. These examples illustrate the way in which the market sanctifies the ownership of land, instruments, and resources at levels exceeding that which the owners themselves can exploit. This model puts self-sustaining producers and yeoman farmers at a disadvantage and, at the extreme, reduces them to economic dependency or ruin, as seen with large-scale dispossession during Solon's lifetime. In our time, many highly "deregulated" and thoroughly monetized economies also handsomely reward sectors of speculative finance and resource monopoly, such as in the areas of investment banking, real estate, and oil-gas production. In monetary terms, the market declares the individuals in control of these assets—whose economic roles are injurious to *homo faber*—to be worth millions more than the average worker who toils every day. Worse yet, this extractive class could use their money to buy speech and influence politics, tilting the game further in their favor. To equate self-directed honest work that improves the world with economic entitlements that suck in rent, interest, surcharge (from enclosing resources), and profit (from exploiting labor), and to allow the latter to be quantitatively superior, is one of the most unforgivable dealings of the free market system.

CONCLUSION

In this chapter, we have examined the key factor of labor in the Olympian convivial model. Overturning the stereotype of ancient Greeks who avoided work, we established the truth of *homo faber* from a close survey of the Olympian sources. Based on these narratives, *homo faber* is someone who searches for meaning and establishes deep social ties through the process of transforming the physical environment. In doing so, *homo faber* must own the wherewithal of production, conceive and execute his own work, enjoy direct exchange with the community, and be able to amplify his strength and talents. A set of social conditions such as wide distribution of resources, open mode of direct exchange, and flexibility in technology and capital were essential for independent producers and yeoman farmers to materialize their *homo faber* aspirations. In addition, we also examined how credit could be provisioned based on principles of love and trust in the *polis* community of interchangeable equals without market or state mechanisms. Last, we contemplated

[400] Michell, *The Economics of Ancient Greece*, 164.
[401] Mossé, *Ancient World at Work*, 95.

the historical development of slavery in ancient Greece, a repulsive phenomenon fueled by Polisism and Oeconomism and exhibiting its roots in extractionism.

The analysis in this chapter reinforces the central thesis of three competing cultures. With the advent of Oeconomism, unequal market relationships weakened the position of *homo faber*: big land owners threatened to replace peasant-farmers in the countryside, large manufacturers exploited slaves for gain, and banking operations pursued private profit at the expense of reciprocal mutual aid and *philia* among citizens. However, the *polis* sought to preserve native male equality by ejecting exploitative, ownership-based commercial relations from the citizenry even while exposing all out-groups to political oppression and economic exploitation. Throughout these changes, the lasting power of Olympianism resisted the advance of the market by preserving *kleros* (land that supported the family farm), buoying small independent workers with favorable *homo faber* conditions, and creating *de facto* if not *de jure* convivial experiences for all, including noncitizens. In this fragmented and heterogeneous cultural landscape, what Athens was becoming in each and every moment, as it is evident now, was a matter that was subject to relentless contestation and contingency.

CHAPTER 4

Unity in Democratic Action

The truth about self-reliance was not only fundamental to economics, but also to politics. At the apogee of Athenian democracy, citizens performed illustrious deeds in variegated facets of life, much like the renowned characters in the epics. As with the Homeric heroes, who carried out political deliberation themselves, the citizens of democratic Athens ran the government largely on their own. In times of war, just like the heroes who jostled opponents in combat, Athenian citizens also fought as hoplites in the army and as rowers in the navy. By taking these matters into their own hands, they eliminated the need for a centralized bureaucracy or professional military force. The same approach applied to games and other contests in which accolades and glory could only be won by those who personally participated and competed.[402]

By treating military service and public life as arenas of identity formation and making them available to all, Greek-style *demokratia* repudiated a division of roles that would allow some to judge and rule, others to fight and defend, and the rest to labor and toil, as the antidemocratic philosophers would advocate. The remarkable fact that all citizens could partake in political decisions and government bodies, taking turns to rule and to be ruled regardless of wealth and profession, must have owed much to the basics of Olympian discourse. Protagoras, for example, defends democracy by arguing that the gods have endowed every human being with the gift of politics.[403] Historically speaking, the body of Olympian truths, transmitted orally throughout the community, taught all Greeks about the origin and history of the cosmos, the norms and ethics of society, and the worth and potential of man. This powerful cultural system, which combined metaphysics (e.g., sacred time and space), sociology (e.g., conviviality and ecumenism), and ontology (e.g., the establishment of identity through action), prepared citizens thoroughly for democratic life.

Furthermore, an economy built around autonomous, independent work complemented politics centered on meaningful individual praxis. At Athens, a combination of concrete economic and legislative measures supported the worker-citizen: first, the economic norms shielded the citizenry from exploitation and abuse; second, the democratic mandate protected the political rights of *homo faber,* including those engaged in manual labor. In the Classical period, farmers, craftsmen, and blacksmiths were the bulwark of the democratic polity. They manned the assembly, deliberated politics, and held political office on an equal footing with the rich and

[402] M. I. Finley and H. W. Pleket, *The Olympic Games: The First Thousand Years* (New York: Viking Press, 1976), 22. Finley noted that the chariot race was exceptional because victory went to the owner rather than the rider, which allowed wealthy men to win glory. Also see further discussion by Margalit Finkelberg, "*Timē* and *Aretē* in Homer," *The Classical Quarterly* 48, no. 1 (1998): 14–28.

[403] Plato, *Protagoras*, 320c–328d

powerful.[404] Pericles, as portrayed by Thucydides, believes in the full compatibility, and even convergence, between *homo faber* and the citizen. "Our public men have, besides politics, their private affairs to attend to, and our ordinary citizens, though occupied with the pursuits of industry, are still fair judges of public matters; for, unlike any other nation, we regard the citizen who takes no part in these duties not as unambitious but as useless" (2.40.2). Pericles' model citizen transforms the material world through economic production, and strengthens the polity through civic collaboration. The unity of social life, economics, and politics in greater life mirrors that of ownership, conception, and execution in productive work; both embody the dynamic of equality and autonomy rather than stratification and dependency.

In these ways, Athenian democracy fed itself off the bundle of metaphysical, ontological, and sociological truths issued by Olympianism. Mass warfare, democratic politics, and public games and festivals all allowed the citizens to distinguish who they were as individuals. To this list, we can now add economic self-reliance, manifested mainly through yeoman-farming and artisan production. With the capacity to do purposeful work as well as manage collective affairs, citizens could make a name for themselves, just like the heroes in Homer. In other words, Athens offered even the poor and the unprivileged a chance to make history, whereby their deeds would be remembered by posterity in songs and legends. In this light, democracy is the materialization of a society for *homo significans*: man born to create meaning.

The Birth of Democracy

The formation of Athenian democracy entailed more than just the design of institutions and social structure. The set of new political truths also spoke to the citizens emotionally, in much the same way the epics move their audience. Being a member of Athens evoked a strong sense of pride, belonging, and togetherness, the same feelings displayed among male companions in the epics. In Homer and other early authors, companion (*hetairos*) is a word that conjures up love, trust, and endearment among those who are like kin and family.[405] Whenever a *hetairos* relationship goes awry, as in the case of Odysseus from time to time in the *Odyssey*, misfortune ensues.[406] Given this precedent, a major function of the Athenian *polis* was to instill love (*philia*) and solidarity in its members and bring them together as an abstract kin group, regardless of whether the members personally knew one another.[407] It is telling that Cleisthenes, the father of Athenian democracy, "made all

[404] Plato, *Protagoras*, 319c–d; Xen. *Memorabilia*, 3.7.6.

[405] For example, Theognis, Achilles in the *Iliad*, and Hesiod (*WD* 709).

[406] See Elmer, *The Poetics of Consent*, 231. The disconnect between Odysseus with his men in the collective process often leads to bad outcomes, where the lack of transparency and trust on the part of Odysseus is largely responsible. By contrast, Achilles despises anyone who says one thing and thinks another (*Il.* 9.312–13). Achilles is true to his words, for he shares all of his thoughts openly with his friends when he rejects Agamemnon's offer. Theognis also condemns the treachery of a true friend (87–92).

[407] To understand the origin of the kinship paradigm that formed the basis of this new polity, we turn to the house of Peleus in Homer, which provides the most memorable and elaborate articulations (albeit still with patriarchal elements against women and slaves). The constitution of the household consists of Peleus, Phoenix, Achilles, and Patroclus, etc., and it illustrates the possibility of artificial, fictive familial ties and

the people his trusted companion (*ton demon proshetairizetai*)."[408] With this emotional appeal, a proper Athenian citizen would develop automatic love and affinity for his brotherly compatriots, while harboring enmity and suspicion toward outsiders. These powerful primordial impulses would guide the behavior of the citizens, overriding other considerations such as material incentives. By enlarging and extending the paradigm of international brotherhood in the epic world to the territorially enclosed albeit larger population, Polisism shifted the truth about what constituted in-groups and out-groups. In the words of Donlan, "[T]he citizen-soldier of the democratic city-state is imprinted with the egalitarian ethic of Odysseus' *hetairoi*-band."[409] Robert Connor also spoke of democracy as a moment when people for the first time begin to profess to the city the kind of loyalty that was formerly promised to friends.[410] In this way, the ideals of love and kinship prized in the earlier sources set the norms for the civic relations among Athenian citizens—the difference being that in the first case, membership was small but cosmopolitan and in the second one, enlarged but local.

Democratic Athens was also without question defined by Olympian values in the way it operated. A number of "aristocrats" like Solon, Cleisthenes, and Pericles, transcending their own class interest, spearheaded radical political reform in the interest of the people. Under such virtuous leaders, no shame befell those who followed. As Hesiod states, "And noble is the man who heeds the advice/ spoken by that kind of man" (*WD* 294–95).[411] Also, a robust civic culture prevailed, encouraging the better-offs to finance and manage city-wide programs for the masses. With the emphasis on sacrifice and benevolence, authority rested on consensus rather than fear. The city protected the underclass from the magistrates and mandated audits for anyone who held office.[412] Moreover, Athens, in stark contrast to Sparta, abstained

---

strong emotional bonds of love and trust among the members. Both Phoenix and Patroclus are nonblood relations, yet they are cherished and cared for like biological family. True to the highest convivial ideals, the long-enduring love (*philia*) facilitates alignment of interests but also accepts differences in the expression of singularity. Both Phoenix and Patroclus, for example, strongly disagree with Achilles' refusal to fight, yet the difference in opinion doesn't affect their affection and love. Within the convivial family, a cycle of giving and returning occurs naturally without being measured or tracked in economic terms—this is what Sahlin would call "generalized reciprocity." Phoenix recalls that Peleus "accepted me with a good will and gave me his love, even as a father loves his own son who is a single child brought up among many possessions. He made me a rich man, and granted me many people." (*Il.* 9.478–83). Phoenix in turn raises and educates Achilles, who vows to share half of his wealth and honor with the elder. Patroclus, the childhood friend of Achilles, accompanies the hero everywhere and later becomes the reason that Achilles dies an early death. Kin members unquestioningly perform critical services like education, elderly care, companionship, emotional support, and even the sacrifice of one's life for each other. The material expenditure toward the long-term well-being of loved ones supersedes just "gifts" exchanged between two separate entities, becoming more like an automatic transfer within the same entity.

[408] Herodotus, 5.66

[409] Donlan, *The Aristocratic Ideal*, 356.

[410] Connor, *The New Politicians*, 100.

[411] All lines of Hesiod are translated by C. S. Morrissey, unless otherwise indicated.

[412] This is not a unique Athenian phenomenon. The rise of law in ancient Greece seems to be related to the desire to prevent excessive power at the top. For example, one of earliest inscriptions comes from Dresos on Crete. It records a law that limits the power of the magistrates. See Kurt A. Raaflaub and Robert W. Wallace, "People's Power and Egalitarian Trends in Archaic Greece," in *Origins of Democracy in Ancient Greece*, ed. Kurt A. Raaflaub, Josiah Ober, and Robert Wallace (Berkeley and Los Angeles: University of

from interfering in the private life of citizens with regard to marriage, childrearing, and profession. In this tolerant, diverse, and largely peaceful city, the "notables" (*hoi gnorimoi*) and their peers hosted symposia and attended the games as they wished, with the people (*demos*) now also taking part in those once-aristocratic activities.[413] By and large, the freedom to live as one wished and the duty to serve in public life were brought into harmony. For the collective drive did not obstruct expressions of individualism; in fact, the building of this free, just, diverse, and equal society multiplied the opportunities for free-born men to "perform" their unique selves during the democratic golden age. Pericles expresses this unity beautifully: "At Athens we live exactly as we please, and yet are just as ready to encounter every legitimate danger" (Thucydides 2.39.1).

Hannah Arendt captured the extent to which this new body politic made possible the self-fashioning of identity through free action—in essence what poets did for the heroes before:

> The polis now gives a guarantee that those who forced every sea and land to become the scene of their daring will not remain without witness and will need neither Homer nor anyone else who knows how to turn words to praise them.[414]

Seen in this light, the actual birth of formal democracy would be unthinkable outside of Olympianism.[415] Instead of abruptly popping up from nowhere,[416] the host of

---

California Press, 2007), 23. In general, "Much early Greek law regulat[es] who may hold which office, for how long, and establishing penalties for infringements." See Ian Morris, "Early Iron Age Greece," in *The Cambridge Economic History of the Greco-Roman World*, ed. Walter, Scheidel, Ian Morris, and Richard Saller (Cambridge: Cambridge University Press, 2007), 238. Zimmern said, "[laws] which go back most certainly to Solon...are those that afford protection to the weak and helpless." See Zimmern, *The Greek Commonwealth*, 135.

[413] For the incorporation of aristocratic values, see Walter Eder, "Aristocrats and the Coming of Athenian Democracy," in *Democracy 2500?: Questions and Challenges*, ed. Ian Morris, Kurt A. Raaflaub, and David Castriota (Dubuque, IA: Kendall/Hunt Pub. Co., 1998), 129f; for the provision of public dining rooms and public occasion for feasting, see Oswyn Murray, "The Affair of the Mysteries: Democracy and the Drinking Group," in *Sympotica: A Symposium on the Symposion* (Oxford: Clarendon Press, 1990), 149–50.

[414] Arendt is quoting Thucydides, 2.41.

[415] Donlan offered the same conclusion: "the *polis* form merely enveloped without radically changing, the political style of the pre-state community" (*The Aristocratic Ideal*, 297). In "The Relations of Power in the Pre-state and Early-state Polities," in *The Development of the* Polis *in Archaic Greece*, ed. Lynette G. Mitchell and P. J. Rhodes (London and New York: Routledge, 1997), 21, Donlan spoke of "fundamental continuities between pre-state and early-state polities." Yet Donlan derived this from examining social and political structures, not cultural elements. Rose entertained the same idea that the "real roots of democracy are to be found in the memories of this meritocratic period (the Dark Age of Homer)," but his analysis of class differs from my cultural approach. See Peter Rose, *Class in Archaic Greece* (Cambridge, UK: Cambridge University Press, 2012), 62.

[416] Ober dated the birth of democracy to the uprising of the Athenian *demos* in 508/7, which has been the traditional date given by George Grote of the eighteenth century. Ober called it a "historical rupture...an epistemic and sociological/ideological moment" that marks the birth of Athenian democracy, though he also acknowledged a "pre-revolutionary history." See Josiah Ober, "I Besieged That Man: Democracy's Revolutionary Start," in *Origins of Democracy in Ancient Greece*, ed. Kurt A. Raaflaub, Josiah Ober, and Robert Wallace (Berkeley and Los Angeles: University of California Press, 2007), 83, 86. My position advocates strong continuity in the process. In my view, the cultural formation of Olympianism had already

institutions considered foundational for *demokratia* can all be traced to the Olympian cultural dispensation. In Dean Hammer's view, the Athenian society moved from the plebiscitary politics of the previous era to a proper city-state democracy in the fifth century.[417] Nor did this unique political configuration emerge in the Aegean due to the obsolescence of religion.[418] The imagination of the gods in fact gave rise to egalitarianism, codependence, reciprocity, and plurality, all of which underpinned the democratic solution of the West. It could even be argued that in some ways Classical Athens significantly improved the core teachings of Olympianism by engraving them into formal structure. For instance, equality between people of different backgrounds as a cultural ideal was more tenuous in the earlier historical context of predominantly spontaneous social interaction. But when institutions serving Olympian goals crystallized at Athens in the fifth century, a person was guaranteed a host of rights by virtue of being a citizen, an all-powerful status that was secure and permanent.

But in major and unforgivable ways, the democracy of the ancient Greeks made a dramatic turn. The Athenian *polis*, the heir apparent to Olympianism, devoted extensive energy to denying resident aliens (*metics*), slaves, and women the rights and opportunities of realizing their full potential. At the pinnacle of Athenian democracy in 451, Pericles introduced a law restricting citizenship to only children from legal marriages between two Athenians. Whereas previously, communal membership was a function of *actions* such as the fulfillment of civic duty, obedience to law, participation in common affairs, and the taking up of a trade, the legal definition of belonging was now predicated on the one-time hereditary circumstance at birth. The new criteria in essence declared that no matter how much someone loved Athens and was willing to serve it, he or she could not be an Athenian citizen unless having been born as one.

Interestingly, we need to only trace back a few generations to see how much mixed marriages and international ties shaped Athens. For example, the mother of Cleisthenes, the founder of Athenian democracy, was the daughter of the tyrant Cleisthenes of Scion. It was after this foreign ruler that the Athenian politician who initiated the famous democratic reform in 508 was named. In this particular case, foreign ancestry, elite status, and monarchial affiliation did not stop Cleisthenes the grandson from bequeathing the enduring legacy of *demokratia* to the ordinary people of his beloved city. Since Pericles' own mother was the niece of this very Cleisthenes, even the general himself could not boast pure Athenian blood within five generations—a testament to the constant indeterminacy or, rather, the unlimited possibility of what individuals might become despite their place of birth.

At the same time, Pericles in his famous funeral oration also defines female virtue as being least mentioned by men (Thucydides, 2.45.2). Indeed, Classical Athens was known for its seclusion of women and their banishment from public

---

prepared the ground for the event of 508/7. Instead of a radical revolution, it makes much more sense to me to attribute the event to numerous democratic precursors in the preceding Dark and Archaic Ages.

[417] Hammer, *The Iliad as Politics*, 161.

[418] On the uniqueness of Greek democracy, Morris explained, "Without God or gods to rule and to reveal, many Greeks concluded that human reason was the only guide to truth." See Ian Morris and Barry B. Powell, *The Greeks: History, Culture, and Society*, 1st ed. (Upper Saddle River, NJ: Pearson Prentice Hall, 2006), 5.

sphere. However, apart from this rhetoric, Pericles himself chose to live with Aspasia, a courtesan (hetaira) from Miletus who was famed not only for her beauty, but also her wise opinions (*The Life of Pericles*, 24). It is natural that the men of Athens who became accustomed to equal peers might also prefer partners who were intelligent and outspoken. In these ways, the exclusive native male political citizenship imposed by the *polis* jarringly perverted the Olympian legacy of inclusion and conviviality.

While robbing foreign residents and women who lived amidst citizens of opportunity and freedom, Athens turned its back most harshly on extraterritorial communities and groups. In another notable episode, Pericles, the architect of the war against Sparta, disavowed in front of the assembly his *xenia* (guest-friendship) with the Spartan king Archidamus, who was approaching Attica with an invading army (Thucydides, 2.18.1-2). Archidamus appeared to be under similar pressure from the Spartans to campaign resolutely and ruthlessly against Athenians (Thucydides, 2.183-5). This zeitgeist contrasts with the supremacy of *xenia* that allowed Glaucus and Diomedes to lay down arms and exchange gifts on the battlefield. Thucydides and contemporary commentators seem all but to admire Perciles' public show of patriotism, treating it as a gesture of placing the common good above personal feelings. However, the severing of *xenia* relations not only wiped out past goodwill but also diminished future prospects of reconciliation and amnesty—measures that restore peace and trust in the long-run. True, in the heat of the war, the Spartans constituted a hostile and aggressive force. Yet just a few decades ago, the same city sacrificed 300 brave men at Thermopylae in 480 BCE to preserve the freedom of Greece. In 510 BCE, the Spartans assisted Athenians in expelling the tyrant Hippias, whose elimination paved the way for the ascent of democracy. Historically, Sparta was the home to the famous Helen and the poet Tyrtaeus. Aside from grand events and figures, a number of Athenian aristocrats must have rubbed shoulders with their Spartan counterparts at athletic games, communal feasts, religious occasions, and other events of celebration and gathering. These shared memories and experiences along with *xenia* would have constantly reinforced the notion that despite temporary quarrels, the Spartans belonged to the same league of mortals after all. But the rise of territorial citizenship in the fifth century in essence postulated that they, the Spartans who were born on foreign soil, could never be regarded like us, the Athenians.

If the Spartans posed some military threats to warrant legitimate self-defense, then the "might-makes-right" doctrine removed any moral pretense in Athenian foreign policy toward other harmless Greek cities under its imperial rule. Hardened by the artificial territorial demarcation between "us" and "them," the Athenian state, which boasted to be the school to all Greece, did not have any sacred respect for non-Athenian lives and refused to believe their well-being could in any way benefit it in return.[419] The divide created by Polisism became so natural that when the besieged Melians invoked the all-embracing gods, their Athenian captors only sneered. Not long ago, in a similar debate regarding the fate of Mytilene, the Athenian assembly narrowly voted to spare their captives only because slaughtering them seemed

[419] We see these notions already solidifying in the Mytilenean debate. Cleon, the imperialist hawk, openly concedes the despotic nature of the Athenian empire, which he jarringly juxtaposes with the security and trust in the daily relations among Athenian citizens (Thucydides 3.37).

costlier. For all we know, the gods—whose images so conspicuously graced Athens with tribute money extorted from the empire—no longer extended their protection beyond the confines of the city (where are the gods in Pericles' glorious Funeral Oration?[420]).[421] With the coming of an invincible rational age, the world full of extraordinary beings first retreated into a city, and then was flattened by commercial forces that rendered everything prosaic and dispensable. By the Hellenistic Period (323–331 BCE), the dust of the three-way contest in our story began to settle, with the definitive rise of Oeconomism as victor. Dynasts and kings, replacing the immortals, extracted tribute, taxes, and military service without apology. Cities that previously celebrated public giving now found themselves at the mercy of the rich's philanthropic whims. Inequality grew, civic spirit dwindled, and internal strife (*stasis*) multiplied.[422] In the year 31 BCE, when the Romans defeated the Greek forces at the battle of Actium, the civilization that was once enchanted with the gods and the heroes had already altered beyond recognition.

[420] For my particular view on the changing nature of religion, see note 144. In the speeches of Pericles, the venerated leader, who was considered an embodiment of Athenian democracy, only mentions Athena once, in reference to the removable gold in her statue (Thucydides 2.13.5).

[421] To be fair, not everyone bought into the glittering opulence of the empire, perhaps some were still afraid of committing hubris and receiving divine retribution. Plutarch from half of a millennium later retrojected a dissenting voice that called Athenian foreign policy under Pericles an outrage and tyranny, and the city fattened by imperial tribute a "gaudy woman, hung around with expensive stones and imagines and thousand-talent temples." See Plutarch, *Life of Pericles*, 12.2.

[422] For the increased number of social conflicts in the Hellenistic era, see Fuks, *Social Conflict in Ancient Greece*, 40–51.

PART II

Olympian Cultural System

Part I outlined the political economy of Olympianism and its conflict with the other two cultures, especially during the Classical period. Part II will elaborate on the values and conceptions that undergirded the Olympian political economy. Before doing so, let us recall the formulation of culture, identity, and action delineated at the very beginning of this book. So far, we have discussed economic behavior and practice (action) as well as outlooks and preferences (identity). The second half of this book will present the discursive truths that unified the notions and ideas behind those actions and identities (culture). Cultural hermeneutics will be applied to Homer and the Archaic poets, this time largely to challenge the opinion that those authors subscribed to an elitist ideology, which stood in opposition to the egalitarianism that later defined the *polis* community of equals. In addition, a number of key historical facts about the development of the Archaic world (800–480 BCE) will be woven into the analysis. While the study continues to suggest that the pre-Classical eras were more "Olympian" in comparison to the later centuries, it must be reiterated that the correspondence was not always one to one. Yet despite the heterogeneity of historical reality, as acknowledged in the Introduction, Olympianism nonetheless was greatly cherished and highly influential before the rise of the *polis*.

CHAPTER 5

Ecumenism, Conviviality, and *Agon*

The core of the Olympian cultural dispensation rests on the concepts of "ecumenism" and "conviviality." Ecumenism is a worldview that treats *every* entity as special and unique, and it is consistent with the truth of sacred time and space discussed in Chapter 1. The unassailable worth of all life calls for joint habitation in a "crowded" world that does not dismiss or violate *anyone*. In this principle alone, Olympianism already sets itself apart from the territorial state, which often regards those outside, as well as the minority groups within, as the lesser *other*. To meet the challenge of cherishing all beings, a second, related truth—one that I call *conviviality*—becomes salient, and it brings about a cluster of interrelated social and cultural norms.[423] The convivial spirit is symbolized by feasting, the phenomenon of festival celebration, which appeals to the senses directly. This very idea offers a contrast to the cold notion from liberalism that regards society as a group of disaggregated and calculating individuals who need the sovereign to protect them. On this basis, ecumenism and conviviality differ from the modern formulations of universal equality and multiculturalism that are germane to the nation-state and the (neo)liberal individual.[424] In the remainder of this chapter, I will elaborate on the discourses of conviviality and ecumenism that are central to Olympianism, which engendered the identifications and actions we have outlined in Part I.

CONVIVIAL FEASTING: A MULTITUDINOUS, INCLUSIVE, HORIZONTAL, AND PLURALIST OCCASION

Feasting, depicted so frequently in ancient Greek sources, is the most apt metaphor for understanding conviviality.[425] Readers of early Greek literature know that besides quarreling or plotting vengeance—qualities that make the Greek gods all too human—they boisterously partake in food, drink, and entertainment together. In Book 1 of the *Odyssey*, for example, Poseidon visits the Ethiopians and "[t]here he sat at the feast and took his pleasure" (1.26). Also, at the beginning of the *Iliad*, the gods go on a trip to party with the Ethiopians (1.423–24). When they return to Olympus, another celebration proceeds for a whole day from dawn to dusk (1.601). This big feast, taking place after an intense moment between Zeus and Hera, the two most foremost gods on Olympus, is all the more striking because it signifies a return to celestial

[423] I borrow this word from Ivan Illich, who described a convivial society without monopolies. See Ivan Illich, *Tools for Conviviality* (London: Marion Boyars, 2001).
[424] Cf. Paul Gilroy, who proposed "convivial living," but placed it within the framework of the nation-state. See *After Empire: Melancholia or Convivial Culture?* (London: Routledge, 2004).
[425] Murray discussed the centrality of feasting and its implied reciprocity and public function. See Oswyn Murray, *Early Greece*, 2nd ed. (Cambridge, MA: Harvard University Press, 1993), 47.

normalcy. Since the gods set the standards for mortals, feasting—conspicuously featured in both epic poems—was to be emulated.

Such celebration not only brings instant gratification, but also, philosophically speaking, normalizes the cultural preference for inclusion, interdependence, horizontal reciprocity, and plurality.[426] First, one cannot feast alone. A single individual cannot reproduce the joy of eating, drinking, and entertaining in company. The rule "the more the merrier," as we say today, also applies, so that others become desirable. Interestingly, we must remember that Zeus, unlike his predecessors Uranus and Cronus who jealously guarded their dictatorial rule, shares Olympus with his children and extended kin—a prerequisite for collective rejoicing. By ending the dark days when one god, or one generation of gods, presided over the world before him, Zeus implements a more multifarious and pluralist order. This ecumenical and polytheist reign implies that the combined wisdom of the group is far greater than the capability of any individual deity who is always imperfect and flawed.[427]

Descending down to the mortal realm, the act of feasting binds gods to humans and brings heaven to earth. In a passage in Book 3 of the *Odyssey*, Nestor explains to his son that a lavish jubilee honors and pleases the goddess Athena (3.418–20). Typically on such an occasion, a ritual sacrifice dedicated to the immortals is followed by the pleasurable partaking of food, drinks, and entertainment, activities that lift man temporarily out of his brutish and nasty existence. Elsewhere in the text, warriors feast abroad (*Il.* 9.89–92, 9.199–222); foreigners feast in their own lands (Cadmeians in *Il.* 4.385–86; Aiolians in *Od.* 10.9); Greeks feast at home (in Odysseus' home in *Od.* 1.136–43; at Nestor's palace in *Il.* 3.33–336; at Peleus' house in *Il.* 11.779); and the villagers depicted on the shield of Achilles feast together (*Il.* 18.491). The narrator does not withhold praise and proclaims "and always the feast is dear to us, and the lyre and dances,/ and changes of clothing and our hot baths and beds" (*Od.* 8.248–49). In Book 9, Odysseus, the one skilled in words, reflects on the experience:

> For I think there is no occasion accomplished that is more pleasant
> than when festivity holds sway among all the populace,
> and the feasters up and down the houses are sitting in order
> and listening to the singer and beside them the tables are loaded
> with bread and meats. (9.5–10)

Through this heartfelt description, the joy of festive gathering becomes visceral.

A truly delightful feast also rationalizes a great degree of redistribution and egalitarianism. Although the attendees may not be identical in achievement, power, and ability, their differences would have to be small enough if they were to sit together at the same table as more or less equals. The Greek word for feasting is *dais*,

[426] Here, I am not presenting the historical facts about feasting in ancient Greece but the concept of feasting as a philosophy.

[427] On this point, see Walter Burkert, *Greek Religion* (Cambridge, MA: Harvard University Press, 1985), 216. This is not to say that gods themselves are just and perfect—they can be callous, selfish, and cause suffering. The point is their interest in all human beings across a wide range of social groups affects the dynamic and perception of power in social life.

and the corresponding verb *daiō* means "to distribute and divide." The etymology highlights the importance of equitable provision. In fact, the line "nor did their hearts lack a fair portion of the equal feast" becomes a formulaic expression for feasting (*Il.* 1.468, 602, 3.66).[428] In the convivial context, the dispersal of resources becomes firmly associated with salubrious pleasure.

With the genuine well-being of others being an end in itself, feasting unsurprisingly draws out mutual goodwill among participants through broad equality and fair redistribution. Abundance, generosity, and the absence of hostility make a good party.[429] Conversely, tension and fear hinder true enjoyment. Worse yet, causes of grievance would destroy all chance of joyous commensality. When Circe entices Odysseus with food and drink, he refuses to oblige until the sorceress frees his companions and transforms them back from swine form to humans. Odysseus explains to his hostess,

> Oh Circe, how could any man right in his mind ever
> endure to taste of the food and drink that are set before him,
> until with his eyes he saw his companions set free? So then,
> if you are sincerely telling me to eat and drink, set them
> free, so my eyes can again behold my eager companions. (*Od.* 10.383–87)

Upon hearing these words, Circe complies with the request (*Od.* 10.458). She releases his men and invites them to the banquet table. The celebration resumes only after genuine reconciliation, at which point the narrator tells us that the hostess now "shines among goddesses" (*Od.* 10.455). For the modern reader, this parable underscores that the exercise of goodwill and elimination of hostility are critical for congenial co-existence.

Equality and Conviviality in Olympus

Likewise, the bickering of Hera and Zeus in Book 1 of the *Iliad* casts a dark shadow over the gods, giving their son Hephaestus cause for dismay. He says,

> This will be a disastrous matter and not endurable
> if you two are to quarrel thus for the sake of mortals
> and bring brawling among the gods. There will be no pleasure
> in the stately feast at all, since vile things will be uppermost. (1.573–76)

Hephaestus tries to restore the mood by urging Hera to acquiesce. But submitting to tyrannical male authority does not conform to the rules of conviviality, nor does the suppression of grievance for the temporary avoidance of conflict.

---

[428] The translation of this line comes from A. T. Murray, trans., *The Iliad, Loeb Classical Library Volume 1* (Cambridge, MA: Harvard University Press; London, William Heinemann Ltd. 1924).

[429] Arthur Adkins concluded: "The godly feast should be the constant way of life for the gods, and no mortal concerns should be permitted to threaten it," See Arthur Adkins, "Homeric Ethics," in *A New Companion to Homer*, ed. Ian Morris and Barry Powell (New York: E.J. Brill, 1997), 709.

Despite patriarchal assertions, the "victims"—the female deities Athena and Hera, in particular—do not obey Zeus in all matters big and small. On the contrary, the two goddesses in the *Iliad* defy the father of the gods by working toward Troy's destruction. At one point, when chided by Zeus, Hera insists that she is entitled to her own course of action:

> Majesty, son of Kronos, what sort of thing have you spoken?
> Even one who is mortal will try to accomplish his purpose
> for another, though he be a man and known not such wisdom as we do.
> As for me then, who claim I am highest of all the goddesses,
> both ways, since I am eldest born and am called your consort,
> yours, and you in turn are lord over all the immortals,
> how could I not weave sorrows for the men of Troy, when I hate them! (*Il.* 18.361–67)

These words show that Hera considers herself to be an equal and independent actor—a belief that propels her to stand up to Zeus. In an episode that underscores this peer dynamic, Hera interferes to stop Zeus from saving his bastard son Sarpedon (*Il.* 16.440–61). In another scene in Book 4, Hera blocks Zeus' plan to broker a settlement between the Greeks and the Trojans. She warns her husband, "Do as you please—but we other gods do not all approve" (*Il.* 4.29). Her interjection implies that without group consensus, no plan can proceed successfully. Indeed, Zeus relents and abandons the idea of ending the war early; in return, Hera makes a reciprocal concession by consenting to the destruction of Troy in the future. Through these compromises, competing preferences from equally worthy advocates are reconciled through horizontal negotiation. All and all, opposing voices—even those from female figures—cannot be cast aside in this collegial world.

These examples of deliberation and consensus-building point to a significant degree of power sharing among the gods. First, they control separate realms and territories, e.g., Poseidon over the sea and Hades the underworld. Second, as individual deities, they stake out a claim to different domains like poetry, love, warfare, and craftsmanship—purviews that are powerful in their own right.[430] Therefore, when Poseidon speaks to Iris about his brother, he unequivocally rejects Zeus' supremacy.

> No, no. Great though he is, this that he has said is too much,
> if he will force me against my will, me, who am his *equal* [my emphasis]
> in rank. Since we are three brothers born by Rhea[431] to Kronos,
> Zeus, and I, and the third is Hades, lord of the dead men.
> All was divided among us three ways, each given his domain. (*Il.* 15.185–90)

[430] Finley and Pleket, *The Olympic Games*, 16.
[431] Spelled Rheia in the original translation according to Greek transliteration.

These words capture the sense of the horizontal equality that characterizes the reign of the Greek gods. As a result, notwithstanding the *de jure* preeminence of Zeus, the gods govern the universe jointly and *de facto* direct the lives of mortals in concert.

The sources speak of Zeus' limitations without reserve. He submits to the Sisters of the Fates, however obscure they are as deities. In another instance, Hera, Poseidon, and Athena form a coalition against Zeus and manage to put him in chains (*Il.* 1.396–406). Headstrong Hera also tricks her mighty husband in a separate incident related by Agamemnon in Book 19. Even the minor sea nymph Thetis puts a check on Zeus' power: she saves Zeus twice, first by rescuing him physically from bondage (*Il.*393–406) and then by avoiding his romantic interest so that her son, who is destined to overthrow his father, would not pose any threat. The shortcomings and inefficacy of Zeus' authority effectively forestall a rigid vertical hierarchy among the gods. In this fashion, a decentralized and pluralist regime takes root in Olympianism.

Feasting and Pluralism

By recognizing that all beings are consequential, the ecumenical and convivial orientation also advances pluralism. Metaphorically speaking, it is easy to see how a large communal feast, unlike a small private dinner, would accommodate guests of varying backgrounds and personalities. It is precisely this proclivity to embrace different races which allows Zeus to mingle with the Ethiopians in the *Iliad* (1.423–24). Diversity also underpins the earthly feasts that are open to foreign visitors and women. Helen, for example, receives Telemachus during a large welcoming dinner (*Od.* 4.121–295); Polycaste, the youngest daughter of Nestor, gives a bath to Telemachus during the latter's visit during a festival (3.465–69). On these convivial occasions, foreigners and women become desirable for joint celebration.

Nor should we think that only the princes and heroes know the art of partying. Our hardworking Hesiod is not any less fond of this "luxury." The Boeotian farmer tells us, amidst his practical tips for eking out a living, "Don't be a boor when many guests have gathered for a feast/ For when the expense is shared, the pleasure's most, the cost is least" (*WD* 722–23).[432] He also urges the listener to "invite your friends to dinner" (*WD* 342). The fact that even a peasant farmer raves about feasting proves its wide appeal.

By contrast, the unusual revelry of the suitors in the *Odyssey* constitutes a perversion precisely because it violates the tenets of inclusion and reciprocity. The suitors invade the home of Odysseus and help themselves to food and wine to the protest of the wife and son. The excluded and harmed people—Odysseus, Telemachus, Penelope, the loyal servants (and to some extent, even the townsmen)—eventually take revenge under a mandate from the gods. In this way, the negative illustration reaffirms the norms of conviviality.

[432] These lines are from Catherine M. Schlegel and Henry Weinfield, trans., *Theogony; and, Works and Days* (Ann Arbor: The University of Michigan Press, 2006). All other lines of Hesiod were translated by C. S. Morrissey.

CONVIVIAL STRIFE

At this point, a critic might object to such a rosy picture. What about the squabbles and vengeance of the Greek gods? Surely they do not only smile at each other at the banquet table? At first glance, many stories of the immortals and the heroes seem to revolve around strife and conflict.[433] Yet, we can interpret these clashes as by-products of an ecumenical and convivial order that has not yet matured. A polytheist world breeds a cacophony of views. So often the gods debate back and forth without reaching a verdict; if they simply followed a clear chain of command with regard to the Trojan War or Odysseus' homecoming, there would be no Homeric epics. Instead, no procedure or office allows a single deity—not even Zeus—to overrule the objections of others. In this world of strong assumptive equality, even a slight gesture of dismissal or insult incites protest. Such commotion would not be very visible in a normalized hierarchy. In this light, conflict stemming from egalitarian impulses is actually indicative of progressive potential.[434] By contrast, the spurious order and manufactured peace of a stratified order—no matter how appealing and convenient for the time being—cannot compensate for internalized inequity.

It should be stressed that contention only escalates into violence when someone abandons diplomacy and employs force—a direct affront to convivial principles. We see this troubling move on the part of Zeus' predecessors and sometimes Zeus himself, such as when he disciplines Prometheus and the other "disobedient" gods. Yet, the Greek narratives by no means endorse the bullying party. In *Prometheus Bound* by the fifth-century tragedian Aeschylus, for example, we witness Zeus' weaknesses and limitations in both morality and power. The brave and heroic protagonist Prometheus defies Zeus not only by stealing the fire for mankind but also by refusing to disclose the name of the one who will overthrow Zeus. By contrast in the *Iliad*, Zeus is "remarkably patient with the repeated attempts to disobey him, and, with two or three exceptions, his utterances to the other gods show a firm but gentle dignity."[435] These stories in general disapprove the use of oppressive force in conflict.

However polemical the gods may be, they live forever; therefore, all of their mistakes are ultimately redeemable. Mortals only live once, so it is absolutely critical that they learn how to avoid inflicting harm. Fortunately, some moments in the epics proffer the wisdom of both defending equality and banishing violence at same time. The instance of the funeral games for Patroclus is a case in point. At the first chariot race, Antilochus protests Achilles' plan to take away his prize, and Menelaus accuses Antilochus of stealing his second-place victory (*Il.* 23.543–85). For both parties, the

---

[433] Hans van Wees asserted that the rampant violence in the Homeric world stems from the constant desire for social recognition from others in a fragmented society. See Hans Van Wees, *Status Warriors: War, Violence and Society in Homer and History* (Amsterdam: J. C. Gieben, 1992), 69.

[434] A potent example can be found in Xenophon's *Hellenica*, regarding Kinadon's conspiracy. Kinadon confesses that he wanted to be inferior to no one in Lacedaimon (III.3).

[435] Cedric Hubbell Whitman, *Homer and the Heroic Tradition* (New York: W. W. Norton, 1965), 225. The relative mildness of the Greek gods becomes most clear when compared to the Biblical God, for the violent and punitive nature of the latter. See Raymund Schwager, *Must There be Scapegoats?: Violence and Redemption in the Bible* (Leominster: Gracewing, 2000), 47ff. Schwager pointed out that in the Bible, there are approximately 1,000 verses of God's acts of punishment, and around 100 passages where God demands killing in his name.

feelings of losing honor (*tîmê*) in public could easily erupt into violence among status-sensitive princes. Yet through gentle dialogue and reconciliatory gestures, the heroes resolve their differences without putting anyone down (*Il.* 23.587–612), just as when Odysseus accepts gifts of apology from Euryalos seeking to mend fences for an earlier taunt (*Od.* 8.408–05). Moreover, at the third funeral game of wrestling, Achilles halts Odysseus and Ajax before they would seriously hurt each other and announces them both as winners (*Il.* 23.735–37). It is important to note that a handsome prize of comparable portion is offered to both participants so that no one feels left out. The pursuit of honor and distinction by social peers, contrary to the opinion of scholars, does not always boil down to a competitive, zero-sum rivalry that is prone to turn violent.[436] In fact, by ensuring that the conferral of distributive honor comes before individual distinction, these games foster consensus and unity.

Greek mythology further glorifies the beauty of a win-win interaction through the story of Pirithous and Theseus. As a proverbial hero, Pirithous, upon hearing about the fame of Theseus, sets his heart on a deadly duel with the latter. But when the two meet, Pirithous admires Theseus so much that they become the best of friends and together go on to perform many spectacular feats.[437] In the Greek repertoire, the means of conflict resolution also include arbitration, which uses diplomacy to preserve maximum *tîmê* (honor) for both sides. In this light, even the later political reform of Solon can be seen as a form of arbitration, because he strives to protect the rich and the poor alike for the sake of the whole city.

Conviviality in its truest and most-developed form is ultimately incompatible with martial violence. Even a war poem like the *Iliad* presents scenes in which characters search for a way out of the endless fighting. Achilles comes closest to grasping the senselessness of a heroism that thirsts for the blood of the imagined enemy and the immolation of precious life: "The Trojans have done nothing to me, why do I want to kill them?" (*Il.* 1.153–54). Even before he becomes profoundly disillusioned with the war, the greatest fighter of the Greeks is known for being soft. For example, after taking over the city Thebe, Achilles does not strip the dead king but buries him with full rites and allows ransom for his wife (*Il.* 6.414–27). It is precisely this tenderness for others—driving him first into an implacable rage at the death of his dear companion Patroclus—that eventually blossoms into majestic compassion for Priam, the father of Patroclus' slayer. Looking at Priam and thinking of his own father, Achilles must have been struck by the precariousness and interdependency of human life: we are all tied to each other in inextricable and irreversible ways, and we all suffer from the effects of others' actions, having chosen none of it ourselves. The great storyteller Homer renders this profound moment through the sound of their sobbing:

> So he [Priam] spoke, and stirred in the other a passion of grieving
> for his own father. He took the old man's hand and pushed him
> gently away, and the two remembered, as Priam sat huddled

[436] Cf. Finley, *World of Odysseus*, 118; James F. McGlew, "Royal Power and the Achaean Assembly at *Iliad* 2.84-393," *Classical Antiquity*, 8, no. 2 (October 1989): 287.
[437] Plutarch, *Theseus*, 30.

> at the feet of Achille[u]s and wept close for manslaughtering
> He[c]tor and Achille[u]s wept now for his own father, now again
> for Patro[c]l[u]s. The sound of their mourning moved in the house. (*Il.* 507–12)

With an elevated understanding of human suffering, Achilles lets go of his anger, for he realizes that "[S]uch is the way the gods spun life for unfortunate mortals,/ that we live in unhappiness, but the gods themselves have no sorrows" (525–26). However brief, Achilles' magnificent gesture of reconciliation underscores the truth that mortals can break the endless cycles of vengeance that constantly stir them. Owing to this remarkable moment in the epic, no matter how much ancient Greece is known to posterity for its martial aggression and incessant warfare, the instantaneous switch from hating to embracing the *other* shall forever remain as part of the Classical legacy. Such an epic moment brings us closer to the question of how we can "value human relationships and cooperation and enable us to challenge one another without resorting to mutual slaughter."[438]

Interestingly, the folklore origin of the Trojan War also helps us critique military violence. Greek myth traces the genesis of the Trojan War to a petty feud among three egomaniacal goddesses.[439] Another version even suggests that Zeus planned it explicitly for the destruction of men.[440] These mythological explanations, which depict the causes of the conflict as trivial, accidental, and nefarious, shed light on the madness and absurdity of a war that kills so many Trojans and Greeks dear to the gods.

Although no systemic invalidation of warfare can be found in the Olympian sources,[441] a number of passages depict combat and strife with horror and disgust. In the *Iliad*, Zeus calls Ares, the war god, most invidious for delighting in strife, war, and bloodshed (*Il.* 5.889–98). When his beloved companion Patroclus dies, Achilles curses strife and wishes it "would vanish away from among gods and mortals" (*Il.* 18.107). In Hesiod's account of the previous generations, Bronze Age and Silver Age men meet utter ruin by turning against each other rather than living in convivial celebration. His *Theogony* names the children of Eris (strife) after ugly and terrible entities: Toil, Oblivion, Famine, Sorrows, Fights, Battles, Murders, Manslaying, Quarrels, and Lies (226–32). The truth about the ugly nature of war, though often superseded by the glorification of martial valor, nevertheless takes up its own place in the Olympian dispensation.

---

438 Frank Adloff, "The Current Responses," in *Convivialist Manifesto: A Declaration of Interdependence*, Global Dialogues 3. Käte Hamburger Kolleg/Centre for Global Cooperation Research (Duisburg 2014).

439 Hard, *The Routledge Handbook of Greek Mythology*, 30.

440 Ibid., 437.

441 On the important topic of peace, I want to pay my respect to Prof. Michael Nagler, who has kindly provided feedback for my manuscript. Our academic discussion aside, it is important to note that even if the ancients failed to curb violence, it does not mean that we are bound to follow their footsteps. Prof. Nagler shows us how we could outdo the Greeks through his commendable work in founding and serving the Metta Center for Nonviolence, an organization that disseminates the method and wisdom of peaceful conflict-resolution.

Last, we should not forget that Greek religion itself, despite canonizing the martial god Ares, provided the major occasion for halting violence, if only for short intervals. During the Panhellenic celebrations, the Greeks proclaimed a divine truce (*ekecheiria*, literally the "holding of hands"), which guaranteed the safety of attendees from near and afar and forbade any act of warfare and aggression.[442] Moreover, adjacent harbors and markets would guarantee the protection of all passersby from piracy and rapine.[443] The desire for convivial life—though it can be dangerous and volatile if not accompanied by necessary wisdom and maturity—can be the source for curbing violence, precisely because we need each other to compete, interact, and gather, as well as to discover and become ourselves.

INDIVIDUAL AND COMMUNITY IN *AGON*

As suggested, the truth of conviviality at its most powerful can unite individuals and dissipate separation or rivalry between them. Returning to the illustration of feasting, it is easy to see how a host who loves his guests will find pleasure in their enjoyment. Such a host would gladly provision them as if provisioning himself. The dynamic of feasting contrasts with the modernist tendency to treat individuals as separate and disaggregated entities.[444] Instead, the truth about the self in the Homeric world of Olympianism features an "I" (*ego*) that is not enclosed, but punctured by a confluence of evolving ties and connections with others (*alter*).[445] This model of the self, which is mediated by ecumenism, conviviality, and a third concept *agon*, is expansive, integrated, and intersubjective.[446]

Prominence of *Agon*

The convivial convergence of individuals paves the way for *agon*, which can be loosely conceived of as a group event that discloses singular identity in public. The ideal of *agon* defines a number of signature Greek activities like political debate, martial combat, games, and the symposium—all of which evince a quintessential aristocratic quality. Those platforms activate the process of individuation through the

---

[442] Glotz, *Ancient Greece at Work*, 113.
[443] Ibid.
[444] It must be stressed that the community here is not an abstract entity that subsumes the individual, but a plural collectivity that resembles Arendt's conception of an arena of singular subjects.
[445] James Redfield, *Nature and Culture in the Iliad*: *The Tragedy of Hector* (Chicago: University of Chicago Press, 1975), 21.
[446] The automatic acceptance of the modern notion of the individual has often limited scholarly debate. See Arthur Adkins, *Merit and Responsibility*: *A Study in Greek Values* (Oxford: Clarendon Press, 1960). Adkins argued that the epics indiscriminately privilege the success of competitive individuals. This thesis has met strong objection from Anthony A. Long, who argued that Homer reprimands egoistic excess as much as he praises competitive excellence. See Long's criticism in "Morals and Values in Homer," *Journal of Hellenistic Studies* 90 (1970): 122. In addition, Finkelberg ("*Timē* and *Aretē* in Homer," 22–28) also criticized Adkins' understanding by arguing that *aretē* overrides *timē* and the former requires the exercise of personal virtue for public purpose, which is very close to my notion of convivial convergence. In any case, Adkins did not explain the source of his "individual," which resembles the modern subject more than the Greek heroic archetype.

reaction of social equals.[447] On those occasions, the gaze and feedback of the *other* endow the contestants with distinction and differentiation. Infused with ecumenical and convivial truths, *agon*, in its uncorrupted form, insists on fairness and transparency so that a person's performance can aptly feed into identity disclosure.[448] By showcasing the virtue and merit of meaningful (noble) action before peers, *agon* automatically sidelines considerations of heritage, wealth, and status, which subtract from or undermine the mission.

Before all else, we must first separate *agon* from "competition" in conventional modern parlance, for the latter is deeply married to the free market ideology that sanctions individual success achieved in a zero-sum fashion. As Debra Hawhee pointed out, in Greek the root meaning of *agon* is gathering or assembly.[449] In contrast, another word, *athlios* (from the verb *athleuein*), refers to the single-minded struggle for victory, which also carries the meaning of being miserable and wretched, perhaps not by coincidence. The two orientations—one of bringing people together (*agon*), the other of pursuing victory at another's expense (*athlios*)—should not be conflated. As for athletic games, for example, while the contestants seek to prevail, those events draw together judges, spectators, and indirectly, the greater community through songs, reports, and commemoration.[450] The same dualism can be found in political debate and poetic gatherings as well, and even to a very unsatisfied degree, combat, which shall soon be discussed. Overall, the forces of *agon* often contain and supersede *athlios*, with the goal of *agon* being public recognition, rather than the individual utility that is the objective of *athlios*.

Collaboration on Agonistic Space

For an ideal *agon*, the funeral games in the *Iliad* offer an exemplary illustration. The special events commence as Achilles invites "sons of Atreus and all other strong-greaved Achaeans" (*Il.* 23.273) to honor his dead friend Patroclus, excluding no one on the basis of rank, standing, or title. As the games proceed, the contestants learn to deal with issues concerning fairness, luck, and pre-existing barriers. First, we encounter an accusation of foul play at the horse race: Menelaus calls Antilochus out for using dangerous brinksmanship, a practice that rigs the game and undermines morale. Antilochus accepts the charge and replies empathetically that:

> Enough now. For I, my lord Menelaos, am younger
> by far than you, and you are the greater and go before me.
> You know how greedy transgressions flower in a young man, seeing
> that his mind is the more active but his judgment is lightweight. Therefore
> I would have your heart be patient with me. I myself will give you
> the mare I won, and if there were something still greater you asked for

---

[447] This is similar to G. H. Mead's idea that identity results from an interplay of role-taking and role-making.

[448] For the importance of participation and mutual emulation, see Finkelberg, "*Timē* and *Aretē* in Homer," 15–16.

[449] Debra Hawhee, "Agonism and Arete," *Philosophy and Rhetoric* 35, no. 3 (2002): 185.

[450] Ibid.

out of my house, I should still be willing at once to give it
to you, beloved of Zeus, rather than all my days
fall from your favor and be in the wrong before the divinities. (23.587–95)

With Antilochus' admission of unseemly behavior, the two potential adversaries trade gifts and reconcile with each other. Neither of them considers it shameful or weak to yield or compromise. The use of proper redress to restore fairness and comity ratifies the salutary function of *agon* to bring people together.

In this heroic gathering, distorting factors such as luck and old age, which cannot be controlled, are ameliorated. During the race, Eumelos' chariot is smashed by Athena, who became angry with him, but Achilles still rewards the hero for his excellent horsemanship, and the proposal is met with enthusiastic approval of all present (*Il.* 23.539).[451] In addition, Achilles also reserves an honorary prize for Nestor, who is too old to compete, with the result that no one is penalized by pre-existing disadvantage (*Il.* 23.620–23). With corrective measures that exude a spirit similar to today's affirmative action, the force of "coming together" subsumes that of "one-on-one sparring," blending competition with co-operation and aligning individual ambition with group cohesion.[452]

The foil to the positive model in the *Iliad* is the ruthless, perverse boxing match in the *Odyssey*. Fearing to lose his portion of alms to the newcomer (who is in actuality the disguised king of Ithaca), the town beggar Iros—urged on by the nefarious suitors—challenges Odysseus to a nasty duel. Iros mulls over his intentions: "I have some bad plans for him:/ hit him with both hands, and spatter all of the teeth out/ from his jaws on the ground, as if he were a wild pig rooting/ the crops" (*Od.* 18.27–30). This unnecessary brawl over food, an amenity made scarce by the suitors although elsewhere abundantly provisioned by the protagonists, turns the competitors into animals, e.g., a wild pig driven by the villainous belly. The senselessness of this artificial winner-takes-all game is plainly manifest to Odysseus. He remarks: "Strange man, I am doing you no harm, nor speaking any,/ nor am I jealous, if someone takes plenty and gives it to you./ This doorsill is big enough for both of us…" (*Od.* 18.15–17). This lowly, nasty competition created by unnecessary deprivation contrasts starkly with the heroic, convivial games in which participants freely vie for symbolic trophies while deepening their friendship with each other.

Agon as Politics

Let us apply the above, somewhat qualified generalizations of *agon* to the *Iliad.* At first glance, the conflict between Achilles and Agamemnon seems to result from a "competition" over personal reward and individual recognition. But Achilles' bitter indictment of the commander-in-chief reveals a deeper grievance—the detrimental breakdown of the agonistic space.

---

451 Here, the text uses the Greek verb *epaineîn*, which is always correlated with approval; see Elmer, *The Poetics of Consent*, 1.

452 For someone like Adkins, who saw the prevalence of competitive values based on individual needs, the scene in which the awards are not strictly based on game results is indeed confusing, see *Merit and Responsibility*, 56, cf. note 509.

> [...] neither
> do I think the son of Atreus, Agamemnon, will persuade me,
> nor the rest of the *Danaans*, since there was no gratitude given
> for fighting incessantly forever against your enemies.
> Fate is the same for the man who holds back, the same if he fights hard.
> We are all held in a single honor, the brave with the weaklings.
> A man dies still if he has done nothing, as one who has done much. (9.314–20)

For Achilles, only a fair and just contest that acknowledges individual excellence and effort could satisfy the heroes who embarked on this expedition together. But by blurring proper distinction, Agamemnon has undermined the basic rules of *agon* that make the war worthwhile. Agamemnon's monarchic ambition of always being the first irrespective of merit becomes transparent when he tells Achilles: "that well you may know/ how much better I am than you, and another man may shrink back/ from likening himself to me and contending against me" (*Il.* 1.185–87). His assertion is repudiated by Homer, who shows that that all princes have ties to the gods and are equally important and special. Indeed, the federation is made up of Greek nobles who joined Agamemnon voluntarily, and it could only hold together on the basis of consensus and mutual respect. Yet Agamemnon has allowed the agonistic principles to collapse, with the result that those who labor hard are being inadequately appreciated and others who put in no effort are handsomely compensated. By underscoring the loss of agonistic integrity, Achilles belies the corollary that proper game rules are responsible for group coherence. From this perspective, the conflict in the *Iliad* is no longer simply a story of interpersonal quarreling: it highlights the import of just distinction for the health of a polity.

Along very similar lines, the principles of *agon* also apply to public address, whereby any one of multiple, diverse opinions gets a chance to be heard. In a purely fair and open debate, the best advice would be adopted in the interest of the group, with due accolades for the speaker and without resentment from the losing advocates. We will examine the nature of the political debate more closely in the next chapter.

Agon and Warfare

The martial poems of Tyrtaeus and Callinus underscore for us how *agon* works in warfare. Irrespective of specific military tactics and weapons used, warriors risk their precious lives in exchange for the gratitude and admiration from the community. A poem by Callinus describes the reception of such men by the public:

> Yet when a hero dies the great and small shed tears
> by a whole people a brave warrior is mourned.
> In life he seems a demigod before the crowd;
> as a marble pillar they look upon his strength,

for all alone he does the great deeds of an army.[453]

These lines provide a vivid visualization of the process in which true heroism acquires meaning through the validation of others.

Even toward the opponent, some basic elements of *agon* in the form of "gentleman combat" cohere in early Greek aristocratic warfare: heroic fighting is always a one-to-one match in Homer, which places individual prowess and courage above manpower and military strategy. In the famous story of "Seven against Thebes," each Argive leader is matched with a Theban champion at one of the seven gates. In the late Archaic period, both the Spartans and the Argives agree to resolve the conflict over Thyrea by sending 300 men each for a fair trial (Herodotus I.82). Moreover, the unwritten codes of heroic warfare granted even the enemy, the antagonistic *other*, certain rights which bespeak compassion and decency. In the world defined by ecumenical gods, the mutilation of the dead was banned and corpses had to be returned after being stripped of armor,[454] as Achilles well learns after slaying Hector. After a battle, winners erected a trophy made of perishable material outside of the city, but this marker of victory would vanish quickly for the fresh start of a new round of contestation.[455] Since the result of *agon* should not be known ahead of time, prior imbalances need to be rectified even if they result from deserving actions in the past. Donlan characterized the epic heroes in the following way: "Past success counted for little; men who displayed great courage over long periods of time might suddenly be accused of outright cowardice because of a momentary hesitation. Seldom, if ever, does a warrior defend himself by appealing to past performance, for worth is always measured by the present moment."[456] These rules, which aim to implement fairness and equality, prevent meaningful combat from degenerating into senseless massacre.[457]

Olympianism not only regulates warfare, but also questions its basic compatibility with conviviality. In the story about Achilles and Penthesileia,[458] the Greek hero becomes fatally attracted to the Amazon queen on the battlefield. At the very moment when he looks into her eyes just as he is striking her down, love for Penthesileia overcomes Achilles instantly, followed by grief for her death. As the tale signifies, the destruction of sacred life for distinction and the need of convivial *agon* for the other is fundamentally incompatible,[459] because a meaningful contest can no longer take place with the annihilation of an admirable and worthy opponent.

Herodotus offers the most penetrating insight on the true state of our mutual interdependence, even as deadly adversaries. In the preface to his magnum opus the *Histories*, Herodotus expresses the wish to immortalize the great deeds of both the

---

[453] Barnstone, *Ancient Greek Lyrics*, 17.

[454] van Wees, "The City at War," 96. Also, Achilles ransoms his captives (*Il.* 21.100ff), and though he slew Eetion, he buried him with honor, and "the nymphs of the mountain planted elms around his tomb" (*Il.* 6.420).

[455] Ibid.

[456] Donlan, *The Aristocratic Ideal*, 5.

[457] Redfield, *Nature and Culture*, 129.

[458] I want to acknowledge Chris Hedges, who gave me this reference during a very interesting conversation.

[459] According to van Wees, a number of wars in the Classical period were due to "more or less symbolic acts of disrespect towards communities or their citizens." See van Wees, "The City at War," 84.

Greeks and the Persians who went to war with each other. From this perspective, the duty to commemorate *agonistic* glory falls upon everyone across the battle line as well as from the past to the future. Following this thinking, we would conclude that the Persians need the Greeks just as the Greeks need the Persians, if only to remember the bravery of one another. Given this profound interdependence, permanent harm and death dealt to the "enemy" once again affronts the logic of convivial *agon.*

Another way internecine warfare diminishes Olympianism is by imposing and limiting choice—the basis of identity formation. The social norms and public opinions in the Greek heroic society seem to leave young men no option but to endanger their precious lives on the battlefield. The *Iliad* lends credence to this view. The character Hector gives us the impression that he is compelled to fight under the pressure of a socially-constructed understanding of heroic masculinity. Even Achilles, who realizes the problematic nature of imperialist wars, finds no other viable path for achieving a more meaningful existence other than being a warrior hero. Such severe limitation in choice is contrary to the core Olympian project of facilitating individuation, for actors who cannot decide otherwise are unable to set themselves apart from everyone else. Nevertheless, we should keep in mind that social pressure, however powerful, does not amount to actual economic and political coercion. In the epic world, Achilles, by withdrawing from the war temporarily, and to some extent Paris, by preferring the gift of love from Aphrodite over martial prowess, both illustrate the possibility of deviating from soldierly duties. Overall, warfare, in which the orientation of *athlios* prevails, represents the most problematic and inconsistent Greek embodiment of *agon* by anchoring the desire for identity expression in destruction.

Agon and Money

As we can see from the discussion so far, *agon* is most concerned with what participants do and how they act, rather than what they have or possess. Whereas status, position, and wealth can be inherited, transferred, or bought, action must be taken by individuals with attendant responsibilities and consequences. The contrast between wealth and deeds resonates especially in the lines Plutarch attributes to Solon:

> Some wicked men are rich, some good are poor,
> We will not change our virtue for their store:
> Virtue's a thing that none can take away;
> But money changes owners all the day. (Plutarch, *Solon* 3.3)

Solon's concern about money highlights the way it confuses true identities because as a quantitative measure, it obscures the purpose, means, and ramifications behind human action. Yet what one intends to accomplish and how one goes about accomplishing it define a person. For example, Solon prays for affluence, but rejects the use of wanton violence (*hubris*) as a means of achieving it.[460] Similarly, Hesiod approves riches obtained from gainful enterprise and condemns those acquired from

---

[460] Solon 13.7 in Lewis, *Solon the Thinker*, 81.

the fist or a lying tongue (*WD* 321–26). Both of them are keenly aware that those money-making methods not only transform individuals but impart the wrong lessons for society. Therefore, Hesiod's good type of strife is a contest that takes place in the arena of honest work and noble action, while the corrupt, perverse kind competes in violence and treachery. Once again, both Hesiod and Solon judge by evaluating intent, means, and implications. Yet calculation—via mechanical quantification that leaves out the complex moral, social, and political dimensions of human action—conceals those factors, with the result of muddling judgment and even inverting right and wrong. This concern is shared by Pindar, who worries that money rewards vice. Consequently, Pindar too insists that the accumulation of riches must be embedded in the traditional Olympian moral framework. "Wide is the might of wealth given of fate, when some mortal man brings it home mingled with unspotted virtue a ministrant providing many friends" (*Pythian* 5.1–5.4).[461] Rejecting infinite accumulation which abstracts the social context, Pindar places deeds and speech that enhance the civic (convivial) body squarely above the power and ownership exercised for domination.

> Some pray for gold, others for boundless land.
> I pray to delight my fellow citizens
> until my limbs are wrapped in earth—a man
> who praised what deserves praise
> and sowed blame for wrong-doers. (*Nemean VIII* 37–41)

From poems such as this one, Leslie Kurke was right to assert that Pindar negotiates a number of "transactions" to embed wealth into the civic ideology and reciprocal politics of Archaic life.[462]

Another frequently cited poem by Theognis, an author often accused of expressing dismay at the "non-aristocrats,"[463] can be understood as a diatribe against the confounding effect of money on agonistic politics. "Even the finest (*esthlos*) man does not mind marrying the daughter of a bad father, if he gives much wealth; nor does a woman refuse to be the bedmate of a bad (*kakos*) but wealthy man, for she would rather be wealthy than good (*agathos*)" (183–92).[464] Theognis' bitterness is not without basis. In a society orbiting around money, good action never attains the apposite glory, accolade, and remuneration, since base deeds can earn equal or more in monetized terms (*chremata polla*). In a fragment, Theognis points out the perversion plainly: "Wealth, with you a man becomes good (*esthlos*) even if he is really bad" (1117–18). Besides decrying the confusion caused by money, Theognis

---

[461] Donlan, *Aristocratic Ideal*, 103.

[462] Kurke, *Traffic in Praise: Pindar and the Poetics of Social Economy* (Ithaca, NY: Cornell University Press, 1991), passim.

[463] Ibid., 80. Donlan saw noble birth as the basis of pre-eminence in Theognis. Yet interpreting "good" as meaning well-born rather than doing good deeds in the heroic tradition seems rather tenuous to me. I am not convinced that the paradigm of action in Homer has completely changed to good birth merely based on this passage. I see the same problem for lines 429–38: "[B]ut by teaching never will you make the *kakos* man an *agathos*," Ibid. The last line could merely mean that it is difficult to learn how to accomplish good deeds in a society with corrupt rules. Overall, these fragments remain too vague and ambiguous to overturn the model of action I have established for the epics.

[464] Cited in Sarah Pomeroy, *Goddesses, Whores, Wives, and Slaves* (New York: Schocken Books, 1975), 35.

says nothing to oppose the masses from serving heroically and acting justly—the proper channel for rising to prominence. Under the spell of convivial thinking, Theognis cannot help but dwell on deeds and their consequences when defining noble/good (*agathoi/esthloi*) and base/bad (*kakoi-deiloi*).[465] To him, decisions and actions that bear upon the community disclose identity.[466] In these pronouncements, individuals are first and foremost being judged in terms of their impact on the polity, rather than their hereditary pedigree or status.

In a similar vein, a common trope in Greek mythology features an abandoned baby of divine stock who grows up to be a hero through daring deeds. Against all odds and without the help of parents and retainers, the young prince of unknown parentage passes a series of tests to prove his true divine pedigree.[467] We have in this category Jason, Bellerophon, Theseus, Paris, Atreus, Thyestes, Orestes, Telamon and Peleus, to name some. In folkloric fashion, these stories decouple heredity from status, and turn status into a function of extraordinary feats.

Free and Voluntary Action

Both material influence and political interference confound the disclosure of identity by obstructing free will. The removal of economic necessity and greed, as well as political ambition and fear, are critical for realizing true intent. Achilles, for example, announces that he can procure riches at home and shows that he can withdraw from fighting without political repercussion. With this freedom to choose, his final decision to die for immortal glory becomes very meaningful.

[465] J. M. Edmonds, *Elegy and Iambus: Being the Remains of All the Greek Elegiac and Iambic Poets from Callinus to Crates, Excepting the Choliambic Writers, with the Anacreontea* (London: W. Heinemann, Ltd., 1931).

[466] The rest of the poem continues to expound on good (*agathos*) and bad (*kakos*) in this way:

> Never yet, Cyrnus, have good men ruined a city; but when it pleases the bad (*kakoi*) to do the works of pride and corrupt the common folk and give judgment for the unrighteous for the sake of private gain and power, then expect not that city to be long quiet, for all she be now in great tranquility, ay, then when these things become dear to the bad (*kakoi*)—to wit, gains that bring with them public ill. For of such come discords and internecine slaughter, and of such come tyrants; which things I pray may never please this city. (43–52)
>
> Cyrnus, this city is a city still, but lo! her people are other men, who of old knew neither judgments nor laws, but wore goatskins to pieces about their sides, and had their pasture like deer without this city; and now they be good (*agathoi*) men, O son of Polypaus, and they that were high (*esthloi*) be now of low estate (*deiloi*). Who can bear to behold such things? Yet they deceive one another even while they smile at one another, knowing the marks neither of the bad nor of the good. (53–60)

Here, Theognis lampoons behaviors that hinder people's ability to participate in public affairs: ignorance of law, lack of judgement, and tarrying outside of the city—the seat for civic engagement. The comment on goatskin is likely magnifying the deficiency in virtue via an outward mark, because no discrepancy ought to exist between character and garb in the epic/heroic tradition. According to Donlan (*The Aristocratic Ideal*, 6), in the Homeric world, external appearance is a reflection of the true self.

[467] Some historians believe that the age of Homer and myth reflect some sort of rank-based society or a society of big men. In such a society, the chiefs have very little coercive power that can be from derived from formal institutions, with the result that personal charisma and ability count more, which is compatible with the features of the myths. This kind of society is quite different from a class society with stable property laws and state mechanisms that generate coercive power and fixed advantages that can be passed on to the next generation.

Historical narratives about the Archaic period demonstrate a world in which the struggle for personal achievement and identity competed with that for economic and political gain. For example, the symposium, which was well attended by aristocrats for the purposes of singing poetry and making music, was remote from political lobbying or economic networking.[468] Similarly, actual historical instances of athletic winners capitalizing on their fame for political office are few and far between, although some did enhance their reputation in the community.[469] In the earliest descriptions in Homer, to be sure, the victors receive prestigious prizes: at Patroclus' funeral games, the prizes include cauldrons, tripods, horses, mules, and oxen, iron, and also, sadly, captured women. However, the heroes do not enter the contest for profit or to make a living. Ajax, Odysseus, and all the other Homeric nobles ride chariots, raced, boxed, and threw the javelin as pastimes and leisure activities. At the time of Herodotus, the prevailing cultural discourse on the games still revolved around honor rather than riches.[470] In a revealing passage by him, a Persian nobleman asks about the prizes offered at Greek festivals and games, and receives the response of a laurel wreath. Upon hearing this answer, the Persian nobleman exclaims, "Alas Mardonius, what sort of men have you led us here to fight, who compete not for money but for honor!" (*Histories* 8.26). This exchange illustrates, at least in one self-projected image of the Greeks, they compete for the love of excellence, not out of greed or necessity. Although in actual history, more games began to hand out cash prizes to the competitors in later centuries as Polisism and Oeconomism advanced,[471] the original ideal never lost its appeal. In its pure form, the games advance the Olympian drive to achieve personal excellence, along with aristocratic amateurism defined by passion, love, and enjoyment.

On the other hand, Pindar has been accused of composing *epinikia*—victory odes for athletic winners—that glorify the rich and powerful. According to Kurke, the Panhellenic games were "a conspicuous arena for demonstrations of the superiority of the ruling class."[472] But we must wonder to what extent Pindar was able to spin his verses when the wider cultural framework so overwhelmingly affirmed conviviality and ecumenism. As a poet living closer to the Classical Age, Pindar tirelessly reenacted mythology in the biographical accounts of the victors.[473] Against this sacred metaphysics, Pindar turned the games into a platform for channeling individualistic impulse into convivial politics and for converting praise for the tyrant to acclamation for the city. It is therefore not surprising that Donlan saw in Pindar "no trace of

---

[468] Murray believed the symposium was as much concerned with entertainment as with politics. See "The Affairs of the Mysteries," 150.

[469] Davies, *Wealth and the Power of Wealth*, 99. Thucydides recorded the one failed attempt of the Olympian winner Cylon to seize tyranny; Cylon seemed to have completely miscalculated the appeal of his victory to the people (1.126.3–4).

[470] For the indubitable religious roots of the original Greek athletic games, the archetype of *agon*, see Finley and Pleket, *The Olympic Games*, 15–16.

[471] Historically speaking, the four original Olympic games offered only wreaths. In later times, winners increasingly received monetary rewards from "prize games." See Finley and Pleket, *The Olympic Games*, 24.

[472] Kurke, *The Traffic in Praise*, 4.

[473] Ibid., Chapter 1 and 2.

conflict between individual achievement…and service to the community."[474] Even Kurke, despite labeling Pindar as a poet of the ruling class, documented how the poet labored to rehabilitate his illustrious patrons into a series of dense, overlapping social relations nested in family kinship, the civic community, and an international peer network. This type of integrated, reciprocal elite subjectivity is highly reminiscent of Olympianism, rather than a culture in which rulers are distant and remote from the people.

The convivial discourse that structured Pindar's oeuvre was nonetheless in tension with the disproportionate power of the tyrants who allegedly befriended the poet. For despite all, the glorification of big men was antithetical to the commitment to an egalitarian and horizontal order, as well as the values of democratic leadership.[475] As Thucydides observed, "[T]he tyrant's first thought was always for himself, for his own personal safety, and for the greatness of his own family" (1.17).[476] Moreover, when a once sacred work like *epinikion* was beginning to be commissioned for money in the fifth century, it laid the groundwork for distorting the agonistic process of identity disclosure.[477] Leonard Woodbury aptly described the shift: "The change meant that the expense of the poet's fee and the choral production was assumed by a wealthy patron, with whom lay the power of decision in regard to all questions relating to the performance of the ode. The Muse, in Pindar's phrase, had grown fond of money and gone to work for the living."[478] In the original Olympian model, art is tasked to serve the community and speak truth to power; yet the influence of wealth compromises the free will of the artist and diminishes the authenticity of artistic production.[479] Nevertheless, under the impetus of Olympianism, most Archaic poems do *not* function as propaganda pieces that eulogize tyranny, at least not without the more dominant message about ecumenism and conviviality. In fact, the Greek *turannoi*, or tyrants, were remarkably civic-minded in the Archaic Age.[480] Some of them, like Cypselus of Corinth, redistributed land,[481] and others, like Pisistratus of Athens, aided the poor against the interest of the rich. Pisistratus' rule in particular paved the way for the advent of democracy in the estimations of many ancient and modern observers.[482] It is therefore unclear whether

---

[474] Donlan, *The Aristocratic Ideal*, 101.

[475] I discuss "tyrant" here as a political ideal type, not how individual tyrants behaved in history. We know many Greek tyrants ruled mildly and were popular, though the office can still be detestable, which is what the Athenians felt toward Pisistratus, for they glorified Harmodius and Aristogeiton who slew his son.

[476] Trans. R. Warner, in Ian Morris and Barry Powell, *The Greeks*, 166.

[477] Kurke, *The Traffic in Praise*, 7.

[478] L. Woodbury, "Pindar and the Mercenary Muse: Isthmian 2.1–13," *Transactions of the American Philological Association* 99 (1968): 535.

[479] Cf. Nagy's forward in *The Traffic in Praise*, where he said that at the time of Pindar, "The craft of song is in danger of shifting from an expression of community to an expression of the individual whose wealth and power threatens the community." See Kurke, *The Traffic in Praise*, ix.

[480] See Wallace, "Solonian Democracy," in *Democracy 2500?: Questions and Challenges*, ed. Ian Morris, Kurt A. Raaflaub, and David Castriota (Dubuque, IA: Kendall/Hunt Pub. Co., 1998), 14–15; Austin and Vidal-Naquet, *Economic and Social History*, 70.

[481] Austin and Vidal-Naquet, *Economic and Social History*, 70.

[482] See Greg Anderson, "Before *Turannoi* Were Tyrants: Rethinking a Chapter of Early Greek History," *Classical Antiquity* 24, no. 2 (2005): 173–222. I am glad that I got to know Greg and have received from him great words of encouragement and wisdom, which helped me persevere through difficult times in the final stages of this book.

Pindar's patrons succeeded more in manipulating Olympianism for their own ends or succumbed more to its enticing truths.[483]

On the topic of elitism, scholars have also suggested that the poetry in this period exhibits a fondness for luxury modeled on the lifestyle of the eastern monarchies.[484] Again, it is too simplistic to see only the appeal of extravagant kingdoms, but not the pushback and resilience of Olympianism. True, there is evidence of greater material prosperity and higher wealth concentration in the early part of the Archaic Age, also called the "Orientalizing period" because Greek art adopted motifs and styles of the Eastern Mediterranean and the Near East. Archaeological record, for example, attests to impressive funerary artifacts such as tall jars (e.g., Late Geometric Kerameikos) and large statues (*kouros* and *kore*) that served as grave markers in the eighth and seventh centuries.[485] Around the same epoch, coinage was introduced into Greece.[486] This new economic device, which allegedly came from Libya, a society that was neither free nor equal, allowed individuals to hoard large amounts of wealth. Taken together, these indicators seem to herald the emergence of a ruling class that would wish to put themselves before the community through the ostentatious display of affluence and exuberance.[487] But as the Archaic period proceeded, the wealth in individual graves—signs of private status—declined, while dedications at sanctuaries and monumental temples located in the middle of the *polis*—display of public piety and loyalty—increased.[488] We should remember that the Greek gods, boosted by religious offerings and buildings, punished hubristic men and cared for all types of people. In addition, even if the elites made those public offerings out of individual desire for power, the fact that they chose to do so via communal channels still added to the perceived significance of the polity.[489] As a result, while money was capable of disrupting Olympian norms, Greek elites like Pindar envisioned ways of skillfully reining it in for communal ends. Similarly, despite the loveliness of oriental luxury, a number of poems from the same group advocate an aesthetics of restraint and decorum with a religious undertone, like this one by Anacreon: "But come, let us no longer pursue this Scythian kind of drinking, with din and uproar over the wine, but drink in moderation between beautiful hymns" (Anacreon Fr. 356(b)). Here indulgence and inordinate consumption are associated with the barbarians, and

---

[483] It is very difficult to say how much the tyrants were able to exploit the symbols of Olympianism to increase their political power in actuality. If anything, the participation in these cultural forms probably pressured them to conform to the core principles of Olympianism, even if only at the rhetorical level. This ambivalent interplay informs the central themes of *The Traffic in Praise*.

[484] Leslie Kurke, "The Politics of ἁβροσύνη in Archaic Greece," *Classical Antiquity* 11, no. 1 (1992): 91–120.

[485] I am aware that Ian Morris made a powerful case for a brief time in the late eighth century when burial was more inclusive and egalitarian. But just to play devil's advocate against myself, and also because the debate is still on, I shall assume this moment was merely an exception, not necessarily the rule. See Ian Morris, *Burial and Ancient Society*.

[486] Scholars estimate that the earlier coins from Lydia, the influential neighbor of Greece, date to the sixth century. See Schaps, *The Invention of Coinage*, 95–96. The earliest issues of Athens, the so-called *wappenmünzen*, date to the sixth century. Ibid., 104–05.

[487] This would be in line with Ian Morris' model; see note 126.

[488] Sara Forsdyke, *Ostracism, and Democracy: The Politics of Expulsion in Ancient Greece* (Princeton and Oxford: Princeton University Press, 2005), 22.

[489] Ibid., 23.

elegance and self-control with the poet and his high-class Greek friends. Even the art of writing, used before to keep track of the possessions of the rulers, returned in the archeological evidence of Archaic Greece primarily as a means to record convivial occasions (e.g., Nestor's Cup, Dipylon Inscription). In these ways, Olympianism in its heyday showed itself adept at either resisting foreign influence or re-appropriating it for its own purpose of maintaining a society of interdependent peers.

Individual Identity Expression

With the image of the gods solidly in their hearts, Solon famously turns down the chance to rule as a tyrant, and Sappho famously prefers the object of her love over dashing chariots and fast ships.[490] What sort of values and tendencies made it possible for those cultural icons to profess such distinctive predilections, particularly Sappho's, which subverted conventional heterosexuality and martial politics? Unmoved by the temptation to dominate and exploit through power and wealth, a conspicuous number of personas in this group turn their gaze inward to explore the self at its most intimate. In this literary tradition, poetic personas dwell on powerful emotions, such as the passion of erotic love, melancholy for the fleeting of youth, and dread of miserable mortality. These personal forms of expression could only persist in a compassionate and tolerant environment that recognizes and safeguards the pluralistic aspects of identity. In fact, with a few exceptions, there was no preaching of social homogeneity or denunciation of deviant behavior with regard to private life in Archaic poetry.[491] It is no coincidence that Sappho can poeticize her burning desire for another woman without reservation: "come to me now and loosen me/ from blunt agony. Labor and fill my heart with fire."[492] With the ecumenical affirmation of all lives and the agonistic commitment to identity differentiation, Olympianism saw to it that diverse forms of individual expression could thrive and be freely indulged in.

Inclusion and Exclusion from *Agon*

Although earlier sources overwhelmingly portray only aristocratic figures in the games, political debate, contests, and other forms of *agon*, no formal rules of exclusion based on wealth or status were enacted (although those who lacked access to training clearly would face disadvantages, a result of economic reality, not ideology). In fact, *agon*'s strong conceptual foundation of inclusion and equality complicates efforts to erect barriers. For instance, in the *Odyssey*, even the reprehensible suitors agree to a fair, merit-based contest of the bow in order to decide who should take Penelope home. The ringleader Antinous, with words "pleasing to all

---

[490] Sappho, Fragment 16.

[491] The Greeks were certainly less forgiving toward women, although this tendency is more dominant in later Classical sources onward; see the discussion on women. Foucault also reminded us that there were specific rules about male sexuality in ancient Greece, but what he observed applies more to the Classical period, which showed the anxiety for legitimate citizenship and property inheritance (though I argue they were driven by Polisism and Oeconomism). I would add that social norms are not the same as real political or economic coercion. In other societies, deviant personal behavior could incur grave penalty, but did not in Greek society.

[492] Barnstone, *Ancient Greek Lyrics*, 44.

of them" (*Od.* 21.143), declares, "Take your turns in order from left to right, my companions all" (*Od.* 21.141). But when Odysseus—still disguised as a vagabond and newcomer—asks for a chance, the same Antinous berates him and threatens to haul him away to be mutilated. Thanks to the prompt interference from Penelope and Telemachus, Odysseus enters the contest and strings the bow, inaugurating his plan to revenge the suitors. Although Odysseus' victory may have more to do with his real princely status, the discourse of *agon* still problematizes the removal of a nameless beggar due to "class." The truth about *agon* is that glory comes from besting strong contenders, not eliminating them.

Although slaves, women, non-natives, and the poor were either kept out or kept at the periphery of agonistic pursuits in many instances (except for female athletes at Sparta and interpolis participants at Panhellenic events), we are still left with parables of *agon* that destabilize these very limitations and restrictions. In the famous tale of Atalanta, the heroine joins the boar hunt and outperforms most of the men. As a result, Meleagros, the host, awards the hide and tusks to Atalanta against the protest that she is a woman and a foreigner. At least in one version of myth, the inclusion of a female outsider and the recognition of her excellence makes the *agon* unforgettable.

It is perhaps in the creative *agonistic* arena that the elevation of privileged native men breaks down the most and the "coming-together" capacity is most realized. Hesiod, the proud peasant who wins a song contest without anyone raising eyebrows, indicates this type of "opening" in *agon* for the plebeian class. The author of *Works and Days* tells us:

> From Aulis I sailed over,
> to compete in the games at Chalcis.
> In honor of noble Amphidamas,
> a great-souled man, his sons
> had established many great prizes.
> May I boast about what happened at Chalcis?
> With my song, the Theogony, I won first prize.
> I was awarded a trophy, a tripod cauldron,
> which I took home. I set it up as a monument,
> dedicated to the Muses of Helicon, on that
> spot by sacred Helicon, where they had breathed into me
> a clear-speaking, inspired voice. (654–59)

The hardworking farmer takes for granted his right to compete and receive due recognition. In this case, the focus on excellence in *agon* indeed readily sublates social differentiation. Similarly, the choral poet Alcman was said by some to be of slave origin (e.g., Heraclides Ponticus fr. 2), yet the sheer strength of his artistic achievement was enough for him to enter the canonical group of nine Greek lyric poets. Sappho, more or less a contemporary of Alcman and Hesiod, likely recited her work in the symposium, a convivial setting that included women and foreigners in the audience.[493] The fact that she, as a female literary persona, left traces at all in Greek literature monopolized by male elites, illustrates again that artistic excellence can prove gender, place of birth, and nationality irrelevant in the creative arena.

In conclusion, as an important Olympian paradigm, *agon* accounts for the type of convivial spirit that guided a wide range of Greek aristocratic activities. Unlike modern economic competition aimed at maximizing utility, agonistic pursuits strive to establish identity via intersubjective recognition. Based on the truth of man as *homo significans*, *agon* upholds convivial and ecumenical principles to facilitate the process of individuation. The fact that marginal groups were excluded in practice is very much a failure to implement *agon* effectively; however, the solution is not to abandon the project but to fight harder for its true realization.

Models of Action: Service to the Community, the Critique of Power, and the Struggle for Individual Excellence

Let us examine how the emphasis on concrete praxis plays out in all aspects of the Olympian culture, a system that distributes power widely and rejects hierarchy and inherited power. In the literature of ancient Greece, deeds that serve the greater good,[494] protest the abuse of power, and strive for individual excellence win the most accolades. The famous interchange between Sarpedon and Glaucon underlines the significance of heroic sacrifice.[495]

> Glaucon, why is it you and I are honoured before others
> with pride of place, the choice meats and the filled wine cups
> in Lycia, and all men look on us as if were immortals,
> and we are appointed a great piece of land by the banks of Xanthos,
> good land, orchard and vineyard, and ploughland for the planting of wheat?
> Therefore it is our duty in the forefront of the Lycians
> to take our stand, and bear our part of the blazing of battle,
> so that a man of the close-armoured Lycians may say of us:
> Indeed, these are no ignoble men who are lords of Lycia,
> these kings of ours, who feed upon the fat sheep appointed
> and drink the exquisite sweet wine, since indeed there is strength
> of valour in them, since they fight in the forefront of the Lycians.
> (*Il.* 12.310–21)

[493] Ewen Bowie argued that a high percentage of the surviving poetry was delivered to an audience outside of the poet's *polis*. See Ewen Bowie, "Wandering Poets, Archaic Style," in *Wandering Poets in Ancient Greek Culture: Travel, Locality, and Pan-Hellenism*, ed. Richard Hunter and Ian Rutherford (Cambridge, UK: Cambridge University Press, 2009), 105.

[494] This includes all Homeric social bonds and obligations, such as those between followers and leaders, host and guests.

[495] This is a passage that comes up frequently for discussion. See Raaflaub and Wallace, "People's Power," 31; Redfield, *Nature and Culture*, 100; Graham Zanker, *The Heart of Achilles: Characterization and Personal Ethics in the Iliad* (Ann Arbor: The University of Michigan Press, 1994), 78.

Although Sarpedon speaks of martial excellence here, the epics do not discount other qualities that benefit the group, such as speaking and debating well in council.[496] For instance, Nestor often reminds young warriors that: "the gods give to mortals not everything at the same time;/ if I was a young man then, now in turn old age is upon me./ Yet even so I shall be among the riders, and command them/ with word and counsel; such is the privilege of the old men" (*Il.* 4.320–24). In another instance, he praises Diomedes for his gift of oratory: "Son of Tydeus, beyond others you are strong in battle,/ and in counsel also are noblest among all men of your own age" (*Il.* 9.37). In peaceful times, skills such as defending justice, persuading with gentle words, and cultivating peace command adulation as well.[497] Even the infamous Thersites episode betrays the significance of noble action (see next chapter). In the aftermath of Thersites' provocation, Odysseus tells the masses: "Sit still and listen to what others tell you,/ to those who are better than you, you skulker and coward/ and thing of no account whatever in battle or council" (*Il.* 2.200–02). Despite Odysseus' imperious tone, he nevertheless reasons that the princes should be obeyed because they surpass others in combat and debate. Another telling moment takes place in Book 11, when Achilles asks Odysseus for news about his son. To the father's eager inquiry, Odysseus replies:

> [H]e would always speak first, and never blunder. In speaking
> only godlike Nestor and I were better than he was.
> And when we Achaeans fought in the Trojan plain, he never
> would hang back where there were plenty of other men, nor stay
> with the masses but run far out in front, giving way to no man
> for fury, and many were those he killed in the terrible fighting.
> (*Od.* 11.511–16)

We should note that Odysseus does not bring up wealth, title, or privilege, but what the young hero does. This report delights the father Achilles, who reckons that his son's noble deeds will attract immortal fame from the people (11.540). Even the wicked suitors in the *Odyssey* know that true nobility is premised upon excellence that rides on the opinions of the community, for they admit:

> But we are ashamed to face the talk of the men and the women,
> for fear some other Achaean, who is meaner than we are,
> might say: far baser men are courting the wife of a stately
> man. They are not able to string his bow. Then
> another, some beggar man, came wandering in from somewhere,
> and easily strung the bow, and sent a shaft through the iron.

---

[496] Nestor, for example, is too old to fight and yet he is known for his oratory skills. Also see Phoenix's speech on the importance of oratory for a good warrior (*Il.* 9.443–44), and Polydamas' speech on the diverse gifts other than warfare from the gods (*Il.* 13.727–35). Earlier we saw how resolving conflicts peacefully is important for a king.

[497] The martial qualities are stressed more in Homer and the "political" ones in Hesiod, which is natural due to the different settings: one is in war and the other against the backdrop of a small agricultural community. They do not necessarily need to indicate a change or difference in values.

So they will speak; and that would be a disgrace on all of us.
(21.323–29)

Here, the suitors take for granted that the public will judge their merit, whereas a society that reinforces rigid heredity would forbid any doubt in the first place. Indeed, even the degenerate elites of Ithaca are convinced that only valiant action can certify their nobility.

The responsibility of proving one's worthiness is especially acute for politicians who make decisions that affect the whole polity. For instance, Hesiod describes his ideal of a capable and accountable leader as someone who speaks gentle words to the people and makes just and prudent decisions in the assembly (*Theogony* 81–90). This model of the gentle and effective king can also be found in the *Odyssey.*

> [A]s of some king who, as a blameless man and god-fearing,
> and ruling as lord over many powerful people,
> upholds the way of good government, and the black earth yields him
> barley and wheat, his trees are heavy with fruit, his sheepflocks
> continue to bear young, the sea gives him fish, because of
> his good leadership, and his people prosper under him. (19.109–14)

Be they the warrior elites of Homer or the venerated kings of Hesiod, those who use the gifts from the gods to strengthen the collective entity, such as defending against enemies and maintaining justice, achieve preeminence.[498] In this model, the possessor of authority is thoroughly and constantly subject to trials of excellence and virtue.

Convivial Body Politic

The duty to build a symbiotic, fair, and just entity falls not only on the leaders but also the people. Achilles' anger at the insouciance of the soldiers belies mature notions of collective rights and responsibility. First of all, the prince's desire for the people to rise up clearly runs counter to a strictly elitist worldview. This same belief prompts Telemachus to reproach the men of Ithaca for turning a blind eye to the crimes of the suitors (*Od.* 2.64–67). Mentor, his friend, chimes in and reiterates the obligation of each community member to take action: "But now I hold it against you other people, how you all/ sit there in silence, and never with an assault of words try/ to check the suitors, though they are so few, and you so many (*Od.* 239–41). The awareness that masses are powerful due to their number is a "secret" that no aristocrat would want to propagate. Even the suitors are anxious, fearing the day when the people will take up arms and rebel. One of them ruminates on this frightening scenario:

[498] Through the protest of Achilles and Thersites, the *Iliad* questions whether the war against the Trojans can indeed be seen as an appropriate community objective. I consider this room for skepticism to be a step in the direction of "concrete progress," a notion put forth by Richard Rorty in response to Foucault's general pessimistic view that individuals can never fight overwhelming structural powers. See Richard Rorty, "The Continuity Between the Enlightenment and 'Postmodernism,'" in *What's Left of the Enlightenment*, ed. Keith Michael Baker and Peter Hanns Reill (Stanford: Stanford University Press, 2001), 19–36.

> But come now, before he [Telemachus] can gather the Achaeans and bring them
> to assembly; for I think he will not let us go, but work out
> his anger, and stand up before them all and tell them
> how we designed his sudden murder, but we could not catch him;
> and they will have no praise for us when they hear of our evil
> deeds, and I fear they will work some evil on us, and drive us
> from our own country, so we must make for another community. (*Od.* 16.376–82)

In this way, the conception of a proactive political body in charge of its own destiny fosters collective action.

As a result of this truth, rulers face outcry when they either extract resources through bribery and extortion, or force compliance by oppressing dissent. Since the people, like Hesiod or Thersites, have to bear the consequences of political decisions, they possess the natural right to demand integrity and competence from the authority. For this reason, abuse committed by rulers is especially egregious, as seen in the remarks of Solon, Hesiod, Achilles, Thersites, Chryses, and Eumaeus. By the same token, the constant vigilance of a concerned public is the best means to ensure good governance.

The pursuit of *agonistic* excellence, the discovery of the unique self, the drive to serve and contribute, and the revolt against unworthy politicians are principal truths of Olympian body politic. A passage from Theognis best summarizes those themes (with the four elements marked out in brackets):

> May no other pursuit arise from me in place of excellence and learning [*agonistic* pursuit of distinction] but ever holding on to this may I enjoy lyre, dance and song [freedom of personal expression], and may I have noble thoughts in company with the noble [contribution to a just community], harming with hurtful deeds neither foreigner nor citizen, but living righteously [avoidance of hubris and abuse]." (789–94)[499]

This set of behaviors establishes what is considered heroic and exemplary in the convivial model. The Olympian code of action breaks down the divide between individual and community, infuses competition with cooperation, and reconciles singularity with collectivity.

The truth about righteous actions can be easily identified in the stories we have discussed. For instance, the haughty commander Agamemnon countenances no slights to his status, but he flounders as the commander by harming group fairness and coherence through self-aggrandizement. Agamemnon's standing is further tarnished by being short on courage and benevolence. Achilles rightly calls out Agamemnon, but his insistence on personal revenge perhaps raises the question whether the best of

[499] Stuart Fraser, *Aristocratic Values in Ancient Greece: Change or Continuity* (Perm: Perm State University Press, 2011), 40. Fraser argued that the Greek aristocratic ideal was continuous from the time of Homer down to the days of the *polis*.

the Achaeans is also failing his communal obligations. The pattern continues in Hesiod—the Boeotian farmer publicly bids the kings to rule justly, but manages his own private life without apology. Hesiod indulges in song, poetry, and the games—"leisurely gratifications"—alongside hard work. Likewise, Xenophanes' chagrin at boxing, pentathlon, or wrestling harbors no moral judgment, but only irritation at their uselessness to the community, for he proclaims, "Small joy would it be for the *polis* if any athlete won by Pisa's banks, for these things do not fatten the treasury of the *polis*" (Fr. 2.15–22D).[500] Everywhere we turn, we see the best of the Greeks occupied with how to serve the community, lead justly, excel individually, and develop existentially.

To return to the very question posed in the beginning of this section, we can now conclude that preeminence in the Olympian model is determined by a series of culturally guided actions. By making identity an index of specific deeds, rather than circumstances of wealth (as is the case in a class society)[501] or heredity and parentage (as with feudalism), Olympianism allows for a type of personhood that is much more self-fashioned and protean.[502] This elaborate conception affords us the best and most consistent overall interpretation of the behavior and thinking evinced in the sources. At the same time, the Olympian paradigm points to a new direction in the contemporary debate on identity by moving it away from nationality, religion, and fixed cultural attributes to self-cultivation, social relationships, and democratic contribution.

CONCLUSION

This chapter began by establishing ecumenism and conviviality as the two key concepts for the Olympian cultural system. Taking feasting as a philosophical metaphor, we identified additional second-order values of multiplicity, egalitarianism, horizontal reciprocity, and diversity that accompanied the two main philosophical programs. Furthermore, we explored the paradigm of *agon* and how it brings the individual and the community together through the disclosure of identity. The ideals of *agon* require inclusive, fair, and transparent social interaction to set the stage for the performance of meaningful action according to one's free will. The force of *agon* can be found in athletic games, political address, warfare, and other convivial contests and gatherings. Although *agon* failed to fully incorporate women, foreigners, and nonelites, its exclusionary tendencies were also being destabilized from within. The cultural discourses of ecumenism, conviviality, and *agon* buttressed exemplary

---

[500] Cited from Donlan, *The Aristocratic Ideal*, 65.

[501] My project in fact moves away from the analysis of class struggle, cf. Rose, *Class in Archaic Greece*, and de Ste. Croix, *The Class Struggle*. I ask Marxists for tolerance because I believe the fundamental issues of injustice, exploitation, and oppression can be more effectively addressed by the cultural approach.

[502] Calhoun pointed out the complete omission of the specific words for nobility of birth and distinctions based on descent, which are so abundant in the writings of later ages. See George M. Calhoun, "Classes and Masses in Homer," *Classical Philology* 29, no. 3 (July 1934): 195. Donlan concurred, saying that "claim to personal excellence on the grounds of lofty ancestry is seldom possible," and that "descent from gods or from other great warriors was both proof of ability and incentive to excel further." See Donlan, *Aristocratic Ideal*, 15, 24.

actions that gave rise to a true democracy defined by individual liberty, horizontal reciprocity, and collective responsibility.

CHAPTER 6

Universal Access to the Gods

MARGINAL GROUPS

In the last chapter, we examined the concepts of ecumenism, conviviality, and *agon,* as well as their attendant tendencies for inclusion, multiplicity, reciprocity, and pluralism. We will now consider how these truths specifically shape the social experience and reception of women, foreigners, opponents, beggars, and slaves in the sources. By and large, Olympianism, though not perfect, bestows dignity on marginal groups and incorporates them into a common universe by stipulating their intrinsic worth and potential before the gods. The ability to invoke the gods corresponds to the latitude of Greek polytheistic religion, which, unlike other belief systems, was open to all—with no priest class, sacred text, compulsory belief, or restrictive membership.[503] Under this unquestioned first principle, even the least privileged people display full potential as worthy and equal subjects, a basic guarantee that supersedes other acquired societal differentiation. In multiple passages, this inalienable relationship with divine beings—neither mediated nor monopolized by elites—emboldens disadvantaged groups in their struggle for equal power and status.[504]

Not only do the Greek gods care for all types of people, but they also take on various human forms—for example, Hera in the form of an old woman to test Jason, Demeter as a child-nurse or housekeeper (*Homeric Hymn to Demeter*), and Athena as a shepherd boy (*Od.* 13.222) and as a little girl (*Od.* 7.19–20). Due to these disguises, there was always the danger of mistakenly dismissing or insulting individuals based on the outward indicators of status, wealth, gender, ethnicity, or citizenship of origin. In fact, the suitors in the *Odyssey* are very much aware of this possibility. When Antinous hurls a footstool at Odysseus the beggar, the rest of them wonder, "[What] if he [Odysseus] is somehow a god from heaven./ For the gods do take on all sorts of transformation, appearing/ as strangers from elsewhere" (*Od.* 17.484–86). Because the gods uphold universal justice and can take on any appearance, no individual or group can easily abuse another without fearing retribution.

Women and Foreigners

Women are dear to the gods and can oblige them directly; many even served as revered priestesses and seers in historical times.[505] In Book 6 of the *Iliad,* Priam's

---

[503] Ibid., 4, 8, 95, 119.

[504] For more on the general openness, such as the absence of a priest class and the ability for anyone—including women and slaves—to lead a sacrifice, see Burkert, *Greek Religion*, 95.

[505] For female participation in Greek religion from a variety of sources, including epigraphy and art, see Matthew Dillon, *Girls and Women in Classical Greek Religion* (London: Routledge, 2002).

wife Hecuba prays to Athena at the behest of her son (*Il.* 286–312). In the story of Meleager, the mother of the hero "called down/ [curses] from the gods upon him, in deep grief for the death of her brother" (*Il.* 9.567). In Book 20 of the *Odyssey*, Penelope prays to Artemis of her own volition (60–90). Most potently, in the same book, a mill woman speaks to Zeus after correctly identifying his sign from the sky, a remarkable feat for a female servant (*Od.* 20.112–19). At the same time, women are often desired by deities, which brings suffering but also elevated status: we find romantic ties between Poseidon and Tyro and (*Od.* 11.235–52), Zeus and Antiope (*Od.* 11.260–63), and Poseidon and Iphimedeia (*Od.* 11.305–07). Concurrently, goddesses frequently show up in female form: Athena in likeness of a young girl (*Od.* 7.20) and Aphrodite as an aged wool-dresser (*Il.* 3.386). These divine bonds and female disguises are reasons for taking women seriously; no one can insult women or dismiss what they say without fear of retribution.[506]

The intimacy with the gods likely contributes to women's higher social standing in Homer and other early sources. In many scenes for instance, women are shown to speak their minds freely. The dazzling Helen first comes to mind: she retorts to Aphrodite (*Il.* 3.398–413), scolds her husband (*Il.* 3.427–36), and counsels her father-in-law (*Il.* 3.178–242). In Book 24 of the *Iliad*, queen Hecuba urges her husband Priam to pray and ask for an omen before he sets out to ransom the body of their son Hector, and Priam readily complies (*Il.* 24.287–300). In the *Odyssey*, the narrator informs us that the wife of Alcinous was given "such pride of place as no other woman on earth is given" (*Od.* 7.67). Before departing for the Trojan War, Odysseus also entrusts his household to his wife Penelope, telling her, "[H]ere let everything be in your charge" (*Od.* 18.266). Penelope does not disappoint: she holds the suitors at bay and reprimands them at every opportunity. The most remarkable passage underscoring the prominence of women is located in Book 11 of the *Odyssey*. Following the advice of Circe, Odysseus travels to the kingdom of the dead and meets an army of illustrious men, including Agamemnon and Achilles. After the warriors, a corps of renowned women greets him. Each boasts of noble lineage and outstanding curriculum vitae (225–332). The long list of female characters in this "who's who" of the famous Greeks underscores the centrality of women among the heroic and the famed.

Certainly, the liberality toward women in the epics can suffer from false starts, reversals, and drawbacks. For example, in Book 21 of the *Iliad*, Telemachus arrogantly orders his mother to leave the family hall where the bard sings and to return to the female quarter where she belongs (21.350). As already mentioned, in Book 1 of the *Iliad*, Zeus threatens to lay hands on Hera if she keeps pestering him about his secret rendezvous (*Il.* 1.567), a demonstration of the degree to which patriarchal domination and male arrogance could surge unchecked. Nevertheless, many more narrative instances in early Greek literature dwell on the formidable power of women and emphasize their critical role rather than their subordination. These testimonies from Homer, along with those in tragedy and myth, have prompted

[506] The trope of a patriarch figure disbelieving a young woman's story of having been with a god is common in myth. Partly for this reason, Gould reminded us that women are often seen with fear and anxiety in myth. See John Gould, "Law, Custom and Myth: Aspects of the Social Position of Women in Classical Athens," *The Journal of Hellenic Studies* 100 (1980): 55.

scholars to surmise a higher, albeit still unequal, status of women before the rise of the city-states.[507]

Foreigners make up another group of the *other*. The prevalent Greek custom of *xenia* demands unreserved hospitality during encounters with travelers, sojourners, and strangers. The welcoming of foreigners, which is enjoined by the gods, is exemplified by Nestor who receives Menelaus and Telemachus (*Od.* 3.34, 4.35), the Phaeacians who host Odysseus (*Od.* 8.61), and Eumaeus who takes in Odysseus (*Od.* 14.56). The willingness to assist outsiders is not predicated on their wealth or status. In several examples raised before, *xenia* is practiced on strangers who are, or seem to be, penniless. In another case, the beneficiary Theoclymenus is a wanted fugitive, yet despite being a clear liability, Telemachus treats him as an honored guest (*Od.* 15.513). Through the guided practice of *xenia*, the initial seed of goodwill often blossoms into enduring friendships that last for generations. For example, in Book 6 of the *Iliad*, the Lycian prince Glaucus and the Greek prince Diomedes cease fighting and exchange gifts after learning that their ancestors were old guest-friends of *xenia* (*Il.* 6.215–34). Likewise, when Nestor discovers Telemachus is the son of his guest-friend Odysseus, he gladly extends his love to the youth (*Od.* 3.346–55). With this religio-cultural custom, even individuals of divergent backgrounds become inclined to forge heartfelt bonds.

Similarly, although Hesiod makes no specific mentions of foreign countries, he exhorts the audience to welcome strangers in accordance with *xenia* (*WD* 225–27). In Hesiod's Olympian geography, the East, which denotes not only the region but also its non-Greek inhabitants, is part of the common universe frequented by the gods who transcend borders. The actual practice of unconditional hospitality, which accentuates the pleasure in meeting and befriending strangers, constantly renegotiates existing political, ethnic, and geographic divisions. It is therefore not by coincidence that before the Persian wars, intracommunal and international alliances from marriage, guest-host friendship, military comradery, and aristocratic fraternities were extremely salient. Conversely, inter-*polis* warfare between "citizen armies" became frequent only after around 520 BCE. Only then did dedications at Panhellenic sanctuaries by "the Athenians," "the Corinthians," and the like begin to outnumber those by families and individuals. This evidence confirms the operation of a cosmopolitan and fluid global order consistent with the Olympian ecumenical outlook before the reification of absolute, fixed territories in the Classical era. Under the watch of the gods who guarded all lands and people eternally, Olympianism fueled the imagination of a universe with overlapping loyalties and friendship that meld different cultures and people together.

The Foe

Impressing generations of readers, the *Iliad*, though primarily narrated from the Greek perspective, not only refrains from demonizing the Trojan enemies, but goes to great

[507] These poems do not imply any kind of feminist paradise, but merely a more liberal and open attitude toward women than in sources from later periods. See Dillon, *Girls and Women*; Sue Blundell, *Women in Ancient Greece* (London: British Museum Press, 1995); and Pomeroy, *Goddesses, Whores, Wives, and Slaves*. The misogyny in Hesiod and Xenophanes are noticeable aberrations from the Olympian ideal types.

lengths to show that they are loved by the gods. We know that Aphrodite adores Paris and Apollo stands by Hector to the end. Even Ares, who promises to help the Greeks at one point, later switches sides to aid the Trojans. The closeness between the gods and the non-Greeks is evident even in linguistics. For example, when Apollo calls out the Trojans, he addresses them as "O you children of Priam, the king whom the gods love" (*Il.* 5.464). Next, when the greatest Trojan fighter Hector appears, we are told, "[T]here entered Hector beloved of Zeus" (*Il.* 6.318). In another scene, Zeus succors the sons of Troy: "[He] lightens upon their right hand, showing them/ portents of good, while Hector in the huge pride of his strength rages/ irresistibly, reliant on Zeus" (*Il.* 9.236–38). Even after the climactic death of Patroclus, while appreciating the enormous pain that drives Achilles to defile Hector's body and sacrifice twelve Trojan captives, Homer nevertheless condemns the acts of mutilation and immolation.[508] Some versions of Greek myth even suggest that the Trojan, Spartan, and Euboean royal lines descend from Electra, Taygete, and Alcyone, the three daughters of the sky-bearing Atlas.[509] This genealogical myth creates the possibility of recognizing the enemy as familiar and respectable kin, counteracting the way whereby most conventional war rhetoric distances and alienates the opponent.

Ecumenical sentiments toward outside groups are also present in Herodotus. In his account of the Persian war, the Spartans feel obliged to atone for the earlier murder of the Persian heralds, an act the author calls "sacrilege."[510] Although the Persians were by then already archenemies of Greece, the gods—particularly Talthybius, the patron hero of the heralds—protected them all the same. As a result, at least in this one case, Herodotus confirms that no Greeks can afford to commit crimes against their adversaries. However limited, these narrative instances offer the rationale for treating all people across political and ethnic lines as sacred and precious.[511]

We can further this analysis by asking if the gods ever act concretely on behalf of the enemy, and the answer is affirmative. In the *Odyssey*, Nestor reports that Zeus made homecoming disastrous for the Greeks because they behaved wantonly during the fall of Troy (the original phrase is that they were "neither discreet nor just" (*ou ti noḗmones oude dikaioi*)) (*Od.* 3.130–35). According to Pindar, Apollo plans the death of Neoptolemus, son of Achilles, because he lawlessly murdered the Trojan king Priam.[512] In the *Sack of Troy* epic, another Greek prince Ajax the Lesser also commits sacrilege against the Trojan princess Cassandra. Forgetting all about the gods in the moment of victory, Ajax forcefully tears Cassandra away from Athena's cultic image which she is clinging onto and then rapes her. If Ajax does not seek refuge later in the

---

508 Homer calls the mutilation of Hector's body shameful (*Il.* 22.395, 23.24) and the intent to kill twelve Trojan victims evil (*Il.* 23.176).

509 Hard, *The Routledge Handbook of Greek Mythology*, 519.

510 Herodotus tries to dispel the belief that the murder of Persian heralds was the cause for the destruction of Athens (7.133–37).

511 The observation in part follows Judith Butler's articulation of human interdependency and shared vulnerability. See Judith Butler, *Precarious Life: The Powers of Mourning and Violence* (London: Verso, 2006). Contrast this with the two other culture-systems. Polisism argues that the prosperity of the *polis* depends only on its citizens, disregarding all noncitizens. The market system simply turns the gaze inward and constructs the autonomous individual (or household) whose welfare is separate from others in the community.

512 Hard, *The Routledge Handbook of Greek Mythology*, 491.

same temple of Athena himself, the Greeks would have to stone him to death, indicating the grave nature of the offense, albeit committed against the defeated.[513] Overall, these tales signal that the divine do not hesitate to punish the Greeks (us) when they brutalize their foes (them).

The two remaining groups of the *other* comprise the lower strata of society: beggars and slaves. The former group suffers from economic destitution, and the latter from the loss of social and political rights,[514] but neither of them is being silenced in the epics.

The Treatment of the Poor

Eumaeus' decision to host Odysseus underscores the degree to which the poor enjoy power and protection from the gods, because all guests and beggars come from Zeus (*Od.* 14.57–58). When Melanthios insults Odysseus for being a vagabond, Eumaeus is outraged and prays for divine vengeance on Melanthios (*Od.* 17.240–47). Later in the same scene, the mendicant Odysseus also references the supernatural when placing a curse on Antinous: "Therefore,/ if there are any gods or any furies for beggars,/ Antinous may find his death before he is married" (*Od.* 17.474–76). In these instances, the belief in transcendent beings allows individuals to contest the social obloquy directed at the poor.

To fully grasp how the attacks on the economically deprived are being thwarted in the epics, we must first turn to Hannah Arendt. Based on the political life in ancient Greece, Arendt outlined several distinct notions of human agency and liability that help to illuminate the philosophy of Olympianism.[515] To her, the action of an individual never achieves its intended purpose due to the confluence of other events directed by others.[516] This truth is even more poignant in Olympianism due to the fact that many different gods modulate human affairs simultaneously. As a result, especially in the Olympian universe, human beings are both actors and sufferers in an interactive, co-created social ecology. Such a view contrasts with the logic of "economic individualism," which presupposes that people single-handedly author their own destinies and therefore deserve the failures that befall them. The falsehood

---

[513] Ibid., 482.

[514] Most studies on slavery tend to focus on the institution itself in real history. For the latest example, see Bradley Keith and Paul Cartledge, eds., *The Cambridge World History of Slavery* (Cambridge: Cambridge University Press, 2011). How slavery functioned as a discursive social construct has not received the same attention (only one partial chapter in the new volume 26–28), which is perhaps not surprising because the practice depends on structured silence. Harris also left out discursive analysis in "Homer, Hesiod, and the 'Origin' of Greek Slavery." William Thalmann's *The Swineherd and the Bow* (New York: Cornell, 1998) is one exception that takes advantage of the small window on slavery that the epics offer us. I do not dispute narrative elements that aid domination and subjugation identified by Thalmann. I merely stress that despite these depictions, the slave figures exhibit political consciousness and individual agency, a fact that must not be overlooked in itself.

[515] Scholars who note the frailty and uncertainty of human life in Greek literature are not lacking. For some obvious examples, see Martha Craven Nussbaum, *The Fragility of Goodness: Luck and Ethics in Greek Tragedy and Philosophy*, rev. ed. (Cambridge, UK: Cambridge University Press, 2001) and Arendt, *The Human Condition*. Here, however, I only use this idea at the general level, rather than looking the more specific differences in different authors and texts.

[516] Arendt, *The Human Condition*, 191.

of economic individualism is highlighted for the discerning modern reader in the scene where Melanthios wrongly judges the disguised Odysseus, thinking that "But since he has learned nothing but mischief, he will not be willing/ to go to work, but would rather go begging all through the district,/ asking for handouts and feeding up his bottomless belly" (*Od.* 17.226–28). The allegation that Odysseus is lazy and gluttonous cannot be further from the truth, as the audience knows well. Since even a noble and famed hero like Odysseus can fall out of grace with the gods and lose all his possessions, it bears upon us to pity him for his destitution.[517]

Hesiod knows how miserable men can be when the gods strike them with financial calamity. He advises the audience to never taunt a man for his deadly poverty that comes from the immortal gods (*WD* 717–18). Yet he does not condemn the possession of riches if they are obtained deservingly through effort: "If your competitive spirit has put a longing/ into your heart for wealth, then do it this way:/ work for it" (*WD* 381–82). These two injunctions bear no contradiction because the duty to do what is right does not go away even if acting fails to achieve what was intended. For Olympian actors, the moral compass is precisely anchored in the courage to pursue meaningful action against indeterminacy and uncertainty.

In the poetry of Hesiod, this truth about human interconnectivity and interdependence is applied directly to the political community, with the emphasis that those in power disproportionately affect the fate of others. The author intimates that an entire people pay for the recklessness of kings (*WD* 263) and those "who render, unto strangers and natives, judgments that are fair,/who do not depart, on a holiday of wickedness, from what is righteous, their city shall flourish, and their people prosper within it" (*WD* 225–27). With these statements, Hesiod reminds us that we constantly suffer from the deeds of other people. The *Iliad* contains a passage on political interconnectedness as well: when bad laws are being passed in the assembly, Zeus angrily sends down a flood so that everyone suffers (*Il.* 16.386–88). The recurring motif of pollution in Greek myth and tragedy functions in the same way: the crime of individuals can spread and contaminate an entire community, as with the plague caused by Oedipus who kills his father and the famine of Greece after the murder of Stymphalos by Pelops.[518] By constantly reminding us of the effect that we have on one another, Olympianism thoroughly politicizes seemingly individual decisions.

The above truth about human agency and responsibility also threads through the poetry of Solon. As John Lewis observed, Solon's notion of causality involves two separate entities that cannot easily be reconciled.[519] The first one, *dike* (justice), governs the *polis* and brings retribution to the whole community when someone commits hubris. In subscribing to this belief, Solon shares Hesiod's view that we suffer together from political decisions that are always collective in nature.

> These things my heart prompts me to teach the Athenians:
> how Lawlessness brings the worst evils to the city, and Lawfulness manifests good order and everything perfect, and often puts fetters on the evil-doers.

[517] For more on this point, see Lucia Cecchet, *Poverty in Athenian Public Discourse: From the Eve of the Peloponnesian War to the Rise of Macedonia* (Stuttgart: Franz Steiner Verlag, 2015), 64.
[518] Hard, *The Routledge Handbook of Greek Mythology*, 531.
[519] Lewis, *Solon the Thinker*, 74–95.

> It smoothes what is rough; quells anger, dims hubris
> and shrivels the flowering bud of arrogant destruction.
> It straightens crooked judgments, calms
> overbearing deeds, stops the deeds of civil strife,
> and stops the anger of grievous strife. It is by this
> that all things to men are perfect and reach their peak. (Solon 4.30–39)[520]

In addition to pointing out what humans are capable of inflicting on one another, Solon introduces *moira* (fate/lot), which governs individual life arbitrarily because of temporal delay, especially with regard to wealth.[521] "One man gets what he deserves right away, another later;/ some flee, and if they escape the onrushing fate of the immortals,/ it comes surely sometime. The innocents pay for the deeds/ of their children or their family thereafter" (Solon 13.29–32).[522] This *moira* described by Solon indeed exacerbates the condition of uncertainty and powerlessness for the individual. Solon's treatment of these two distinct forces of human life, as it turns out, reinforces the philosophy of collective yet inconsistent causation. First, because we are intimately linked to one another, any individual act will have an impact on the whole community (justice: *dike*). Secondly, humans do not individually author their own destiny in the sense of getting what they deserve (fate/lot: *moira*). As a result, we should feel compassion toward those who suffer misfortune and be wary of those basked in power and success. At the same time, as Lewis pointed out, the increased unpredictability of the gods—compared to in Homer—increases human fear of divine retribution,[523] with the result that we paradoxically must direct more attention to our actions. With the gods keeping track of crimes and handing out collateral punishment, we must not only steer clear of hubris individually, but also address failings and injustice en masse.

In the mind of Odysseus, the most wily of the Greek heroes, not only are mortals far from omnipotent, they are constantly at the mercy of uncontrollable circumstances, a condition opposite that of economic individualism.

> Of all creatures that breathe and walk on the earth there is nothing
> more helpless than a man is, of all that the earth fosters;
> for he thinks that he will never suffer misfortune in the future
> days; while the gods grant him courage, and his knees have spring
> in them. But when the blessed gods bring sad days upon him,
> against his will he must suffer it with enduring spirit.
> For the mind in men upon earth goes according to the fortunes
> the Father of Gods and Men, day by day, bestows upon them. (*Od.* 18.130–37)

The frailty and powerlessness of humans who inhabit a universe ruled by the gods is pervasive in Homer as well as Hesiod and Solon. Because the gods and other

---

520 Lewis, *Solon the Thinker*, 56.
521 Ibid., 77ff.
522 Ibid., 75.
523 Ibid., 15, 92.

individuals direct our lives, a radically different understanding of poverty emerges: men do not necessarily become indigent because of in-born evil or bad traits (e.g., sloth, shamefulness, or lack of entrepreneurship), but because of the conditions collectively produced by society. This logic turns economic individualism on its head by shifting the responsibility for poverty from individual members to society as a whole.

The *Odyssey* further rejects the validity of economic outcome as a manifestation of human nature by constantly detaching merit from class. In the story, the suitors who look down on the beggar Odysseus meet divine vengeance. By contrast, the swineherd Eumaeus and the cowherd Philoetius, who honor Odysseus despite his apparent indigence, emerge as protagonists. By showcasing the righteousness of honoring the bottom classes, the narrative arc in the second half of the *Odyssey* unequivocally bends toward those who struggle with economic hardship.[524] The sharp contrast between the true excellence (*arete*) of the servants, authenticated by mettle and kindness, and the hollow rank of the suitors, tarnished by greed and vice, underscores the moral of the story. Owing to these representations, we can viscerally grasp the ineffectiveness of wealth and status as measures of identity and character.

Slaves

In the Olympian world, even slaves freely call on the gods for assistance. In greeting his incognito master, Eumaeus—the swineherd who has been purchased by Odysseus' father—states: "Stranger, I have no right to deny the stranger, not even/ if one came to me who was meaner than you. All vagabonds/ and strangers are under Zeus, and the gift is a light and a dear one/ that comes from us" (*Od.* 14.56–61). Emboldened by theological teaching, even this servant who fears his master (*Od.* 14.60–61) takes it upon himself to defend an unknown beggar independently—a decision of great moral courage. Next in the speech, Eumaeus turns to his own personal situation, declaring himself worthy of fair compensation as that gods have borne witness to his hard work (*Od.* 14.61–66). He then moves on to bemoan the Trojan War, an event that in theory concerns only the nobles. Even so, Eumaeus critically reflects on the campaign by pointing out that many are dying for the few (*Od.* 14.68–71). Most significantly, fortified by the gods who represent early ideas of justice, this member of the servile class vehemently rebukes the avaricious suitors who are nobles, "[They] have no regard for anyone in their minds, no pity./ The blessed gods have no love for a pitiless action,/ but rather they reward justice and what men do that is lawful" (*Od.* 14.82–84). The poem indeed fulfills Eumaeus' wish as Odysseus eventually executes the suitors.

---

[524] Donlan listed their heroic deeds: Eumaeus observes the rules of being a host; Odysseus, Telemachus, Eumaus, and Philoetius fight shoulder to shoulder; Eumaeus and Philoetius cast their spears at the enemy; Eumaus receives an honorable wound. Donlan further stressed that "by emphasizing the bonds of comradeship between men of royal blood and slaves, and by showing men of no rank in heroic postures the poet appears to have made a clear statement that excellence and achievement result not from birth and breeding only but from intrinsic worth…. It is most tempting indeed to see social commentary in the fact that the real heroes…are men of the lower classes and not aristocrats." See Donlan, *The Aristocratic Ideal*, 243.

On a number of issues, Eumaeus lacks no opinions of his own and is not afraid to express them openly, much *unlike* a typical fearful and apathetic servant.

However, the figure of an independent, free-thinking slave did not impress William Thalmann, who thought that Homer merely makes Eumaeus parrot his master's agenda.[525] While Thalmann's interpretation has merit, the ease with which a slave character, undeterred by his inferior and dependent status, engages with broad, complex issues, should not be taken for granted. In fact, what the epic does take for granted is that Eumaeus shows keen interest in matters well beyond his immediate survival. Even if we assume that the narrator conveniently aligns his position with that of his master, the episode nonetheless endows a voice from below with depth and intelligence. In this manner, the assurance of powerful divine beings emboldens even a socially inferior figure to attempt critical deliberation.

Besides featuring the heroic Eumaeus, who speaks and acts as if he were his own master, Homer also raises profound questions about slavery itself. Who can forget the words of Hector who foresees the day when the enemies will drag away his beloved wife?

> For I know this thing well in my heart, and my mind knows it:
> there will come a day when sacred Ilion shall perish,
> and Priam, and the people of Priam of the strong ash spear.
> But it is not so much the pain to come of the Trojans
> that troubles me, not even of Priam the king nor He[cuba],
> not the thought of my brothers who in their numbers and valor
> shall drop in the dust under the hands of men who hate them,
> as troubles me the thought of you, when some bronze-armored
> Achaean leads you off, taking away your day of liberty,
> in tears; and in Argos you must work at the loom of another,
> and carry water from the spring Messeis or Hypereia,
> all unwilling, but strong will be the necessity upon you. (*Il.* 6.447–58)

Through the mind of Hector, whose wife the bronze-armored Achaeans will indeed haul away, the epics present the horrors of slavery in full emotional depth. The compassion and empathy for the victims owe to the divine ecumenical gaze, which readily surpasses ethnic and political differences.

Unfortunately, Olympianism sublimates deleterious martial violence into a glowing badge of virility. Despite Hector's deep fear for his wife Andromache and his son Astyanax, he passionately fights on in hopes of defeating other husbands and fathers. A peaceful world in which manhood is not hypostatized through killing is beyond his imagination. For he explains that he would feel deep shame before the Trojans, if he were to shrink aside from the fighting (*Il.* 6.441–43). Immersed in patriotism, Hector never doubts the logic of war, but only prays for his own success. The tight link forged between violence and masculinity amounts to the most disturbing semiotic maneuver in Olympianism.[526] In this respect, we see the gods

[525] Thalmann, *Swineherd and the Bow*, 91–93.

[526] For a detailed discussion of the warrior ethic and its problematic nature, see Redfield, *Nature and*

clearly inflaming and relishing warfare, which undermines the doctrines of ecumenism and conviviality that they themselves so beautifully convey.

If the immortals in the epics sometimes incite combat in the name of glory and justify the subsequent capture of human booty, by contrast, they unequivocally deplore the enslavement of people for economic gain. In the stories told by Odysseus as the Cretan, he recounts the well-deserved punishment of the profit-driven Phoenician slave trader at the hand of Zeus.

> There for the fulfillment of a year I stayed with him,
> but when the months and when the days had come to completion,
> with the circling back of the year again, and the seasons came on,
> then he took me on his seafaring ship to Libya,
> with lying advices, that with him we could win a cargo, but in fact
> so he could sell me there and take the immense price for me.
> I went with him on his ship, forced to, although I suspected
> all, on a North Wind that was favorable and fair, above
> the middle of Crete, but Zeus was plotting these men's destruction.
> (*Od.* 14.292–300)

And surely enough, "The men were thrown in the water,/ and bobbing like sea crows they were washed away on the running/ waves all around the black ship, and the god took away their homecoming" (*Od.* 14.307–09). Here, the Phoenicians' pursuit of "immense price" is associated with deception and treachery, which contrast sharply with the transparency and honor that characterize heroic warfare. Consequently, we see Zeus striking down the acquisitive perpetrators without mercy. After the perfidious Phoenician, the same happens with the Thesprotian men (*Od.* 14.340–59). Once more, the gods intervene and rescue the Cretan Odysseus before he nearly falls victim to slavery again (*Od.*14.348–59). Similarly, when Eumaeus recalls his past, he stresses that Artemis struck down the Phoenician woman who sold him for a "price beyond counting" (*Od.* 15.452). In these scenarios of enslavement driven by the pure desire for economic acquisition, the narrator rebukes the unscrupulous "entrepreneurs" who subject human beings to the profit calculus.

Perhaps we could say that Odysseus only denounces the human traffickers — imagined or real—who attempt to enslave *him*, but not the institutional practice of slavery as a whole; after all, he owns Eumaeus and Eurycleia and executes his maids without apology at the end of the *Odyssey*. While the epics certainly fall short of making any grand abolitionist statement, the difference in the attitudes toward the various modes of slavery nonetheless matters. For instance, in the domestic sphere, insulated from economic imperatives, the relationship between masters and slaves can approach family kinship in the epic world. We recall that Odysseus, however much still a patriarch, earns the loyalty of Eumaeus and feeds the latter's expectation of just recompense (*Od.* 14.61–66). In another scene, the swineherd is likened to a loving father when he rushes to kiss Odysseus' son Telemachus (*Od.* 16.15–29). When Odysseus enlists Eumaeus and the cowherd Philoitios for the final battle, he promises

Culture, 100ff.

them, "Then I shall get wives for you both, and grant you possessions/ and houses built next to mine and think of you in the future/ always as companions of Telemachus, and his brothers" (*Od.* 21.214–16). In the case of the maids who slept with the suitors, Odysseus hangs them for personal revenge, whether justified or not. He slaughters the aristocratic suitors just as ruthlessly without any consultation or formal procedure, as if they were his private property. As we can see, unlike economic slavery, which is purely evil and lacking any redeeming quality, the depictions of master and slave interaction in the household far away from the market are more ambivalent. The question that results from this ambiguity is not that a more intimate face-to-face setting can ameliorate slavery, but rather, how enslavement could exist at all among people who love, cherish, and depend on one another like family.

We can therefore conclude that Olympianism favors authentic interpersonal relationships over anonymous venal transactions. Social relations authenticate identities, whereas commercial transactions only assist the accumulation of abstracted wealth, although both could absorb elements of domination and inequity. Nevertheless, by refusing to treat people as economic units, Olympianism is at odds with the goal of a standardized labor market that facilitates the commercialization of human skills and capacity on a broad scale. Westermann concurred, stating from a historical perspective: "[S]laves in the Homeric period were obtained by capture in war and by casual and sporadic raids, rather than organized stealing of men, women, and children."[527] We have already seen how the core values of Olympianism problematize martial combat, the main source of slavery in the earlier periods,[528] and we should duly note how much market and state forces facilitate institutional slavery. While all three culture systems overlapped at the time when slavery overtook Greek society, the difference in their intended purposes and perfected state should be duly kept in mind.

Mass and Elite

The previous chapter outlined the Olympian dispensation through ecumenism and conviviality. These two foundational truths put forth a vision in which all lives are valued and are regarded as essential to collective well-being. This chapter so far has presented numerous illustrations in which socially marginalized groups are supplied with the raison d'être that strengthens their bid for equal status and recognition in this belief system. For the second half of this chapter, I apply the same analysis to the more exclusive circle of native men in literary representation. I ask whether the same principles of reciprocity, codependence, and egalitarianism—the second-order values that stem from ecumenism and conviviality—also prevail in the dynamic between those who lead and those who follow, or between the elites and the masses. I focus, in particular, on the political culture embodied in the Homeric epics, which most scholars believe reflect either one or several historical societies, or a conflation of

---

[527] See my rebuttal to the more recent opinion of Edward Harris in notes 111 and 121. William Linn Westermann, *The Slave Systems of Greek and Roman Antiquity* (Philadelphia: American Philosophical Society, 1955), 2.

[528] See the discussion in the earlier section Agon and Warfare.

them or their features, within the years ranging from 1300 to 800 BCE.[529] This period, which precedes the rise of the *polis* and corresponds the most to Olympianism, has often been perceived as less developed due to the absence of institutions associated with the state and the market. However, with the lens of Olympianism, I offer a radical reassessment of this era by highlighting the cultural rules and operations that display strong proto-democratic properties.

Scholars who take the *Iliad* and the *Odyssey* as evidence for a real society generally assert that the poems reflect and promote the interest of an aristocratic class.[530] This *communis opinio* faults religion for political oppression by highlighting the role divine heritage plays in establishing the status and authority of the luminaries. This view, however, is reductive and incomplete because it only sees agency in how elites "exploit" transcendent beliefs but not how they acquiesce to theological constraints. The use of cultural hermeneutics will challenge the presumption that the Homeric world conveys the ideologies of a rigid class society. For this perspective, I will revisit the three features considered most indicative of elite domination in the epics by other scholars: the supremacy of Agamemnon, the beating of Thersites,[531] and the passivity of the masses.[532] Upon close analysis, we discover that the very same religious terms embraced by the elites also endow the unprivileged with significant rights and agency. These "discursive resources" at the disposal of the non-patrician group weaken the roots of elitism and increase the likelihood of advancing pluralism and inclusion, two major pillars of democratic politics.

---

[529] The dates and nature of the Homeric world remain controversial; see Morris, "Use and Abuse of Homer," 81–82. The precise dating is not important for my study here, nor is historical accuracy of events and institutions; my focus is on the explication of cultural truths.

[530] Wallace, "Solonian Democracy," 13; Finley concluded, "A deep horizontal cleavage marked the world of the Homeric poems" and "Only the aristocrats had roles" (*World of Odysseus*, 53). See Thalmann for a more class-based reading of the *Odyssey*. According to Thalmann, the work "represent(s) mainly the perspective of an aristocracy that was asserting its interests amid disputes—with significant though not complete success" (*Swineherd and the Bow*, 6). Donlan took the counter position in *The Aristocratic Ideal* (237–48).

[531] The episode in which Thersites the commoner defies Agamemnon and suffers physical blows from Odysseus as a result has rightly attracted much attention in the history of Classical scholarship. See Siep Stuurman, "The Voice of Thersites: Reflections on the Origins of the Idea of Equality," *Journal of the History of Ideas* 65, no. 2 (April 2004): 171–89, for detail. I shall provide a basic summary of the article for the reader. In the nineteenth century, British liberal statesman William Gladstone saw some elements of freedom of speech and limited democracy in the evidence (178), while German classicist Ulrich von Wilamowitz-Moellendorff dismissed Thersites altogether as a useless coward (179). The negative reading has been followed by de Ste. Croix, George Thomson, Vidal-Naquet and Finley, who all found Homer unsympathetic to Thersites (180). However, other recent scholarship also followed the Gladstone tradition by positing Thersites as a democratic figure. The third group of scholarship focuses on the underlying tension and critique of the aristocratic code in the text. Last, treating the character Thersites as a literary device, some Classicists argued that he provides comic relief, i.e., the function of Thersites is more cathartic than subversive. For the last interpretation in particular, see William G. Thalmann, "Comedy, Scapegoats, and Heroic Ideology in the Iliad," *Transactions of the American Philological Association* 118 (1988): 1–28. My argument, however, draws on the understanding of the gods to generate a democratic reading that highlights the resources for contesting elite power.

[532] See Morris, "Use and Abuse of Homer," 123; Finley, *World of Odysseus*, 82; van Wees, *Status Warriors*, 80f.

Among Heroes

Agamemnon, the top commander of the Greek army in the *Iliad*, initially comes off as the supreme ruler *par excellence*, and scholars attribute his political prowess to the gods with good reason.[533] Nestor, the revered elder, offers a clear testimony by declaring that "never equal with the rest is the portion of honor/ of the sceptered king (i.e., Agamemnon) to whom Zeus gives magnificence" (*Il.* 1.278–79). In addition, when Agamemnon convenes an assembly, the narrator diverges into the history of the marvelous scepter he wields, telling us that it has been passed down in his family from Zeus (*Il.* 2.100–08). This detail, emphasized by Homer, insinuates Agamemnon's good standing with the god, which could very well serve as the basis of his outstanding status and authority. So far, the evidence hews to the image of a chieftain being held in high regard because of the special ties to the supernatural.

On the other hand, those same gods who endorse Agamemnon also undermine his authority by bestowing other heroes with favors and gifts. The standoff between Agamemnon and Achilles is difficult to resolve precisely because the commander-in-chief is not more special than other princes who are also in the gods' good graces.[534] In other words, Agamemnon's divine ties are insufficient to win him any exceptional prerogative in this group, because all princes (including those on the Trojan side) by default trace their descent from or possess some connection to one deity or another.

The wide dispersion of divine patronage reflects the simple fact that there are many gods who care for many individuals—the ecumenical foundation of the Greek polytheist religion. For example, when Agamemnon angrily shouts at Achilles, "You are the most hateful to me of Zeus-nurtured kings (*diotrepheôn basilêôn*)!",[535] there is acknowledgement that Achilles is also cherished by Zeus. In fact, Zeus' later intervention on behalf of Achilles forces Agamemnon to concede, "Worth many/ fighters is that man [Achilles] whom Zeus in his heart loves, as now/ he has honored this man and beaten down the Achaean people" (*Il.* 9.116–18). In addition, Agamemnon is not the only one who carries a scepter. Achilles readily uses one when he swears a vengeful oath in its name to remind everyone that the people (the sons of the Achaeans) carry it in their hands when they dispense justice on behalf of Zeus (*Il.* 1. 233–46). In another instance, the narrator refers to all princes as "scepter-bearing kings" (*Il.* 2.85). The dispersal of the royal signet is another indication that no single individual can monopolize divine sanction.

The difficulty of establishing a vertical ranking among nominally equal and autonomous princes results in a more collegial and horizontal constellation throughout. Even Agamemnon feels the pressure to repudiate anyone who seeks unilateral domination. At his most enraged moment, he decries his nemesis Achilles

---

[533] Morris concluded: "Homer frequently alludes to the source of the *basileis*' authority: the will of Zeus" ("Use and Abuse of Homer," 123).

[534] In the epics, office itself carries little weight when not matched by excellent action. When Achilles reproaches Agamemnon, he stresses the importance of the latter's deeds over that of the title: "You wine sack, with a dog's eyes, with a deer's heart. Never/ once have you taken courage in your heart to arm with your people/ for battle, or go into ambuscade with the best of the Achaeans/… King who feeds on your people, since you rule nonentities" (*Il.* 1.225–31). In Book 9 of the *Iliad*, Diomedes also censures Agamemnon's incompetence.

[535] *Il.* 1.176, translated in Peter Rose, *Class in Archaic Greece*, 110.

as "a man who wishes to be above all others,/ who wishes to hold power over all, and to be lord of all, and give them their order" (*Il.* 1.287–89). Yet here Agamemnon is guilty of precisely what he accuses Achilles—it is he, not another, who is behaving like a tyrant. Agamemnon's dictatorial manner prompts Nestor, the conciliatory elder, to lay bare the power fragmentation in the Greek army. The veteran councilor, who defers to Agamemnon throughout the poem, admits that the honor the commander-king receives from Zeus is only one side of the story; on the other hand, Achilles is also formidable because he was born from a goddess. Unable to resolve the quarrel on the basis of celestial pedigree, Nestor ultimately circumvents the conundrum by omitting the gods from the equation altogether. He ultimately declares for Agamemnon, because, so he says, the latter rules over more men (*Il.* 1.281). Nestor's makeshift answer, however, does not settle the dispute. First, Nestor himself, the third-party arbitrator, lacks the nominal or actual authority to adjudicate the matter.[536] Indeed, both sides happily ignore the elder's recommendation to reconcile. Additionally, the development of the plot further discredits Nestor's one-sided pronouncement. We know that Achilles' goddess mother successfully convinces Zeus to avenge the dishonor of a "much better man than [Agamemnon] is" (*Il.* 2.239).[537] Zeus consequently humbles the mighty king, heedless of how many men Agamemnon controls. As Zeus' plan unfolds, Agamemnon concedes his folly and calls himself a victim of madness (*Il.* 9.119). In the opinion of Walter Donlan, this fanciful excuse is indicative of the extent to which social normality was breached by Agamemnon's violation of collective authority.[538] Whatever divine favor he previously vaunted, it does not spare him of public humiliation and political setback.

Most importantly, Agamemnon's lordship over subordinates, which alludes to the use of force and threat,[539] does not sit well with the Olympian heroic code that extols individual excellence and community service.[540] Excellence and service are valued in the Olympian dispensation because only they bring immortal glory (*kleos aphthiton*) that endures on the lips and in the mind of future generations. Although a hero would not abjure material reward or political power as earthly or unworthy (since Olympianism rejects inward asceticism, as we have already discussed in Chapter 1),

---

[536] Hanna Roisman pointed out that although Nestor is esteemed in the poem, his advice often fails to persuade others and his predictions turn out to be untrue, see Hanna Roisman, "Nestor the Good Counselor," *The Classical Quarterly* 55, no. 1 (May 2005): 18–21.

[537] We should not take for granted the success of Thetis, which might very well speak to the seriousness of the injustice suffered by Achilles. Many heroes suffer defeat and lose their lives in the battlefield without intervention from their divine fathers, for example, in the case Sarpedon, who is also a son of Zeus.

[538] Donlan, *The Aristocratic Ideal*, 259.

[539] The text implies that Agamemnon collects underlings through the use of force. See Hammer, *The Iliad as Politics*, 83. By contrast, Achilles attracts followers on the basis of friendship. Ibid., 81.

[540] Scholars have disagreed on which one is more important. Arthur Adkins, for instance, held that the elites cared for their own individual success, thus they embody competitive values. See note 444. Donlan, buying into the dominance of *oikos*—a historical development external to the epics—shared this opinion. He mused, "In general, private considerations tend to override public concerns in Homer" (*The Aristocratic Ideal*, 8). Long represented the other side, arguing that the elites cooperated for the communal good (though not defining what kind of community: *polis* or another). See Long, "Morals and Values in Homer." Stuart Fraser also shared this view. He identified the intracommunity network as a framework for encouraging aristocrats to care for the people. See Fraser, "Aristocratic Values in Ancient Greece." I oppose this bifurcation altogether and seek to unite them through the concept of conviviality.

he would also not confuse *kleos aphthiton* with its tangible by-products.[541] This everlasting fame, the only solace to death, is intrinsically immaterial and transcendental. In this matrix of heroic values, Agamemnon's command of underlings cannot be converted into the type of esteem that wins adulation from other heroes. After discounting Agamemnon's manpower, we are back to square one: a world of contesting claims that cannot be neatly sorted into a vertical order.

Overall, because an array of gods love an array of men and women, any flaunting of divine backing automatically invites others to follow suit. In Agamemnon's case, the gods who bestow the wondrous scepter to him (*Il.* 2.101–09) also easily chastise and punish him on behalf of others. Overall, in an ecumenical world, power and authority tend to decentralize, fragment, and counter-balance. As a result, the general of the Greek army cannot expect automatic and unconditional compliance, as the wrath of Achilles amply illustrates.

Thersites and the Role of Common Men

If elites cannot successfully establish a clear pyramidal ranking among themselves, can they at least boast undisputed superiority over the masses? Citing the beating of the commoner Thersites in the *Iliad* as a potent example, a number of scholars have concluded that the hero-warriors, or "nobility," exercise domination over the people, or the *demos*.[542] However, a close study of theological themes and context contradicts this presumed rigid division and the existence of two highly unequal classes. Religious discourse, in particular, delegitimizes and obstructs the potential formation of an abusive hereditary class.

The beating of Thersites, the *locus classicus* for proving elite domination, becomes complicated when scrutinized with the tools of cultural hermeneutics. For those who are unfamiliar with this episode in Book 2, it begins with Agamemnon gathering his army to announce falsely that the war is over. After the soldiers rush to the ships, Odysseus herds them back and bids them to fight on. Amidst the chaos and commotion, a soldier named Thersites delivers a passionate speech against the princes, but then receives a beating by Odysseus to the cheer of the spectators. It is true that the narrator highlights the outrageous manner and ungainly appearance of Thersites as soon as he enters on stage, tarnishing our immediate impression of the outspoken critic (*Il.* 2.213–17). But aside from this portrayal, the disruption caused by

---

[541] Seaford commented that "Achilles puts life, honor and fame above wealth." See Richard Seaford, *Money and the Early Greek Mind* (Cambridge: Cambridge University Press, 2004), 56. We can see this economic disinterest in Achilles' rejection of Agamemnon's extravagant gifts (9.317–69). In this, Achilles reveals that his goal is not to amass as many goods as possible (but only in the sense that they represent honor and distinction), or else he would have happily bargained with Agamemnon. Donlan summarized this distinction, using "greed" to indicate material acquisition for its own sake. He stated "The acquisition of wealth... was not prompted by greed: such a mainspring belongs to market economies... The clear and definite impression of the Homeric age's attitude towards wealth is that it was regarded both as the tangible proof of a man's excellence and a means of increasing reputation and standing, not as a primary goal in itself" (*The Aristocratic Ideal*, 4).

[542] For example, Finley, *World of Odysseus*, 111–12; Morris, "Use and Abuse of Homer," 123; van Wees, *Status Warriors*, 80, 83f; Raaflaub, "Homeric Society," 634, despite arguing for the significance of the *demos* in "People's Power and Egalitarian Trends in Archaic Greece." For a longer list, see N. Postlethwaite, "Thersites in the 'Iliad,'" *Greece & Rome* Second Series 35, no. 2 (October 1988): 123.

Thersites inadvertently divulges the inclusive and open mode of politics in the *Iliad*. First, the presence of Thersites and other soldiers in the assembly—the important decision-making body of the Greek army—is taken for granted. Second, the fact that Thersites speaks is significant: none of the nobles interrupts or stops him until his speech becomes dangerous. Homer himself says that Thersites had launched diatribes in the past; however, this time his blazing condemnation of the campaign threatens the elites heavily invested in the war effort. In this political system, no fixed rules regulate public speech or confine it exclusively to the province of the princes.

We should not generalize from this one instance alone, but other examples of commoners participating in political debate abound. In Book 2 of the *Odyssey*, all the long-haired Achaeans arrive at the assembly summoned by the heralds at the bequest of Telemachus, and various attendees who feel moved to speak simply rise up to do so (*Od.* 2.7–256). Some of the speakers like Mentor and Halitherses have no epithets or patronym that indicate aristocratic status. In Book 19 of the *Iliad*, Achilles returns to the Greek camp and right away convenes a meeting that is marked by its inclusiveness. According to the narrator: "And even those who before had stayed where the ships were assembled,/ they who were helmsmen of the ships and handled the steering oar,/ they who were stewards among the ships and dispensers of rations, even these/ came then to assembly" (*Il.* 19.42–45). In contrast to these exemplary assemblies that are open to everyone, the evil suitors in the *Odyssey* allow no one to sit with them when they convene (*Od.* 16.361), creating a feeling of illegitimacy for their secluded meeting. On the Trojan side, even at one executive council, a man named Dolon—son of a herald with swift feet, a dreadful face, and no particular celestial distinction—spontaneously proposes an idea and receives great praise (*Il.* 10.314–31). In all these instances, the narrator describes the presence of the plebian class in public deliberation as normal and natural.

In addition, the political process in the *Iliad* successfully foregrounds the perspectives and voices from below. In Book 12, the Trojan soldier Polydamas is determined to speak out, although he is fully aware that his commander Hector does not always take being contradicted well (215). In this exchange, Homer lets Polydamas, "better in words [than Hector]" (*Il.* 18.253), to deliver the correct and sensible interpretation of Zeus' omen, to the concurrence of Trojan soldiers present. Such a scene shows that even an ordinary man is capable of intelligent ideas. Hector, by rebuking Polydamas' heartfelt advice, appears rash and conceited. Hector's close-mindedness contrasts sharply with two prior times wherein he heeds to the "blameless" Polydamas and gains victory on the battlefield (*Il.* 12.60–115, 13.725–53). At the climactic assembly in Book 18, Hector arrogantly brushes aside the injunction of the commoner Polydamas (285–96), and then says: "Fool, do not declare these sentiments any longer among the people,/ for no Trojan will obey—for I will not allow it" (295–96).[543] The silencing of Polydamas deprives the Trojans of the opportunity to consider a different course of action. Refusing to listen, Hector rushes out to meet Achilles and is killed in combat. As for the Trojan soldiers who dismiss Polydamas at Hector's urging, Homer calls them "fools, since Pallas Athene had taken away the wits from them" (*Il.* 18.311). By making the leader appear foolhardy

[543] Elmer, *The Poetics of Consent*, 137f.

when suppressing dissent, Olympianism in effect advocates inclusion and openness in decision-making.

In addition, Polydamas' final vow to say "what he thinks best" echoes Nestor's comments in Book 9. When it comes to speeches, Nestor stresses it is the substance that matters. Although always deferential almost to the point of being obsequious toward Agamemnon, Nestor nonetheless asserts that the commander must also be tolerant of differences.

> It is yours therefore to speak a word, yours also to listen,
> and grant the right to another also, when his spirit stirs him
> to speak for our good. All shall be yours when you lead the way. Still
> I will speak in the way it seems best to my mind. (*Il.* 9.100–03)

Here, the criteria for speaking in public are the speech's authenticity and pertinence, not the speaker's position or status. Most significantly, Nestor understands that a welcoming and liberal debate benefits all and sundry: "When many assemble together follow him who advises/ the best counsel, for in truth there is need for all the Achaeans/ of good close counsel" (*Il.* 9.74–76).

The nonhierarchical nature of political deliberation manifests itself throughout Homer. Walter Donlan tallied all the cases of someone making a proposal to the group in the *Iliad.* He discovered that the injunctions of Agamemnon and Hector, leaders of both armies, are frequently overturned, while those of the subordinates are often adopted.[544] The spontaneous and lively dynamic reflects a fluid and competitive order rather than that of fixed command and authority. Along the same line, David Elmer characterized the decision-making in the *Iliad* as one of consensus because it abets compromise and cooperation.[545] Specifically, Elmer pointed out that members of this culture can yield and concede without being seen as weak.[546] This mechanism harmonizes and reconciles divergent, even opposing positions, reinforcing the values of multiplicity, interdependence, and egalitarianism that undergird Olympianism. Because multiple deities and heroes act and decide together, the synergy of their views and perspectives is bound to be superior to those of a single being.

Having highlighted the tolerant and inclusive political culture that made Thersites' disruption possible in the first place, let us now turn to his speech. As scholars have noted, this fearless soldier and Achilles are kindred spirits in terms of their populism.[547] Both of them evaluate leadership critically, because they are keenly aware of its impact on group cohesion and justice. Thersites bluntly tells Agamemnon, "It is not right for/ you, their leader, to lead in sorrow the sons of the Achaeans" (*Il.* 2.233–34). His disgust at Agamemnon's poor treatment of others (*Il.* 2.225–34) pinpoints to the root cause of Achilles' grievance. Despite past quarrels,[548] Thersites defends Achilles gallantly: "[N]ow he has dishonored Achilles, a man much better/ than he is" (*Il.* 2.239–40). Most significantly, Thersites believes in the power

[544] Donlan, *The Aristocratic Ideal*, 252.
[545] Elmer, *The Poetics of Consent*, 4f.
[546] Ibid., 5.
[547] Ibid., 99fn47.
[548] Homer says Thersites was always abusing Odysseus and Achilles (*Il.* 2.220).

of the masses and urges them to rise up and rebel against a selfish and incompetent leader like Agamemnon (*Il.* 2.235–38). Replete with charged political ideas, the speech of Thersites cannot be dismissed as the mere senseless grumbling of an outcast. We have reason to assume that Achilles expects his other comrades to stand up in solidarity with him as Thersites does. Very early on, Achilles proclaims that the "sons of the Achaeans...administer/ the justice of Zeus" (*Il.* 1.237–39)—a remark that recognizes the true sovereignty of the people. Achilles shows his respect for them concretely through action: when the plague strikes, he calls all the Greeks to a meeting and offers to protect Calchas so the seer can speak freely (*Il.* 1.54). After the death of Patroclus, he summons the assembly again—here the narrator stresses that even stewards and helmsmen came—to formally announce in front of them that he will put aside the grudge against Agamemnon (*Il.* 19.40–68). With these words and gestures, Achilles, although a high-born prince of divine blood, takes the people into account when making decisions.

Yet the passive stance of the masses disappoints and estranges the hero who has labored hard on their behalf. Their failure to stand up for him prompts him to withdraw from politics and society. Achilles bitterly explains: "I will not fight for the girl's sake, neither/ with you nor any other man, since you [plural] take her away who gave her" (*Il.* 1.298–99). In another place, he complains that if the Greeks were not such cowards, Agamemnon would not have been able commit such outrage (*Il.* 1.231–32). Despite being let down by his compatriots, Achilles never ceases to care for them. When a major Greek defeat occurs later after his abstention from battle, the illustrious hero is overcome by guilt: "I was no light of safety to Patroclus, nor to my other/ companions, who in their numbers went down before glorious Hector,/ but sit here beside my ships, a useless weight on the good land" (*Il.* 18.102–04). In this light, though Thersites is being publicly humiliated and ridiculed while Odysseus strikes him, the ugly soldier actually resembles Achilles in that he fiercely speaks his mind and stands up for the group as a whole. Given their attention to collective action and group justice, if we take Achilles as seriously as the *Iliad* wants us to, then we cannot dismiss Thersites as a comic rabble-rouser.

In addition to the above considerations, the truth regime of Olympianism also decisively rebukes the princely bullies of Thersites. In Olympian culture, authority derives from wisdom and knowledge imparted by the gods. We see this quality in Achilles who learns of his fate from his divine mother, or in Hesiod who receives instructions from the Muses—both men achieve preeminence in part because they are privy to special information. By contrast, those who spurn or are ignorant of the will of the gods eventually court disaster, regardless of their worldly station. Such downfalls are usually told to the audience beforehand, but only revealed to the victims when it is too late. In narratological terms, a temporal lag is inserted between the primary narrator, who lays out future outcomes, and the focalizer, who learns the same facts only much later.[549] Given this device, we should always watch for the pending catastrophe, and the *Iliad* clearly endangers Agamemnon in this manner.

[549] For a more extensive discussion of these terms and their application, see Irene J. F. de Jong, *Narrators and Focalizers: The Presentation of the Story in the Iliad* (Amsterdam: B. R. Grüner Pub. Co., 1987).

The justice meted out by the gods is often delayed rather than timely. Book 1 opens with Agamemnon committing a major act of impiety by bullying the priest Chryses. While to the Achaeans, the gods seem to idle around as Chryses returns home in tears, the narrator informs us that Apollo shall avenge Chryses by sending a plague to the Greeks. In this episode, Agamemnon's utter blindness will cost him dearly.[550] Soon, we witness Agamemnon again threatening the seer Calchas for divulging the real reason behind the plague. In the subsequent confrontation between him and Achilles, Agamemnon takes away Briseis by force. Here, even the obsequious Nestor intervenes, urging Agamemnon to back down and "let her be, a prize as the sons of the Achaeans gave her/ first" (*Il.* 1.276–77). Nestor's reasonable suggestion is blatantly ignored. Once more, Agamemnon triumphs momentarily, perhaps because he is a Zeus-nurtured king, but the audience learns about Athena's promise to take revenge on behalf of Achilles. After having been reassured of divine backing, Achilles bluntly points out Agamemnon's shortcoming—the failure to keep in mind the past and the future (*Il.* 1.343)—a fatal flaw in anyone, and much more so in a leader. The poem proceeds to narrate the labor of Achilles' mother Thetis, who obliges Zeus to ensure Greek defeat so long as Achilles withdraws in order to prove that her son is indispensable. In the scene of entreaty, the goddess first grabs Zeus "underneath the chin with her right hand" and then reminds him of his indebtedness to her, all before demanding the father of the gods to "give honour to my son short-lived beyond all other/ mortals" (*Il.* 501, 505–06). Zeus' consent to the plan, which materializes after much time has passed, ultimately forces Agamemnon to bow down his proud head and offer elaborate concessions in order to win Achilles back (*Il.* Book 9). Since the gods often humble arrogant mortals not by inflicting instant harm but by delivering punishment at a later juncture, Thersites' momentary defeat calls for patience in judgment.

In the larger narrative context, the injury suffered by Thersites—that is, being beaten by Odysseus and lampooned by other heartless soldiers—advances Zeus' design to devastate the Greeks. As usual, Agamemnon is kept in the dark, while the narrator apprises us of the insidious plan:

> but the ease of sleep came not upon Zeus
> who was pondering in his heart how he might bring honor
> to Achilles, and destroy many beside the ships of the Achaeans.
> Now to his mind this thing appeared to be the best counsel,
> to send evil Dream to Atreus' son Agamemnon. (*Il.* 2.2–6)

By testing the soldiers as a result of this devious dream, Agamemnon commits political and moral blunders which "presupposes that popular support (for withdrawing from the war)…can be overridden."[551] The narrator does not hesitate to

[550] The rejection of the seer's wise advice is a common motif in this group of literature. One can think of Teiresias, who is brushed aside when he tries to persuade Pentheus to obey Dionysus in the *Bacchae*, or when he warns Creon that the gods are angry with him in the *Antigone*.

[551] Elmer, *The Poetics of Consent*, 90. The author contrasted this with the way Odysseus and Achilles rally the soldiers by acknowledging their will to go home but reminding them of their pledge to sack Troy (*Il.* 2.284–300, 16.205–06). What Agamemnon does is more along the lines of manipulation rather than

call Agamemnon a fool who is completely ignorant of Zeus' intentions (*Il.* 2.38). When the soldiers take delight in the thrashing of Thersites, the most outspoken critic of the war, they are also unaware that Zeus "was indeed to visit tears and sufferings/ on Trojans and Danaans alike in the strong encounters" (*Il.* 2.39–40). Armed with this knowledge, however, we readers do not want to laugh with the soldiers,[552] nor should we regard Thersites' call for rebellion foolish.

Proponents of elitism might also point to Odysseus' speech calling for obedience in order to rein in the masses.[553] Yet we shall assess his intervention in the same interpretive framework of larger, delayed events. In this scene, Odysseus lectures the homesick and war-weary soldiers: "Surely not all of us Achaeans can be as kings here./ Lordship for many is no good thing. Let there be one ruler,/ one king, to whom the son of devious-devising Kronos/ gives the scepter and right of judgment, to watch over his people" (*Il.* 2.203–06). With this affirmation of one-man rule, Odysseus manages to instill order and discipline into the soldiers,[554] but the reader is once more aware of additional information in the background: we recognize that Odysseus is effectively gathering his fellow Greeks for the carnage Zeus has planned. More to the point, by using violence and intimidation against Thersites and the army, Odysseus already disobeys Athena, who instructs him to "speak to *each man* in words of gentleness" (*Il.* 2.180). Athena's insistence on "words not swords" coheres with the ideal noble king in Hesiod's poetry. Such a leader uses a "sweet voice" to solve disputes, i.e., through persuasion and consensus (*Theogony* 96–97). By betraying these cultural norms, the monarchical endorsement of Odysseus comes off as highly problematic.

Moreover, Odysseus' authoritarian message is at odds with the horizontal configuration of the Greek federation. In fact, the most wily of the Greek heroes does not practice what he preaches, for Odysseus considers himself equal to the king and disobeys the "monarch" whenever convenient. In Book 4, Odysseus angrily refutes the accusation of cowardice from Agamemnon in the manner of a peer (*Il.* 4.350–55), forcing the commander-in-chief to retract the charge (*Il.* 4.357–63). Later, in Book 14, Odysseus condemns Agamemnon's decision to retreat (*Il.* 14.83–102). In behavior and manner, Odysseus countenances no position of inferiority and treats Agamemnon like a colleague rather than a superior.

In the overall picture, the gods have no qualms putting down the powerful in the conflicts that rile up mortals. When Achilles opposes Agamemnon, essentially resisting autocratic power, Zeus helps the "subordinate." In the case of Agamemnon "testing" the will of the soldiers using deceit and threat, Zeus undermines the commander-in-chief. Given the typical stance of the gods and the unseemly treatment

---

persuasion.

[552] Gregory Nagy suggested that in this episode, the epic poet gets the last laugh on Thersites, who functions like a blame poet. See Gregory Nagy, *The Best of the Achaeans: Concepts of the Hero in Archaic Greek Poetry* (Baltimore: Johns Hopkins University Press, 1979), 262. Perhaps Epos does, but we as the audience may not want to, given the series of events that follow.

[553] For example, Raaflaub, "Homeric Society," 634.

[554] However, Feldman reminded us that Odysseus was not delivering a lecture on political theory, but restoring military concord. See Abraham Feldman, "Homer and Democracy," in *The Classical Journal* 47, no. 8 (1952): 338.

of Thersites, we should wonder if Odysseus' temporary triumph actually spells a reverse lesson.

One might pause here and ask why innocent soldiers should die for the guilty, that is, why Zeus sends them to a bloodbath out of spite for Agamemnon. This unjust outcome can only be explained by the truth of inescapable interconnectedness and interdependence we outlined earlier: humans can die and suffer without "deserving it," as a result of the decisions and choices of others (either men or gods). This messiness contrasts with the ability of actors to plan and effect outcomes in the utilitarian model. Yet, despite the fact that life is unpredictable and chaotic, the conclusion is not paralysis or inaction. On the contrary, the foremost imperative in the Olympian world is to act irrespective of the end.[555] As Arendt argues, actions are "independent of victory and defeat and must remain untouched by any eventual outcome by their consequences for better or worse."[556] Hector, for example, reiterates at death his life-long desire to do something memorable, so that his name will not fade into oblivion (*Il.* 22.303–05). Those who read Homer will indeed remember the most about his courage in defending Troy, not his ultimate defeat. Especially through songs and poetry, action acquires a life of its own and becomes its own end in the Olympian world.

From the perspective of taking maximum action, each Greek soldier must hold his leader accountable, because bad decisions at the top drag everyone down together, as we have seen in Agamemnon's refusal to negotiate with Chryses or his seizure of Achilles' prize. These examples show that no one can avoid evil completely on an individual basis, but only en masse through concerted effort. The *Iliad* hints at this moral priority. Although the soldiers should not pay the price of life for Agamemnon, they clearly also do nothing to stop him from wronging Chryses, Achilles, or Thersites. Using this logic, rather than blaming the bad temper of Achilles,[557] or the bad manners of Thersites for "stirring things up," one might cite the lack of solidarity and collective action as the true cause of the conflict. The speeches of Achilles and Thersites indeed stress the interdependent and connected nature of the body politic and insinuate the right, and even obligation, for every Greek to protest and rebel when necessary. Seen in this light, although the soldiers suffer unjustly as collateral damage, they can certainly be faulted for failing in the responsibility to act together.

Let us review the series of readings that work against an elitist interpretation of the Thersites episode. Homer first normalizes inclusive and porous political debate, then fills Thersites' speech with useful insight, and finally highlights the glaring hubris on the part of the elites. Given these narrative features, we cannot easily surmise that the poem or the culture it embodies exemplifies the ideology of

555 We can also think of Oedipus, who takes responsibility for things that are not strictly his fault and becomes a hero in the process.

556 Arendt, *The Human Condition*, 205.

557 It is true that the narrator suggests that the anger of Achilles caused many to die in the first few lines of the *Iliad*, but soon the focus shifts to the anger of Apollo, which was incited by Agamemnon. In addition, Donlan argued that Agamemnon's offer to reconcile with excessive gifts later is actually insulting in the cultural context. See Donlan, *The Aristocratic Ideal*, 330–33. If we accept Donlan's argument, then Achilles is less guilty for not returning to the Greek army right away.

aristocratic domination. On the contrary, the moral and cultural leanings urge ordinary people to demand accountability from their rulers.

The Masses

Leaving behind the famous characters of the *Iliad*, let us proceed to dispute the third argument for elite supremacy in Homer: the obscurity of the *demos* (the Greek terms that generally correspond to "the people").[558] The claim that Homer ignores the *demos* to the point of oblivion can no longer hold.[559] Instead, recent studies focused on analyzing warfare have suggested that the role of the "albeit less visible" multitude is not at all negligible.[560] For instance, entire armies of Greeks or Trojans often assail, resist, and fight as one (*Il.* 15.306, 15.312, 15.277). Furthermore, Achilles prepares his soldiers—all 2,500 of them—with an impassioned oration that fills their hearts with desire for battle (*Il.* 16.198-211). Later, he includes them in his prayer (*Il.* 16.240–48), and his best friend Patroclus urges them to honor their commander on the battlefield (*Il.* 16.268–75). Although the masses often elude the spotlight, they nevertheless partake in military campaigns that are collective in nature. In one instance, the Cretan leader Idomeneus proclaims on behalf of his men, "[A]ll of us know how to wage war" (*Il.* 13.223) and "The warcraft even of sad fighters combined turns courage" (*Il.* 13.237); at another time, the two Ajaxes, Ajax the lesser and the Great, urge their soldiers that "this is work for all" (*Il.* 12.269–71). Even in terms of appellations, Donlan reminded us that "the rank and file are also given the epithet *aristoi*, and that they, too, are called 'Heroes.'"[561] These narrative details unequivocally position the common soldier at the center of the war effort.

Besides warfare and political deliberation (the latter we discussed through a close reading of the Thersites episode in the previous section), the people (*demos*) are also active in a number of ways. Throughout the poem: they are seen to divide spoils (*Il.* 11.704); listen to the leader (*Od.* 7.11); honor the rulers and pay for their wickedness accordingly (*Il.* 5.78, *Od.* 261); gather for a project (*Il.* 20.166); express opinions to constrain individuals (Od. 14.239; 16.75), among other deeds.[562] To this list, we can also add feasting, already described extensively in Chapter 5. As Susan Sherratt's article on Homeric feasting confirms, virtually everyone at some time or other join a feast.[563] The joyful group celebration begins with ritual animal sacrifice which involves burning fat for the gods and apportioning meat to humans. On those sacred

---

[558] Donlan, *The Aristocratic Ideal*, 225. Donlan concluded that *demos* in Homer usually denotes all the free inhabitants of a community, sometimes minus the elites.

[559] For the traditional opinion that people in the *Iliad* had no power, see Elmer, *The Poetics of Consent*, 3.

[560] Raaflaub and Wallace, "People's Power and Egalitarian Trends," 25ff; Hans van Wees, "The Homeric Way of War: The Iliad and the Hoplite Phalanx," *Greece and Rome* 41, no. 1 (April 1994): 2; Joachim Latacz, *Kampfparänese, Kampfdarstellung und Kampfwirklichkeit in der Ilias, bei Kallinos und Tyrtaios* [Battle Phenomena, Representation and Reality in the *Iliad* through Callinus and Tyrtaeus] (München: Zetemata 66, 1977).

[561] Donlan, *The Aristocratic Ideal*, 19, 19n37, e.g., *aristori*: *Il.* 2.577–78; 5.780; 12.89, 197; 13.128; heroes; *Il.* 2.110, etc. 12. 165; 15.230, 261; 19.34.

[562] These examples are taken from Donlan, *The Aristocratic Ideal*, 288–89.

[563] Susan Sherratt, "Feasting in Homeric Epic," in *Hesperia: The Journal of the American School of Classical Studies at Athens* 73 no. 2, Special Issue: The Mycenean Feast (April–June 2004): 302, 304.

occasions, economic resources are abundantly redistributed to the community for coming together and enjoying one another's company. By showing people being active in those political, social, and religious capacities, the society Homer portrays is certainly not at all one where the masses are completely insignificant.

Most importantly, since the right to invoke the gods is not alienable, religious recourse becomes a guarantee for all, including the underprivileged. Very simply, because anyone can sacrifice and pray, anyone can plea with the gods. In fact, at one point during the war, both Greek and Trojan soldiers implore Zeus to end the conflict by taking the life of Menelaus or Paris, the two men who sparked off the epic war in the first place (*Il.* 3.320–23). In this moment, we can see a group consciousness awakening for peace that would benefit the rank and file soldiers the most. Furthermore, even the less princely characters are formidable on an individual level, because every single one of them has ties to divinity or royalty.[564] The aforementioned commoner Thersites, for example, is a descendent from the Aetolian royal family in another myth.[565] The swineherd Eumaeus' father is the king of Syria.[566] The charioteer Myrtilus is the son of Hermes.[567] Finally, Patroclus and Menesthios, Achilles' personal attendants, are the grandson of the nymph Aegina[568] and the son of the river-god Spercheios, respectively.[569] Even the reviled monster Polyphemus was fathered by Poseidon. With celestial lineage being so readily available, divine association functions like a basic birthright in the Homeric world.[570]

Even without high-born blood, a commoner can always speak and act like a hero, as Polydamas does in the *Iliad* and the cowherd does in the *Odyssey*. Alternatively, one can receive special messages from the gods as Hesiod does, or seek divine patronage as singers (*aoidoi*), seers, heralds, and craftsmen do.[571] The last resort would be to call on the Furies, as the beggar Odysseus or the adulteress Clytemnestra does. The fact that even Clytemnestra, who keeps a lover and murders her husband, is entitled to formidable deities who contest her killing, is all the more remarkable in a culture that otherwise displays strong patriarchic leanings. Altogether, in the absence

---

[564] In the story of Hercules, the hero accidentally kills a page boy, who turns out to be of noble birth, being a relative to the king (Hard, *The Routledge Handbook of Greek Mythology*, 280). Euryalos, the lieutenant of Diomedes, also turns out to be a noble. Sthenelos, a charioteer and comrade of Diomedes, has noble blood as well. In the story of Theseus, the villain Skeiron, who forces passers-by to wash his feet and then kills them, has been made by local tradition to be of royal descent as a great-grandson of the primordial king Lelex in Pausania (Hard, *The Routledge Handbook of Greek Mythology*, 343).

[565] Homer never explicitly labels Thersites as a commoner, although anyone who is a hero would broadcast his distinguished lineage openly. Those in favor of him being a prince note that Thersites mentions taking prisoners (*Il.* 2.231; Elmer, *The Poetics of Consent*, 93n23). Thersites allegedly joined the Calydonian boar hunt, which is reserved for "the best men of Hellas," see Elmer, *The Poetics of Consent*, 94. Other traditions have survived. Thersites is apparently the cousin of Diomedes; see Alfred Feldman, "The Apotheosis of Thersites," in *The Classical Journal January* 42, no. 4 (January 1947): 219–20. According to some myths, Thersites is a member of the Aetolian royal family who joined his brothers, the sons of Agrios, to depose Oineus, the king of Calydon, their aged uncle. Unlike most of his brothers, he escaped the retribution; see Hard, *The Routledge Handbook of Greek Mythology*, 467.

[566] *Od.* 15.413. Penelope calls the swineherd *dios huphorbos* (divine swineherd) (*Od.* 17. 507).

[567] Hard, *The Routledge Handbook of Greek Mythology*, 503.

[568] Ibid., 532.

[569] Ibid., 533.

[570] Feldman, "Homer and Democracy," 339.

[571] Hephaestus is the patron god for all craftsmen, and Hermes for heralds.

of compulsory belief, fixed doctrines, and recorded texts, the underprivileged can create almost an unlimited repertoire of stories to invoke and oblige higher beings.

Given the above observations, it is highly possible that the obscurity of the masses in Homer does not stem from class bias, but a rejection of abstract social categories, which in fact curbs individualization.[572] We should keep in mind that the birth of reified groups that lump unique people together and define them in terms of unchanging essence happened in a very specific moment in the modern era.[573] Seen from this angle, Greek epics, which take a keen interest in the unfolding of personal biography, resist the imposition of generalized common identity (beyond mere appellation and basic physical description).[574] In other words, the narrative lens of Homer might only be able to fixate on singular beings, every one of them unique, special, and greater-than-life, but is unable to conceptualize homogenous groups. This hypothesis gives further reason for why we should not mistake particularized epic technique for class-based contempt. In this regard, the epic genre, by featuring distinctive characters, is loyal to the program of *homo significans*, which aims to establish meaning and significance in every short yet sacred mortal life—the highest end in the Olympian dispensation as well as Greek democracy. By contrast, such a mission is constantly obstructed when the market reduces different individuals to arithmetic calculations and when the territorial state defines our identity with predetermined loyalty and enmity.

Hesiod Re-examined

We now bring up another plebeian figure, Hesiod (who dates very closely to Homer), as an illustration of a formidable commoner. Already, Hesiod subjects authority to scrutiny in his poems with a sense of natural entitlement.[575] We know right away that the Muses have taken Hesiod under their tutelage and taught him special knowledge. Moreover, the goddesses bestow upon him a scepter of laurel as a token of their endorsement, a sacred object that signifies the power of both Zeus and Apollo (*Theogony* 30). A king like Agamemnon, for example, holds one just like it during assembly (*Il.* 2.101). The conferral of heavenly wisdom and article on Hesiod, a mere peasant-farmer, is another potent illustration of how Olympian ecumenism overrides distinctions of social class.

With the backing of the Muses, Hesiod takes matters into his own hands when authorities fail, completely undeterred by his lowly social-economic standing or lack

---

[572] For a very similar view, see McGlew, "Royal Power and the Achaean Assembly," 290.

[573] Benedict Anderson would argue that the conceptualization of the nation became only possible after the rise of new technology like print media and other means of mass communications. I believe the *polis* also required a similar "technological foundation." If we accept this argument, we should not assume that the epic poets knew how to represent a whole group of people, but deliberately chose not to in order to speak for the "elites."

[574] In general, historians find the notions of ethnicity, class, and gender to be weak in the epics. To me, those modern categories are "modern" precisely because they require an imagination that subsumes unique individuals, a technique that is not prominent in the epics.

[575] Lloyd-Jones traces the justice in Hesiod to similar concepts in the *Iliad* and the *Odyssey*. See Lloyd-Jones, *Justice of Zeus*, 35.

of credentials. Much like Eumaeus, Hesiod concerns himself explicitly with political issues. To the corrupt kings, he warns:

> O Kings, even you
> yourselves can understand
> this (invisible taloned) Justice:
> it is said that the immortals are near
> to us humans,
> when by crooked judgments
> we grind each other down,
> taking no need of the gods' divine vengeance.
> The ground can nourish many,
> and thirty thousand Angels of the golden age roam over it.
> For mortal human,
> Zeus made them the immortal watchers.
> They keep close watch
> over legal disputes and merciless deeds.
> Clothed in nothing but air,
> they stalk the land everywhere. (*WD* 248–55)

Invoking the presence of the powerful deities, the author not only communicates to the ruler what his subjects expect from him, but also demands it.

Hesiod's faith in justice, strengthened by Greek religious truths, reflects key facets of Olympian culture. His poem *Works and Days*, for example, instructs his delinquent brother on how to achieve a prosperous and righteous life now, rather than seek awards in remote afterlife. On farming, Hesiod offers tips on when to prune the vines and cultivate the grapes (*WD* 569–70), how to thresh and mill grain, and how and when to press grapes into wine and dry them into raisins (*WD* 597–614). On social interaction, Hesiod urges his brother to treat neighbors fairly and provide hospitality to foreigners (*WD* 327, 349). For wealth, Hesiod tells his brother Perses to work tirelessly instead of employing treachery (*WD* 297–316, 32–35). These pieces of advice represent not only ethical ideals but also rational decisions, because in Hesiod's mind, righteousness, however gradual, triumphs over the calculation of gain or loss, however immediate. Hesiod's outlook matches the conceptions of Olympian time and space, which focus on the present but also take into account long-term consequences. Immersed in the sacred time and space that is both immediate and abiding, Hesiod subscribes to distinctive notions of truth and justice that are firmly grounded in Olympian metaphysics.

While information on the basics of the Greek Archaic society in which Hesiod lived is scant, we can treat him as more or less representative of the general farming populace. For the ruling class, a political subject like Hesiod would be difficult to subdue but very easy to "offend." Historically speaking, the Greek peasants were not subject to heavy exploitative taxation or compulsory army service, both of which are mechanisms of the "big state." The unavailability of regular revenue and military apparatus denied elites a secure base of institutional domination, enabling more spontaneous collective action. While Archaic Greece has been seen as somewhat anarchist and primitive,[576] the people living in this early period have a stellar record of rising up to effect political change. Take for example Athens, our best documented city: the *demos* famously defended the city against a coup attempted by Cylon in 632 (Thucydides 1.126), outfitted Pisistratus with bodyguards in 561 (Herodotus 1.59), and overthrew Isagoras and his Spartan army in 510 (Herodotus 5.72). These acts were directly carried out by ordinary people, without approval from authorities or permission from the courts. State power grew in the Classical period only after institutional rubrics got firmly integrated into the democratic regime, e.g., the popular assembly managed public finances as well as military operations. Overall, the archetypical figures in Hesiod and Homer, as well as the governing pattern in the Archaic period, point to a kind of political subject that is fiercely desirous of self-rule. A community made of such individuals would resist heavy-handed, authoritarianism rule and prefer a regime of horizontal democratic praxis.

CONCLUSION

In this chapter, we first surveyed the ways in which the Olympian dispensation supplies useful truths to women, strangers, adversaries, slaves, and the poor in their struggle for recognition and power. Through the mediation of transcendent beings, these out-groups acquire nobility, dignity, and voice in ancient Greek narratives. Particularly through the construct of collective causality, Olympianism provides the philosophical fodder for combating economic individualism. On this basis, the Olympian cultural paradigms—despite operating side-by-side with patriarchy, slavery, and militarism in the historical context—abets a social order that celebrates alterity. The ensuing political order is inevitably decentralized and spontaneous, with a wide distribution of decisions and power. Individuals shaped by this culture recognize the benefit of compromising, cooperation, and consensus via acts of mutual assistance and goodwill. This convivial ideology contrasts sharply with the doctrine of the invisible hand, which commends the self-interest of competitive and atomistic individuals who consider others as either hostile or inconsequential.

Next, a careful cultural reading demolishes the long-held supposition of a deep chasm between rulers and masses in the epic world, a quasi-historical period that most matches the ethos of the Olympian dispensation. This new appraisal denies the preponderance of an elitist outlook in Homer, and argues instead for the presence of populist tendencies that are grounded in religious ecumenism. In this configuration, even if princes wish to seize power individually or as a class, the awareness of the gods and the desire for convivial *agon* would bring them back to the community.[577] This conclusion can be valid even if a narrator like Homer at times lapses into being the mouthpiece for the elites. Overall, in this new reading, while the distinction

[576] Foxhall, "A View from the Top," 61. Recently some scholars have begun to see Archaic Greece as being quite revolutionary, although still somewhat of a precursory stage for the Classical Age.

[577] Some argue that the egalitarianism of the Archaic Age is only about elites sharing power with other elites, but such a theory fails to appreciate the cultural discourse of Olympianism. As Walter Eder asserted, the aristocrats made political structures more egalitarian in their competition with each other, without knowing that this process would eventually hand power over to the people, which is how Olympianism is supposed to work. See Eder, "Aristocrats and the Coming of Athenian Democracy," 122–23.

between the heroes and the rest of the population still exists—marring any sense of absolute equality—the holders of power are checked and constrained by the religious discourse that emphasizes service, reciprocity, and leadership. The demands placed on authority greatly facilitated the eventual historical transition to formal democracy and popular government at Athens.

FINAL CONCLUSION

New Conjunction and Glimmering Stars

The journey we have embarked on to search for Olympianism, the vision of how humans can flourish without the market and the state, is now near its end. In the Olympian world driven by the imagination of extraordinary beings, no moment or place is ever prosaic and homogenous, but always unique and extraordinary. Moreover, due to the belief that immortals live forever and yet intervene in human affairs, actors engage with the present while taking into account the lasting impact of their deeds. This temporal and spatial outlook propels individuals to put aside immediate calculations and to undertake thoughtful decisions that are optimal over time and in the aggregate.

The overview of the Olympian political economy unfolded with an analysis of property in Part I. In Chapter 2, we investigated the Olympian paradigms of *kleros*, *temenos*, the commons, and the gift, tracing the ways they directed the allocation and adjudication of goods and resources. This set of economic norms combined to promote equity, autonomy, service, and social well-being. In this model, even knowledge, though immaterial and intangible, was treated like a divine gift from the gods to be accessed as a common good. Yet as the power of market forces advanced from the seventh to the fifth centuries, we began to observe the phenomena of debt bondage/enslavement, mortgage alienation, and the professionalization of knowledge, which were all signs indicating the atrophy of Olympianism vis-à-vis the market system.

Turning to labor, Chapter 3 presented the concept of *homo faber*. This cultural truth elevated work to a process that made men god-like by injecting dignity, control, autonomy, and solidarity into the laboring experience. Under the influence of *homo faber*, democratic Athens sustained a large number of independent contractors, skilled craftsmen, self-employed specialists, sole proprietors, and yeoman farmers. Those citizen producers, the biggest group in Athenian democracy and the bulwark of its way of life, collectively met the city's economic needs through means of equal exchange, horizontal coordination, and reciprocal aid. Against this background, surplus wealth in the form of loans circulated horizontally for mutual assistance among citizens. The investment in the people forwarded the notion that real prosperity and security comes from human flourishing, not monetary aggregation. At the end of this investigation, we witnessed the undermining of the Olympian labor ideal by the historical turn toward imperialism and slavery, which were buttressed by Polisism and Oeconomism, two cultures that advanced structural exclusion and disparity.

Part II of this book provided an elaboration on the cultural dispensation of Olympianism. With the assurance that the gods protect even marginal figures and the desire for festival living, members of Olympianism learned the dialectics of ecumenism and conviviality, the philosophies that advance universal inclusion and mutual thriving. A detailed survey of literary sources confirms the prominence of these two cultural truths as well as their corollary principles of inclusion, multiplicity, tolerance, and horizontality. This set of values facilitated the flowering of a decentralized, collegial, and spontaneous order, which left an indelible mark on the social interactions and power relations in ancient Greek societies. Furthermore, Oympianism set the groundwork for *agon*, a type of public contest centered on the performance of extraordinary *action* in an open, transparent arena that brought the community together. In this platform, meaningful praxis authenticates individual identity, shunting aside considerations of wealth, status, and other fixed attributes. Altogether, ecumenism, conviviality, and *agon* provided the rationale for the economic system reviewed in Part I. This body of discourses, framed in relation to immortal and extraordinary beings, produced an identity/subjectivity that is conscious of the *other* and at home with a diverse, rhizomic, and horizontal social makeup. From this general disposition, an aristocracy in the true original sense of the Greek word came into being. Unlike the nobilities who invested heavily in heredity, prerogatives, and extraction in other periods, the Greek upper class oriented itself toward excellence, leadership, and service, distinctions which did not undermine democratic workings.

DISENCHANTMENT

As Olympianism receded in the fifth century, market and state institutions stepped in to fill the void. However, the two younger systems never completely destroyed their noble predecessor, which continued to shape the essential fabrics of Greek society down to late antiquity. Particularly noteworthy is Polisism's perversion of Olympian ecumenism through geographic delimitation: the new territorial sovereign state, while cherishing all citizens unconditionally, treated those outside of its border (and to a lesser extent, noncitizens within it) as the inferior *other*. At the same time, Oeconomism diluted the spirit of mutual thriving and civic solidarity, despite benefitting from the ethics of *homo faber* and the trust and stability provided by the *polis*. More interestingly, both cooperation and tension underpinned the relationship between Polisism and Oeconomism. On one hand, capitalist enterprises thrived when compliant dependent labor became readily available via Polisism's institutionalization of a noncitizen underclass, but on the other hand, the egalitarian framework of the city-state also hampered the prospects for endless profit. In these ways, although the union of legal-judicial exclusions and utility-maximizing rationales attenuated the older Olympian dispensation, the three systems also complemented and infiltrated one another. The cracks, overlap, and incongruence created opportunities for localized struggle, contestation, and negotiation in nearly every instance, a dynamic that imperils any static teleological reading of ancient Greece.

The truth about the Greek polytheist gods which was the basis of Olympianism was dealt a heavy blow by the advent of rational thinking from 600 BCE onward. The damage done to old belief, however, was not ostentatious. In fact, life in the fifth and fourth centuries BCE did not display any dramatic rupture at first glance: the gods continued to be worshipped in the temples, their festivals lavishly celebrated, their stories recited in front of the population,[578] and irreverence toward them nominally cost Socrates his life. Yet, the sacred order determined by the immortals and heroes no longer steered the learned men who were major cultural makers: members of the intelligentsia like Thucydides and Aristotle left out the Homeric gods in their writings without apology. When individuals could cast aside fundamental belief as a matter of personal choice, ancient Greece entered a "secular age" (as defined by Charles Taylor), despite the continued outward appearance of ritual and worship.[579]

With the withering of Olympianism, Athenians experienced the metaphysical, sociological, and ontological consequences of cultural morphosis. In place of ecumenism, Polisism denied equal considerations to noncitizens who were not born from Athenian parents. At the same time, forces of Oeconomism subjected goods, services, labor, and surplus to enclosure, expropriation and exploitation through clever, though shallow, calculation. These alternating world views clashed with each other and left the cultural firmament in a state of constant toss-up. While the Greeks could not fully capture and reflect on this subtle yet profound turmoil, for it was happening on the ground beneath their feet, *we* can. The exposure of this commotion and the rescue of Olympianism invites us all to imagine and fight for better possibilities.

SECOND DISENCHANTMENT

Understanding the cultural struggle that unfolded in ancient Greece allows us to conceptualize our current age in new ways. Christianity, which in some ways also sustained a borderless, noncommercial world in the Middles Ages—albeit one with unforgivable hierarchy, intolerance, and hypocrisy—was severely crippled during the second wave of rationalization unleashed by the Enlightenment. Since then, modern secular knowledge has been fueling the nation-state and the global market, which have rapidly taken over the world, propagating their own normative and institutional directives. The success of these two systems is contrasted with the underdevelopment of Olympianism in the contemporary age. For we have yet to fully build an up-to-date, all-encompassing narrative that can dispute and render obsolete the ideologies behind national borders and universal commodification. Nascent and partial forms of this third configuration, however, are already all around us. They can be seen in non-Western traditions that embody reciprocity and consensus, grassroots movements that bolster civil society and community, popular uprisings that deplore the violence of capital and the state, the struggle for emancipation that began in the Age of Revolution, and last but not the least, a growing international alliance for building global inclusion and solidarity. With new Olympian forces gathering strength by the day in defiance of the other two systems, we arrive now at another critical crossroads. The difference is that after more than two millennia of time for the dust to settle, we may finally be able to grasp what occurred in Ancient Greece and use the lessons from hindsight for the challenges that confront us now.

---

[578] Robin Osborne, *Classical Greece, 500-323 BC* (New York: Oxford University Press, 2000), 16.

[579] For the specific understanding of the concept of a secular age, see Taylor, *A Secular Age*.

MATURATION, RENAISSANCE, EMANCIPATION, AND A CALL TO ACTION

As a work of history, this new account of Ancient Greece shatters the notions of fixed geographic entity and linear historical progression; Greece was not uniform and its history did not move constantly in one direction. In this light, rather than seeing human society as converging steadily toward the cementation of the state and the market with the West leading the way, more composite and dynamic accounts can be constructed. It is entirely possible, for example, to see humanity as moving through different stages of maturation, with the industrial revolution and its excess being a painful time of adolescence marked by gains but also folly and hubris.[580] It is also possible to see the rhythm of human history, particularly in Europe, punctuated by cycles of what might be metaphorically described as death and rebirth. The Renaissance of the sixteenth century, which revived ancient culture, was a rebirth that led to giant leaps in progress.[581] Now the restoration of Olympianism can initiate another round of awakening. Last but not least, it is still plausible to see the rediscovery of Olympianism as a new chapter in the project of emancipation that began during the Enlightenment and yet remains unfinished.[582]

There is a lot that we can do to expedite the rebirth, maturation, or the completion of the Enlightenment project apart from just learning another interesting way to think about history and society. Since Olympianism depends on the building of a very specific identity, we should consciously transform each and every moment of our being accordingly. For instance, even for quotidian matters like buying an apple or a pair of socks, we should ask if the items were produced by dignified and masterly workers in a joyful process, since their well-being and happiness are intrinsically linked to our own. By visualizing the pain and suffering, the soul-killing monotony and toil behind any quick savings, we would recognize the desirability of conscientious products and be willing to support them economically. Beyond individual purchases, we also need to empower people-centered, independent, artisan production by augmenting direct exchange, expanding access and resources for independently operated businesses, and building international infrastructure that facilitates knowledge and information sharing. This economic initiative, similar to the idea behind fair-trade programs that help small producers, their communities and environment, can be scaled up with the requisite organization, communication, and most importantly, a decisive shift in value and awareness. Engagement through cumulative collective action is also key: we need groups and organizations that fight for Olympian values in the management of land, labor, money, and knowledge at the local, national, and global level. Some ideas are community land trust funds that circumvent private property, open-access platforms that defy copyrights, public benefit corporations that challenge the profit motive, ownership regimes that enable

[580] This is a very fascinating view proposed by Charles Eisenstein, see *Sacred Economics: Money, Gift, and Society in the Age of Transition* (Berkeley, CA: Evolver Editions, 2011).

[581] The credit of thinking about this project in relation to another round of the Renaissance goes to Helmut Staubmann, who expressed this idea after hearing my presentation in the department of Sociology at University of Innsbruck on September 12, 2016.

[582] I am grateful to my wonderful mentor and friend, Max Preglau, for this point of view and for earning my respect for the commitment to social democracy. While I personally would like to see a much more radical rupture, I think we agree on a lot, after putting aside differences in terminology and semantics.

worker collaboration and self-management, and large-scale transnational trade pacts drafted on the basis of labor rights and environmental protection. Perhaps most importantly, the realm of traditional politics should never be forsaken. Any governing body that claims to serve the people under a democratic mandate must not only create infrastructure for Olympian projects, but also social programs that increase abundance and reduce scarcity, such as universal health care, basic income, public housing, free education, elderly care, etc.

New Epistemology

Finally, the body of accepted axioms that doggedly reinforce society's orientation toward the capitalist market and nation-state must be thoroughly reexamined. Our current intellectual moorings have flaunted the superiority of reason at the expense of emotions, spiritual imagination, and aesthetics[583] which made it easy to regard the universe as purely physical and mechanical, and beings as merely biological and chemical. Out of this disenchanted landscape, life in the state of nature came to be viewed—to paraphrase the famous Thomas Hobbes—as nasty, brutish, short, and prone to selfishness and violence. The cultural dispensation of Olympianism shows an utterly different orientation. The Greeks conjured a world in which the universe is sacred, human association tends to be win-win, and individuals aspire to be extraordinary and heroic. Although derived from a series of mythic and fictional tales rather than scientific findings and facts, the Olympian outlook was fully capable of explicating and advancing social justice and human dignity with clarity and efficacy. Moreover, at the level of personal appeal, Olympianism provides what is most deficient in contemporary secular liberalism: "meaning, belonging, a vertical dimension to human life, a hope against mortality."[584] The Olympian subjectivity unites the personal and political by satisfying the yearning for individual recognition in the context of coming together. Given these outcomes, this book urges not a return to some utopian past or a renewal of Greek paganism, but a thoughtful and open conversation about what type of truth narratives should operate as the foundation of our society—for they function as self-fulfilling prophesies.

The very attempt of remaking a cultural system cannot possibly be carried out by a single person. Collectively, we need to boldly pursue the ruptures in and alternatives to our current epistemological regime. On that front, many of my contentions have been endorsed by recent findings in biology, anthropology, sociology, and economics, and they are accompanied by increasingly more audible movements that demand dramatic revision and overturn of old disciplinary assumptions.[585] At the same time, more imaginative thinkers have begun to theorize system-wide change by advocating and designing the so-called solidarity, peer-to-peer, and sacred economies. All these efforts, when linked explicitly to the mission of addressing urgent problems and

---

583 The intelligence of emotions has been increasingly affirmed by scientists. For a contemporary philosophical treatise on the importance of human emotion, see Martha Nussbaum, *Upheavals of Thought: The Intelligence of Emotions* (Cambridge: Cambridge University Press, 2001).

584 Ross Douthat, "The Crisis for Liberalism," *The New York Times*, November 19, 2016.

585 I shall mention a few names like David Graeber, E. O. Wilson, Elinor Ostrom, and movements like Rethinking Economics, Commons Transition, and solidarity economics.

improving immanent conditions, echo the best intellectual tradition from Chinese Confucianism, Greek democracy, and European Enlightenment, which spurred periods of great progress and efflorescence.

More than anything else, should we decide to embrace Olympianism, we could finally stop obsessing over teleology, which is the provenance of the gods, and focus on our obligation to act, which is the lot assigned to mortals. For as it turns out, we as humans invent our own truths, which in turn create the realm we inhabit. This catalytic power is in itself capable of changing the world overnight—if we so will it. And that will, which can be buried so deep, should be seized now so it can instill in us the mettle, wisdom, and imagination for a new beginning. From this perspective, to us mere mortals who do not control the past or the future, history is the sum of infinite thresholds in our consciousness. Each orientation toward a different truth can make a hell of heaven, a heaven of hell. As the Ancient Greeks knew very well, when we thrust ourselves into the great unknown, holding onto only the awful grace of the gods (δαιμόνων δέ που χάρις βίαιος), we paradoxically open ourselves to the most radical hopes and possibilities.

Abbreviations

Il. The *Iliad*

Od. The *Odyssey*

Routledge Mythology *The Routledge Handbook of Greek Mythology*

WD *Works and Days*

Primary Sources

Aeschines, *Against Timarchus*

Aeschylus, *Persians*

Aristotle, *Constitution of the Athenians* (*Athenaion Politeia*)

Aristotle, *Politics, Rhetoric*

Augustine, *Confessions*

Callinus (Barnstone, *Ancient Greek Lyrics*)

Demosthenes

Against Aristocrates

Against Midias

Against Nicostratus

Against Phaenippus

Against Pantaenetus

Herodotus, *The Histories*

Hesiod, *Theogony*

Hesiod, *Works and Days*

Homer, *Iliad*

Homer, *Odyssey* (Lattimore New York: Harper Perennial, 1965, 1967)

Lysias in Van Wees 2000

Pausanias, *Description of Greece*

Philostratos: Life of Apollonius of Tyana: 5.20 in Acton's *Poiesis*

Pindar, *Pythian Odes*

Plato, *Laws*

Plato, *Protagoras*

Plato, *Republic*

Pliny, *Natural History*

Plutarch, *Life of Agis*

Plutarch, *Life of Pericles*

Plutarch, *Life of Solon*

Plutarch, *Lives of Ten Orators,* [*Lysias, Lycurgus*]

Plutarch, *Theseus*

Plutarch, *Timoleon* XXIII

Polybius, *The Histories*

Pseudo Xenophon or the Old Oligarch, *Constitution of Athens* (*Athenaion Politeia*)

Solon in Lewis, *Solon the Thinker*

Sappho

Theognis

Thucydides, *The History of the Peloponnesian War*

Xenophanes, fragments of poetry

Xenophon, *Cyropaedia*

Xenophon *Hellenica*

Xenophon, *Memorabilia*

Xenophon, *Oeconomicus*

Xenophon, *Ways and Means*

Currency Units

Drachma (silver, 4.33 grams)

Obol (6 per drachma)

Mina (100 drachmas)

Talent (6,000 drachmas)

The standard wage in late fifth-century Athens was one drachma a day for a skilled worker.[586]

[586] Burford, *Craftsmen in Greek and Roman Society*, 138.

REFERENCES

Acton, Peter Hampden. "Industry Structure and Income Opportunities for Households in Classical Athens." In *The Ancient Greek Economy: Markets, Households and City-states*, edited by Edward M. Harris, David M. Lewis, and Mark Woolmer, 149–65. New York: Cambridge University Press, 2016.

———. *Poiesis: Manufacturing in Classical Athens*. Oxford: Oxford University Press, 2014.

Adkins, Arthur W. H. *From the Many to the One: A Study of Personality and Views of Human Nature in the Context of Ancient Greek Society, Values, and Beliefs*. Ithaca, NY: Cornell University Press, 1970.

———. "Homeric Ethics." In *A New Companion to Homer*, edited by Ian Morris and Barry Powell, 694–714. New York: E.J. Brill, 1997.

———. *Merit and Responsibility: A Study in Greek Values*. Oxford: Clarendon Press, 1960.

Adloff, Frank. "The Current Responses." In *Convivialist Manifesto: A Declaration of Interdependence*. Global Dialogues 3. Duisburg: Käte Hamburger Kolleg/Centre for Global Cooperation Research, 2014.

Anderson, Benedict. *Imagined Communities: Reflections on the Origin and Spread of Nationalism*. London: Verso, 2006.

Anderson, Greg. "Before *Turannoi* Were Tyrants: Rethinking a Chapter of Early Greek History." *Classical Antiquity* 24, no. 2 (2005): 173–222.

Anderson, Perry. *Passages from Antiquity to Feudalism*. London: NLB, 1974.

Arendt, Hannah. *The Human Condition*, 2nd ed. Chicago: University of Chicago Press, 1998.

Aristotle. *The Nicomachean Ethics*. Translated by H. Rackham. Cambridge, MA: Harvard University Press, 1999.

Arnheim, M. T. W. *Aristocracy in Greek Society*. London: Thames & Hudson, 1977.

Augustine, and R. S. Pine-Coffin. *Confessions: Saint Augustine*. New York: Penguin Books, 1961.

Austin, M. M., and Pierre Vidal-Naquet. *Economic and Social History of Ancient Greece: An Introduction*. Berkeley, CA: University of California Press, 1977.

Baldry, H. C. *The Unity of Mankind in Greek Thought*. Cambridge, UK: Cambridge University Press, 1965.

Baldwin, John R. *Redefining Culture: Perspectives across Disciplines.* Mahwah, NJ: Lawrence Erlbaum Associates, 2006.

Barnstone, Willis. *Ancient Greek Lyrics.* Translated and annotated, 4th ed. Bloomington, IN: Indiana University Press, (1962) 2010.

Barthes, Roland. "The Death of the Author." In *Image, Music, Text.* Translated by Stephen Heath. New York: Hill and Wang, 1977.

Beekes, Robert. *Etymological Dictionary of Greek*, vol 1. Leiden: Brill, 2010.

Blundell, Sue. *Women in Ancient Greece.* London: British Museum Press, 1995.

Bothmer, Dietrich von. "The Subject Matter of Euphronios." In *Euphronios, Peintre: Actes De La Journée D'étude Organisée Par L'Ecole Du Louvre Et Le Département Des Antiquités Grecques, Étrusques Et Romaines Du Musée Du Louvre, 10 Octobre 1990* [Euphronios Painter: Proceedings of the Workshop Organized by L'Ecole Du Lourvre and the Department of Greek and Etruscan and Roman Antiquities], edited by Euphronios and Martine Denoyelle, 13–22. Paris: Documentation française, 1992.

Bourdieu, Pierre. *Outline of a Theory of Practice.* Cambridge, UK: Cambridge University Press, 1977.

Bowie, Ewen. "Wandering Poets, Archaic Style." In *Wandering Poets in Ancient Greek Culture: Travel, Locality, and Pan-Hellenism*, edited by Richard Hunter and Ian Rutherford, 242–305. Cambridge, UK: Cambridge University Press, 2009.

Bradley, Keith, and Paul Cartledge, eds. *The Cambridge World History of Slavery*, vol. 1. Cambridge, UK: Cambridge University Press, 2011.

Bremmer, Jan. "Atheism in Antiquity." In *The Cambridge Companion to Atheism*, edited by Michael Martin, 11–26. New York: Cambridge University Press, 2007.

Bresson, Alain. *The Making of the Ancient Greek Economy.* Translated by Steven Rendall. Princeton and Oxford: Princeton University Press, 2016.

Burford, Alison. "The Builders of the Parthenon." *Greece & Rome, Second Series* 10, Supplement: Parthenos and Parthenon (1963): 23–35.

———. *Craftsmen in Greek and Roman Society.* Ithaca, NY: Cornell University Press, 1972.

———. *Land and Labor in the Greek World.* Baltimore, MD: Johns Hopkins University Press, 1993.

Burke, Edmund M. "The Economy of Athens in the Classical Era: Some Adjustments to the Primitivist Model." *Transactions of the American Philological Association* 122 (1992): 199–226.

Burkert, Walter. *Greek Religion.* Cambridge, MA: Harvard University Press, 1985.

Burns, Timothy. "The Problematic Character of Periclean Athens." In *On Civic Republicanism: Ancient Lessons for Global Politics*, edited by Geoffery Kellow and Neven Leddy, 15–40. Toronto: University of Toronto Press, 2016.

Burtt, J. O., trans. *Minor Attic Orators in Two Volumes, 2*. Cambridge, MA: Harvard University Press; London, William Heinemann Ltd., 1962.

Butler, Judith. *Frames of War: When Is Life Grievable?* London: Verso, 2009.

———. *Precarious Life: The Powers of Mourning and Violence*. London: Verso, 2006.

Calhoun, George M. "Classes and Masses in Homer." *Classical Philology* 29, no. 3 (July 1934): 192–208.

Carmichael, C. M. "Public Munificence for Private Benefit: Liturgies in Classical Athens." *Economic Inquiry* 35, no. 2 (1997): 261–70.

Cartledge, Paul. "Raising Hell? The Helot Mirage—A Personal Review." In *Helots and Their Masters in Laconia and Messenia: Histories, Ideologies, Structures*, edited by Nino Luraghi and Susan E. Alcock, 12–30. Washington, D.C.: Center for Hellenic Studies, 2003.

Cecchet, Lucia. *Poverty in Athenian Public Discourse: From the Eve of the Peloponnesian War to the Rise of Macedonia.* Stuttgart: Franz Steiner Verlag, 2015.

Chakrabarty, Dipesh. *Habitations of Modernity: Essays in the Wake of Subaltern Studies*. Chicago: University of Chicago Press, 2002.

———. *Provincializing Europe: Postcolonial Thought and Historical Difference.* Princeton, NJ: Princeton University Press, 2000.

Christ, Matthew R. "Liturgy Avoidance and Antidosis in Classical Athens." *Transactions of the American Philological Association* 120 (1990): 147–69.

Clay, Jenny Strauss. *Hesiod's Cosmos*. Cambridge, UK: Cambridge University Press, 2003.

Cohen, David. *Theft in Athenian Law (Munchener Beitrage zur Papyrusforschung und antiken Rechtsgeschichten*. Munich: Beck, 1983.

Cohen, Edward. *The Athenian Nation.* Princeton, NJ: Princeton University Press, 2000.

———. *Athenian Economy and Society: A Banking Perspective*. Princeton, NJ: Princeton University Press, 1992.

———. *Athenian Prostitution: The Business of Sex*. New York: Oxford University Press, 2015.

———. "An Unprofitable Masculinity." In *Money, Labour, and Land: Approaches to the Economies of Ancient Greece*, edited by Paul Cartledge, Edward E. Cohen, and Lin Foxhall, 100–12. London: Routledge, 2002.

———. "Works and Days: Tracing the Path to Arete." In *Brill's Companion to Hesiod*, edited by Franco Montanari, Antonios Rengakos, and Christos Tsagalis, 71–90. Leiden; Boston: Brill, 2009.

Connor, Robert W. *The New Politicians of Fifth-century Athens*. Indianapolis and Cambridge: Hackett Publishing Company, 1992.

Crawley, Richard. *The Landmark Thucydides: A Comprehensive Guide to the Peloponnesian War*. Edited by Robert B. Strassler. New York: Free Press, 1996.

Dal Lago, Enrico, and Constantina Katsari. *Slave Systems: Ancient and Modern.* Cambridge, UK: Cambridge University Press, 2008.

Davies, John Kenyon. "Classical Greece: Production." In *The Cambridge Economic History of the Greco-Roman World*, edited by Walter Scheidel, Ian Morris, and Richard P. Saller, 333–61. Cambridge, UK: Cambridge University Press, 2007.

———. *Wealth and the Power of Wealth in Classical Athens*. Salem, NH: Ayer Co, 1992.

De Jong, Irene J. F. *Narrators and Focalizers: The Presentation of the Story in the Iliad.* Amsterdam: B.R. Grüner Pub. Co., 1987.

De Ste. Croix, G. E. M. *The Class Struggle in the Ancient Greek World: From the Archaic Age to the Arab Conquests*. Ithaca, NY: Cornell University Press, 1981.

Desmond, William D. *The Greek Praise of Poverty: Origin of Ancient Cynicism.* South Bend, IN: University of Notre Dame, 2006.

Diamond, Jared. *Guns, Germs, and Steel: The Fates of Human Societies*. New York: Norton, 2005.

Dietler, M., and Brian Hayden. *Feasts: Archaeological and Ethnographic Perspectives on Food, Politics, and Power*. Washington, D.C.: Smithsonian Institution Press, 2001.

Dillon, Matthew. *Girls and Women in Classical Greek Religion*. London: Routledge, 2002.

Dodds, Eric. R. *The Greeks and the Irrational*. Berkeley and Los Angeles: University of California Press, 1951.

Donlan, Walter. *The Aristocratic Ideal and Selected Papers*. Wauconda, IL: Bolchazy-Carducci, 1999.

———. "Dueling with Gifts in the *Iliad*: As the Audience Saw It." *Colby Quarterly* 29, no. 3 (1993): 155–72.

———. "The Homeric Economy." In *A New Companion to Homer*, edited by Ian Morris and Barry Powell, 649–67. New York: E.J. Brill, 1997.

———. "Homeric τέμενος and the Land Economy of the Dark Age." *Museum Helveticum* 46, no. 3 (1989): 129–45. doi:10.5169/seals-36081.

———. "The Relations of Power in the Pre-state and Early-state Polities." In *The Development of the* Polis *in Archaic Greece*, edited by Lynette G. Mitchell and P. J. Rhodes, 21–25. London and New York: Routledge, 1997.

———. "Social Vocabulary and Its Relationship to Political Propaganda in Fifth-century Athens," *Quaderni Urbinati*, no. 27 (1977): 95–111.

———. "The Tradition of Anti-aristocratic Thought in Early Greek Poetry." *Historia: Zeitschrift für Alte Geschichte* [Historia: Journal for Ancient History], Bd. 22, H. 2 (2nd Qtr., 1973): 145–54.

Doran, Timothy. "Review of *Die Wirtschaft Spartas*, by Lukas Thommen." *Bryn Mawr Classical Review*, September 29, 2015.

Dorjahn, A. P. "Homeric Foemen." *The Classical Weekly* 40, no. 2 (Oct. 21, 1946): 10–12.

Dougherty, C., and Leslie Kurke. *The Cultures within Ancient Greek Culture: Contact, Conflict, Collaboration*. Cambridge, UK: Cambridge University Press, 2003.

Douthat, Ross. "The Crisis for Liberalism." *The New York Times*, November 19, 2016.

Duara, Prasenjit. *Rescuing History from the Nation: Questioning Narratives of Modern China*. Chicago: University of Chicago Press, 1995.

Dué, Casey. "Learning Lessons from the Trojan War: Briseis and the Theme of Force." *College Literature* 34, no. 2 (2007): 229–62.

Eagleton, Terry. *Ideology*. London: Verso, 1991.

Easterling, P. E., and J. V. Muir, eds. *Greek Religion and Society*. Cambridge, UK: Cambridge University Press, 1985.

Eder, Walter. "Aristocrats and the Coming of Athenian Democracy." In *Democracy 2500?: Questions and Challenges*, edited by Ian Morris, Kurt A. Raaflaub, and David Castriota, 105–40. Dubuque, IA: Kendall/Hunt Pub. Co., 1998.

Edmonds, J. M. *Elegy and Iambus: Being the Remains of All the Greek Elegiac and Iambic Poets from Callinus to Crates, Excepting the Choliambic Writers, with the Anacreontea*. London: W. Heinemann, 1931.

Ehrenberg, Victor. *The People of Aristophanes, A Sociology of Old Attic Comedy*. Oxford: B. Blackwell, 1951.

Eisenstein, Charles. *Sacred Economics: Money, Gift, and Society in the Age of Transition*. Berkeley, CA: Evolver Editions, 2011.

Eliade, Mircea. *The Sacred and the Profane*. New York: Harper & Row, 1959.

Elmer, David F. *The Poetics of Consent: Collective Decision Making and the Iliad*. Baltimore, MD: The Johns Hopkins University Press, 2013.

Euphronios, and Martine Denoyelle. *Euphronios, Peintre: Actes De La Journée D'étude Organisée Par L'Ecole Du Louvre Et Le Département Des Antiquités Grecques, Étrusques Et Romaines Du Musée Du Louvre, 10 Octobre 1990* [Euphronios Painter: Proceedings of the Workshop Organized by L'Ecole Du Louvre and the Department of Greek and Etruscan and Roman Antiquities]. Paris: Documentation française, 1992.

Evans, Nancy. *Civic Rites: Democracy and Religion in Ancient Athens*. Berkeley, CA: University of California Press, 2010.

Feldman, Abraham B. "The Apotheosis of Thersites." *The Classical Journal* 42, no. 4 (January 1947): 219–20.

———. "Homer and Democracy." *The Classical Journal* 47, no. 8 (May 1952): 337–45.

Feyel, Christophe. *Les artisans dans les sanctuaires grecs aux époques classique et hellénistique à travers la documentation financière en Grèce* [The Artists in the Greek Sanctuaries in the Classical and Hellenistic Periods in the Financial Documents of Greece]. Athens: Ecole française d'Athènes, 2006.

Fine, John V. A. *Horoi: Studies in Mortgage, Real Security, and Land Tenure in Ancient Athens*. Baltimore, MD: American School of Classical Studies at Athens, 1951.

Finkelberg, Margalit. "*Timē* and *Aretē* in Homer." *The Classical Quarterly* 48, no. 1 (1998): 14–28.

Finley, M. I. *The Ancient Economy*. Berkeley, CA: University of California Press, 1973.

———. "Aristotle and Economic Analysis." *Past and Present*, no. 47 (1970): 3–25.

———. "Athenian Demagogues." *Past and Present*, no. 21 (1962): 3–24.

———. *Democracy Ancient and Modern*. New Brunswick, NJ: Rutgers University Press, 1973, rev. ed. 1996.

———. *Economy and Society in Ancient Greece*, edited by Brent D. Shaw and Richard P. Saller. London: Chatto & Windus, 1981.

———. "Homer and Mycenae: Property and Tenure." *Historia: Zeitschrift für Alte Geschichte* [Historia: Journal of Ancient History], Bd. 6, H. 2 (April 1957): 133–59.

———. *Studies in Land and Credit in Ancient Athens, 500-200 B.C.: The Horos Inscriptions*. New Brunswick, NJ: Transaction Books, 1985.

———. *The World of Odysseus*, 2nd ed. Middlesex: Penguin Books, 1979.

Finley, M. I., and H. W. Pleket. *The Olympic Games: The First Thousand Years*. New York: Viking Press, 1976.

Fontenrose, Joseph. "Work, Justice, and Hesiod's Five Ages." *Classical Philology* 69, no. 1 (January 1974): 1–16.

Forsdyke, Sara. *Exile, Ostracism, and Democracy: The Politics of Expulsion in Ancient Greece*. Princeton and Oxford: Princeton University Press, 2005.

Foucault, Michel. *The Birth of the Clinic: An Archaeology of Medical Perception*. New York: Vintage Books, 1994.

———. *Discipline and Punish: The Birth of the Prison*, 2nd Vintage Books ed. New York: Vintage Books, 1995.

———. *The History of Sexuality*, Vintage Books ed. New York: Vintage Books, 1990.

Fowler, Barbara Hughes. *Archaic Greek Poetry: An Anthology*. Madison, WI: University of Wisconsin Press, 1992.

Foxhall, Lin. "Technology in Context: Questioning the Transformative Powers of Olive and Vine Cultivation." In *La main-d'oeuvre agricole en Méditerranée archaïque: statuts et dynamiques économiques* [The Agricultural Work Force in the Ancient Mediterranean: Statues and Economic Dynamics], edited by Julien Zurbach, 110–53. Athens and Bordeaux: École française d'Athènes, 2015.

———. "A View from the Top: Evaluating the Solonian Property Classes." In *The Development of the* Polis *in Archaic Greece*, edited by Lynette G. Mitchell and P. J. Rhodes, 61–74. London and New York: Routledge, 1997.

Fraser, Stuart. *Aristocratic Values in Ancient Greece: Change or Continuity*. Perm: State University Press, 2011.

French, A. *The Growth of the Athenian Economy*. New York: Barnes & Noble, 1964.

Fuks, Alexander. "Redistribution of Land and Houses in Syracuse in 356 B. C., and Its Ideological Aspects." *The Classical Quarterly* 18, no. 2 (1968): 207–23.

———. *Social Conflict in Ancient Greece*. Jerusalem: Magness Press, the Hebrew University, 1984.

Gabrielsen, Vincent. *Financing the Athenian Fleet: Public Taxation and Social Relations*. Baltimore, MD: Johns Hopkins University Press, 1994.

Gallant, T. W. "Agricultural Systems, Land Tenure, and the Reforms of Solon." *The Annual of the British School at Athens* 77 (1982): 111–24.

Gallego, Julián. "Farming in the Ancient Greek World: How Should the Small Free Producers Be Defined?" *Studia Humaniora Tartuensia* 8.A.3 (2007): 1–21.

Garlan, Yvon. *Slavery in Ancient Greece*. Reviewed and expanded ed. Ithaca, NY: Cornell University Press, 1988.

Garland, Robert. *The Piraeus: From the Fifth to the First Century B.C.* London: Duckworth, 1987.

Garnsey, Peter. *Famine and Food Supply in the Graeco-Roman World: Responses to Risk and Crisis*. Cambridge, UK: Cambridge University Press, 1988.

Geertz, Clifford. *The Interpretation of Cultures: Selected Essays.* New York: Basic Books, 1973.

Gilroy, Paul. *After Empire: Melancholia or Convivial Culture?* London: Routledge, 2004.

Glotz, Gustave. *Ancient Greece at Work: An Economic History of Greece from the Homeric Period to the Roman Conquest*. Hildesheim: Georg Olms, (1926) 1987.

Golding, Martin P., and William A. Edmundson. *The Blackwell Guide to the Philosophy of Law and Legal Theory*. Malden, MA: Blackwell Publishing, 2005.

Gould, John. "Law, Custom and Myth: Aspects of the Social Position of Women in Classical Athens." *The Journal of Hellenic Studies* 100 (1980): 38–59.

———. "On Making Sense of Greek Religion." In *Greek Religion and Society*, edited by P. Easterling and J. V. Muir, 1–33. Cambridge, UK: Cambridge University Press, 2002.

Graeber, David. *Debt: The First 5,000 Years*. Brooklyn, NY: Melville House, 2011.

Graham, A. J. *Colony and Mother City in Ancient Greece*. Oxford: Manchester University Press, 1999.

Greenhalgh, P. A. L. "Patriotism in the Homeric World." *Historia* 21 (1972): 528–37.

Hall, Jonathan M. "Approaches to Foundation Accounts." In *Greek Colonisation: An Account of Colonies and Other Settlements Overseas*, vol 2., edited by Gocha R. Tsetskhladze, 383–426. Boston: Brill, 2008.

———. *Ethnic Identity in Greek Antiquity*. Cambridge, UK: Cambridge University Press, 1997.

———. *Hellenicity: Between Ethnicity and Culture*. Chicago: University of Chicago Press, 2002.

———. *A History of the Archaic Greek World: Ca. 1200-479 BCE*. Malden, MA: Blackwell Publishing, 2007.

Hammer, Dean. *The Iliad as Politics: The Performance of Political Thought*. Norman: University of Oklahoma Press, 2002.

———. Review: "Ideology, the Symposium, and Archaic." *The American Journal of Philology* 125, no. 4 (Winter 2004): 479–512.

Hansen, Mogens Herman. "A Note on the Growing Tendency to Underestimate the Population of Classical Attica." In *Three Studies in Athenian Demography*. Historisk-filosofiske Meddelelser 56. Copenhagen: Royal Danish Academy of Sciences and Letters, 1988.

———. "The Theoric Fund and the *graphe paranomon* against Apollodorus." *Greek and Byzantine Studies* 17, no. 3 (1976): 235–46.

Hanson, Victor Davis. *The Other Greeks: The Family Farm and the Agrarian Roots of Western Civilization*. New York: Free Press, 1995.

Hard, Robin. *The Routledge Handbook of Greek Mythology*. London and New York: Routledge, 2004.

Harris, Edward. "Did Solon Abolish Debt-bondage?" *The Classical Quarterly* 52, no. 2 (2002): 415–39.

———. "Homer, Hesiod, and the 'Origin' of Greek Slavery." *Revue des Études Anciennes* 114, no. 2 (2012): 345–66.

———. "Introduction: Markets in Classical and Hellenistic Greece." In *The Ancient Greek Economy: Markets, Households and City-states*, edited by Edward M. Harris, David M. Lewis, and Mark Woolmer, 1–40. New York: Cambridge, 2016.

———. "The Legal Foundations of Economic Growth." In *The Ancient Greek Economy: Markets, Households and City-states*, edited by Edward M. Harris, David M. Lewis, and Mark Woolmer, 116–46. New York: Cambridge University Press, 2016.

Harris, Edward. "A New Solution to the Riddle of the *Seisachtheia*." In *The Development of the* Polis *in Archaic Greece*, edited by Lynette G. Mitchell and P. J. Rhodes, 55–60. London and New York: Routledge, 1997.

———. "When Is a Sale Not a Sale? The Riddle of Athenian Terminology for Real Security Revisited." *Classical Quarterly*, New Series 38, no. 2 (1988): 351–81.

———. "Workshop, Marketplace and Household: The Nature of Technical Specialization in Classical Athens and Its Influence on Economy and Society." In *Money, Labour and Land: Approaches to the Economies of Ancient Greece*, edited by Paul Cartledge, Edward E Cohen, and Lin Foxhall, 67–99. London: Routledge, 2002.

Hawhee, Debra. "Agonism and Arete." *Philosophy and Rhetoric* 35, no. 3 (2002): 185–207.

Herman, Gabriel. *Morality and Behaviour in Democratic Athens: A Social History.* Cambridge, UK: Cambridge University Press, 2006.

———. *Ritualised Friendship and the Greek City*. Cambridge, UK: Cambridge University Press, 1987.

Hesiod. *The Homeric Hymns and Homerica*, with an English translation by Hugh G. Evelyn-White. Cambridge, MA: Harvard University Press; London, William Heinemann Ltd., 1914.

Hesiod, and C. S. Morrissey. *Theogony: Works and Days*. Vancouver: Talonbooks, 2012.

Hesiod, and Glenn W. Most. *Hesiod.* Cambridge, MA: Harvard University Press, 2006.

Hesiod, and M. L. West. *Works and Days*. Oxford: Clarendon Press, 1978.

Hodkinson, Stephen. "Land Tenure and Inheritance in Classical Sparta." *The Classical Quarterly*, New Series 36, no. 2 (1986): 378–406.

———. *Property and Wealth in Classical Sparta*. London: Duckworth and the Classical Press of Wales, 2000.

Homer, and Richmond Lattimore. *The Iliad.* Chicago: University of Chicago Press, 1951.

———. *The Odyssey of Homer*. New York: Harper Perennial, 1967, Reprint 1991.

Horden, Peregrine, and Nicholas Purcell. *The Corrupting Sea: A Study of Mediterranean History*. Oxford: Blackwell Publishers, 2000.

Huang, Yang. 黄洋,《古代希腊土地私有制的确立与城邦制度的形成》[The Establishment of Private Property and the Rise of the Polis in Ancient Greece)《复旦学报》[Fudan Journal of the Humanities and the Social Sciences] 1 (1995): 46–51.

Humphreys, S. C. *Anthropology and the Greeks*. Oxon: Routledge, (1978) 2004.

Hunter, R. L., and Ian Rutherford. *Wandering Poets in Ancient Greek Culture: Travel, Locality, and Pan-Hellenism.* Cambridge, UK: Cambridge University Press, 2009.

Illich, Ivan. *Tools for Conviviality*. London: Marion Boyars, 2001.

Isager, Signe, and Jens Erik Sydsgaard. *Ancient Greek Agriculture*. London: Routledge, 1992.

Jameson, Michael H. "Agriculture and Slavery in Classical Athens." *The Classical Journal* 73, no. 2 (December 1977–January 1978): 122–45.

———. "On Paul Cartledge, 'The Political Economy of Greek Slavery.'" In *Money, Labour and Land: Approaches to the Economies of Ancient Greece*, edited by Paul Cartledge, Edward E Cohen, and Lin Foxhall, 167–74. London: Routledge, 2002.

Jeffery, J. H. "The Pact of the First Settlers at Cyrene." *Historia: Zeitschrift Für Alte Geschichte* [Historia: Journal for Ancient History] 10, no. 2 (1961): 139–47.

Jones, A. H. M. "The Economic Basis of the Athenian Democracy." *Past and Present*, no. 1 (1952): 13–31.

Kallet, Lisa. *Money, Expense, and Naval Power in Thucydides' History 1-5.24.* Berkeley, CA: University of California Press, 1993.

Karanika, Andromache. *Voices at Work: Women, Performance, and Labor in Ancient Greece*. Baltimore, MD: John Hopkins University Press, 2014.

Kjosavik, Darley Jose. "Methodological Individualism and Rational Choice in Neoclassical Economics: A Review of Institutionalist Critique." *Forum for Development Studies*, no. 2 (2003): 205–44.

Knox, Bernard. "Always to Be Best: The Competitive Spirit in Ancient Greek Culture." The Professor John C. Rouman Classical Lecture Series at the University of New Hampshire, Durham, October 13, 1999.

Knox, Ronald, and Joseph Russo. "Agamemnon's Test: *Iliad* 2.73-75." *Classical Antiquity* 8, no. 2 (October 1989): 351–58.

Kron, Geoffrey. "Classical Greek Trade in Comparative Perspective." In *The Ancient Greek Economy: Markets, Households and City-states*, edited by Edward M. Harris, David M. Lewis, and Mark Woolmer, 356–80. New York: Cambridge University Press, 2016.

———. "The Distribution of Wealth at Athens in Comparative Perspective." *Zeitschrift für Papyrologie und Epigraphik* [Journal for Papyrology and Epigraphy] 179 (2011): 129–38.

Kurke, Leslie. *Coins, Bodies, Games, and Gold*. Princeton, NJ: Princeton University Press, 1999.

———. "Crisis and Decorum in Sixth-century Lesbos: Reading Alkaios Otherwise." *Quaderni Urbinati di Cultura Classica, New Series* 47, no. 2 (1994): 67–92

———. "The Politics of ἁβροσύνη in Archaic Greece." *Classical Antiquity* 11, no. 1 (1992): 91–120.

———. *The Traffic in Praise: Pindar and the Poetics of Social Economy*. Ithaca, NY: Cornell University Press, 1991.

———. "VIII. The Cultural Impact of (on) Democracy: Decentering Tragedy." In *Democracy 2500?: Questions and Challenges*, edited by Ian Morris, Kurt A. Raaflaub, and David Castriota, 155–69. Dubuque, IA: Kendall/Hunt Pub. Co., 1998.

Kyrtatas, Dimitris J. "Domination and Exploitation." In *Money, Labour and Land: Approaches to the Economies of Ancient Greece*, edited by Paul Cartledge, Edward E. Cohen and Lin Foxhall, 140–55. London and New York: Routledge, 2002.

Larson, Jennifer. *Understanding Greek Religion*. London and New York: Routledge, 2016.

Latacz, Joachim. *Kampfparänese, Kampfdarstellung und Kampfwirklichkeit in der Ilias, bei Kallinos und Tyrtaios* [Battle Phenomena, Representation and Reality in the Iliad through Callinus and Tyrtaeus]. München: Zetemata 66, 1977.

Lattimore, Richmond, *Greek Lyrics*, 2nd ed. Chicago: University of Chicago Press, 1960.

Lewis, John. *Solon the Thinker: Political Thought in Archaic Athens*. London: Duckworth, 2006.

Lincoln, Bruce. *Gods and Demons, Priests and Scholars: Critical Explorations in the History of Religions*. Chicago: University of Chicago, 2012.

Lind, L. R. "Economic Man in Ancient Athens." *The Classical Journal* 35, no. 1 (October 1939): 27–38.

Lis, Catharina, and Hugo Soly. *Worthy Efforts: Attitudes to Work and Workers in Pre-industrial Europe*. Leiden: Brill, 2012.

Liverani, Mario. "The Near East: The Bronze Age." In *The Ancient Economy: Evidence and Models*, edited by Joseph Gilbert Manning and Ian Morris, 47–57. Stanford, CA: Stanford University Press, 2005.

Livingstone, Niall, *Athens: The City as University*. London: Routledge, 2016.

Lloyd-Jones, Hugh. *Justice of Zeus*, 2nd ed. Berkeley, CA: University of California Press, 1983.

Long, Anthony A. "Morals and Values in Homer." *The Journal of Hellenistic Studies* 90 (1970): 121–39.

Lu, Houliang. *Xenophon's Theory of Moral Education*. New Castle upon Tyne: Cambridge Scholars Publishing, 2015.

MacDowell, Douglas M. *The Law in Classical Athens*. Ithaca, NY: Cornell University Press, 1978.

Mann, Christian. *Die Demagogen und das Volk. Zur politischen Kommunikation im Athen des 5. Jahrhunderts v. Chr.* (= KLIO. Beiträge zur Alten Geschichte. Beihefte. Neue Folge; Bd. 13) [The Demogagues and the People: Political communication in fifth-century Athens]. Berlin: Akademie Verlag, 2007.

Manning, Joseph Gilbert, and Ian Morris, eds. "Introduction." In *The Ancient Economy: Evidence and Models*, 1–44. Stanford, CA: Stanford University Press, 2005.

Manville, Philip Brook. *The Origins of Citizenship in Ancient Athens*. Princeton, NJ: Princeton University Press, 1990.

Marcuse, Herbert. *Art and Liberation: Collected Papers of Herbert Marcuse*. Abingdon: Routledge, 2007.

Martin, Michael. *The Cambridge Companion to Atheism*. New York: Cambridge University Press, 2007.

McGlew, James F. "Royal Power and the Achaean Assembly at *Iliad* 2.84-393." *Classical Antiquity* 8, no. 2 (October 1989): 283–95.

McGowan, John. *Hannah Arendt: An Introduction.* Minneapolis: University of Minnesota Press, 1998.

Meiggs, Russell, and David M. Lewis. *A Selection of Greek Historical Inscriptions to the End of the Fifth Century B.C.* Oxford: Clarendon, 1969.

Michell, H. *The Economics of Ancient Greece*, 2nd ed. New York: Barnes and Noble, 1957. First published in 1940 by Cambridge University Press.

———. "Land Tenure in Ancient Greece." *The Canadian Journal of Economics and Political Science / Revue canadienne d'Economique et de Science politique* 19, no. 2 (May 1953): 245–53.

Migeotte, Léopold. *The Economy of the Greek Cities: from the Archaic Period to the Early Roman Empire*. Translated by Janet Lloyd. Berkeley, CA: University of California, 2009.

Mikalson, Jon D. *Ancient Greek Religion*, 2nd ed. Chichester, UK: Wiley-Blackwell, 2010.

Millett, Paul. "The Economy." In *Classical Greece, 500-323 BC*, edited by Robin Osborne, 23–51. New York: Oxford University Press, 2000.

———. *Lending and Borrowing in Ancient Athens*. Cambridge, UK: Cambridge University Press, 1991.

Möller, Astrid. "Classical Greece: Distribution." In *The Cambridge Economic History of the Greco-Roman World*, edited by Ian Morris, Walter Scheidel, and Richard P. Saller, 362–84. Cambridge, UK: Cambridge University Press, 2007.

Morris, Ian. "Antithetical Cultures." In *Archaeology as Cultural History: Words and Things In Iron Age Greece*. Malden, MA and Oxford: Blackwell, 2000.

———. "Archaeology as a Kind of Anthropology (A Response to David Small)." In *Democracy 2500?: Questions and Challenges*, edited by Ian Morris, Kurt A. Raaflaub, and David Castriota, 229–39. Dubuque, IA: Kendall/Hunt Pub. Co., 1998.

———. “The Athenian Economy Twenty Years after the Ancient Economy.” Review of *Athenian Economy and Society: A Banking Perspective*, by Edward E. Cohen, *Classical Philology* 89, no. 4 (1994): 351–66.

———. *Burial and Ancient Society: The Rise of the Greek City-state*. Cambridge, UK: Cambridge University Press, 1987.

———. “Early Iron Age Greece.” In *The Cambridge Economic History of the Greco-Roman World*, edited by Walter Scheidel, Ian Morris, and Richard Saller, 211–41. Cambridge, UK: Cambridge University Press, 2007.

———. “Gift and Commodity in Archaic Greece.” *Man*, New Series 21, no. 1 (March 1986): 1–17.

———. “Hard Surfaces.” In *Money, Labour and Land: Approaches to the Economies of Ancient Greece*, edited by Paul Cartledge, Edward E. Cohen, and Lin Foxhall, 8–43. London: Routledge, 2002.

———. “The Strong Principle of Equality and the Archaic Origins of Greek Democracy.” In *Dêmokratia: A Historical and Theoretical Conversation on Ancient Greek Democracy and Its Contemporary Significance*, edited by Josiah Ober and Charles Hedrick, 19–48. Princeton, NJ: Princeton University Press, 1996.

———. “The Use and Abuse of Homer.” *Classical Antiquity* 5, no. 1 (April 1986): 81–183.

Morris, Ian, and Barry B. Powell. *The Greeks: History, Culture, and Society*, 1st ed. Upper Saddle River, NJ: Pearson Prentice Hall, 2006.

Mossé, Claude. *The Ancient World at Work*. New York: Norton, 1969.

Murakawa, Kentarô. “Demiurgos.” *Historia: Zeitschrift für Alte Geschichte* [Historia: Journal for Ancient History], Bd. 6, H. 4 (October 1957): 385–415.

Murray, A. T., trans. *The Iliad, Loeb Classical Library Volume 1*. Cambridge, MA: Harvard University Press; London, William Heinemann Ltd., 1924.

Murray, Oswyn. “The Affairs of the Mysteries: Democracy and the Drinking Group.” In *Sympotica: A Symposium on the Symposion*, edited by Oswyn Murray, 149–61. Oxford: Clarendon Press, 1990.

———. *Early Greece*, 2nd ed. Cambridge, MA: Harvard University Press, 1993.

Nagy, Gregory. *The Best of the Achaeans: Concepts of the Hero in Archaic Greek Poetry*. Baltimore: Johns Hopkins University Press, 1979.

Naphtali, Lewis. “Solon’s Agrarian Legislation.” *The American Journal of Philology* 62, no. 2 (1941): 144–56.

Nevett, Lisa. "A Real Estate 'Market' in Classical Greece? The Example of Town Housing." *The Annual of the British School at Athens* 95 (2000): 329–43.

Nguyen, Marie-Lan. "Female Workers Making Bread and a Flute Player Sets the Work Pace." Boeotian terracotta figurine, 525–475 BC, from Thebes. Louvre Museum. Wikimedia Commons. https://commons.wikimedia.org/wiki/File:Bakers_kneading_Louvre_CA804.jpg.

Nussbaum, Martha Craven. *The Fragility of Goodness: Luck and Ethics in Greek Tragedy and Philosophy*, revised ed. Cambridge, UK: Cambridge University Press, 2001.

———. *Upheavals of Thought: The Intelligence of Emotions*. Cambridge, UK: Cambridge University Press, 2001.

Ober, Josiah. *Athenian Legacies: Essays on the Politics of Going on Together*. Princeton, NJ: Princeton University Press, 2005.

———. "Conditions for Athenian Democracy." In *The Making and Unmaking of Democracy: Lessons from History and World Politics*, edited by Theodore K. Rabb and Ezra N. Suleiman, 2–22. New York: Routledge, 2013.

———. *Democracy and Knowledge: Innovation and Learning in Classical Athens*. Princeton, NJ: Princeton University Press, 2008.

———. *Fortress Attica: Defense of the Athenian Land Frontier 404–322 BC*. (*Mnemosyne, Supplementum 84*). Leiden: Brill, 1985.

———. "I Besieged that Man: Democracy's Revolutionary Start." In *Origins of Democracy in Ancient Greece*, edited by Kurt A. Raaflaub, Josiah Ober, and Robert Wallace, 83–104. Berkeley and Los Angeles: University of California Press, 2007.

———. *Mass and Elite in Democratic Athens: Rhetoric, Ideology, and the Power of the People*. Princeton, NJ: Princeton University Press, 1989.

———. "Chapter Five: Quasi Rights: Participatory Citizenship and Negative Liberties." In *Athenian Legacies: Essays on the Politics of Going on Together*, 92–127. Princeton, NJ: Princeton University Press, 2005.

———. "Wealthy Hellas." *Transactions of the American Philological Association* 140, no. 2 (January 2010): 241–86.

Oliver, James H. "Herodotus 4.153 and *SEG* IX 3." *Greek, Roman and Byzantine Studies* 7, no. 1 (1996): 25–29.

Osborne, Robin. "Archaic Greece." In *The Cambridge Economic History of the Greco-Roman World*, edited by Walter Scheidel, Ian Morris, and Richard P. Saller, 227–301. Cambridge: Cambridge University Press, 2007.

———, ed. *Classical Greece, 500-323 BC*. New York: Oxford University Press, 2000.

———. "Early Greek Colonization? The Nature of Greek Settlement in the West." In *Archaic Greece: New Approaches and New Evidence*, edited by N. Fisher, H. van Wees, and Debora Dickmann, 251–69. London: Boedeker, 1998.

———. *Greece in the Making, 1200-479 BC*. London: Routledge, 1996.

Papazarkadas, Nikolaos. *Sacred and Public Land in Ancient Athens*. Oxford: Oxford University Press, 2011.

Parke, Herbert W. *Festivals of the Athenians*. Baltimore, MD: Johns Hopkins University Press, 1977.

Parker, Robert. *Polytheism and Society at Athens*. Oxford: Oxford University Press, 2005.

Pelling, C. B. R. *Plutarch and History*. London: Classical Press of Wales, 2002.

———. "Plutarch's Adaptation of His Source-material." *Journal of Hellenic Studies* 100 (1980): 127–40.

Perelman, Michael. *The Invention of Capitalism: Classical Political Economy and the Secret History of Primitive Accumulation*. Durham, NC: Duke University Press, 2000.

Persson, Karl Gunnar. *An Economic History of Europe: Knowledge, Institutions and Growth, 600 to the Present*. New York: Cambridge University Press, 2010.

Pipes, Richard. *Property and Freedom*. New York: Alfred A. Knopf, 1999.

Plutarch. *Lives of Ten Orators, Lysias (Plutarch's Morals, vol. 5.)*. Translated by William W. Goodwin, 1878.

Polanyi, Karl. "On the Comparative Treatment of Economic Institutions in Antiquity with Illustrations from Athens, Mycenae, and Alalakh." Reprinted in *CITY INVINCIBLE: A Symposium on Urbanization and Cultural Development in the Ancient Near East*, University of Chicago, 1960, 329–350. Accessed April 10, 2015. http://kpolanyi.scoolaid.net:8080/xmlui/handle/10694/501.

Pomeroy, Sarah. B. *Goddesses, Whores, Wives, and Slaves*. New York: Schocken Books, 1975.

Postlethwaite, N. "Thersites in the 'Iliad.'" *Greece & Rome* Second Series 35, no. 2 (October 1988): 123–36.

Prasch, Robert E. "How Is Labor Distinct from Broccoli? Some Unique Characteristics of Labor and their Importance for Economic Analysis and Policy." In *The Institutionalist Tradition in Labor Economics*, edited by Dell P. Champlin and Janet T. Knoedler, 146–58. Armonk, NY: M.E. Sharpe, 2004.

Pritchard, David M. *Public Spending and Democracy in Classical Athens*. Austin: University of Texas Press, 2015.

———. *Sport, Democracy and War*. Cambridge, UK: Cambridge University Press, 2013.

Pritchett, Kendrick W. *The Greek State at War*. Berkeley, CA: University of California Press, 1974.

Purves, Alex C. *Space and Time in Ancient Greek Narrative*. Cambridge and New York: Cambridge University Press, 2010.

Raaflaub, Kurt A. "Homeric Society." In *A New Companion to Homer*, edited by Ian Morris and Barry Powell, 624–67. New York: E.J. Brill, 1997.

———. "Power in the Hands of the People: Foundations of Athenian Democracy." In *Democracy 2500?: Questions and Challenges*, edited by Ian Morris, Kurt A. Raaflaub, and David Castriota, 31–66. Dubuque, IA: Kendall/Hunt Pub. Co., 1998.

Raaflaub, Kurt A., and Robert W. Wallace. "People's Power and Egalitarian Trends in Archaic Greece." In *Origins of Democracy in Ancient Greece*, edited by Kurt A. Raaflaub, Josiah Ober, and Robert Wallace, 23–48. Berkeley and Los Angeles: University of California Press, 2007.

Radin, Margaret Jane. *Contested Commodities*. Cambridge, MA: Harvard University Press, 1996.

Randall, Richard H. "The Erechtheum Workmen." *American Journal of Archaeology* 57, no. 3 (July 1953): 199–210.

Reden, Sitta von. *Exchange in Ancient Greece*. London: Duckworth, 1995.

Redfield, James M. *Nature and Culture in the Iliad: The Tragedy of Hector*. Chicago, University of Chicago Press, 1975.

Rhodes, Peter John, and Robin Osborne. *Greek Historical Inscriptions: 404-323 BC*. Oxford: Oxford University Press, 2003.

Rice, Eugene F. *The Foundations of Early Modern Europe, 1460-1559*. New York: Norton, 1970.

Roisman, Hanna. "Nestor the Good Counselor." *The Classical Quarterly* New Series 55, no. 1 (May 2005): 17–38.

Roisman, Joseph. *Ancient Greece from Homer to Alexander*. West Sussex, UK: Wiley-Blackwell 2011.

Rorty, Richard. "The Continuity between the Enlightenment and 'Postmodernism.'" In *What's Left of Enlightenment?: A Postmodern Question*, edited by Keith Michael Baker and Peter Hanns Reill, 19–36. Stanford, CA: Stanford University Press, 2001.

Rose, Peter W. *Class in Archaic Greece*. Cambridge, UK: Cambridge University Press, 2012.

———. *Sons of the Gods, Children of Earth: Ideology and Literary Form in Ancient Greece*. Ithaca, NY: Cornell University Press, 1992.

Rosivach, Vincent J. "Redistribution of Land in Solon, Fragment 34." *The Journal of Hellenic Studies* 112 (1992): 153–79.

Rostovtzeff, Michael Ivanovich. *The Social & Economic History of the Hellenistic World*. Oxford: Clarendon Press, 1941.

Runciman, W. G. "Origins of States: The Case of Archaic Greece." *Comparative Studies in Society and History* 24, no. 3 (July 1982): 351–77.

Said, Edward W. *Orientalism*, 1st Vintage Books ed. New York: Vintage Books, 1979.

Sapirstein, Philip. "Demographics and Productivity in the Ancient Athenian Pottery Industry." *In Athenian Potters and Painters III*, edited by John Oakley, 175–86. Oxford and Philadelphia: Oxbow Books, 2014.

Satlow, Michael L. *The Gift in Antiquity*. Chichester, UK: Wiley-Blackwell, 2013.

Schaps, David M. *The Invention of Coinage and the Monetization of Ancient Greece*. Ann Arbor, MI: University of Michigan Press, 2004.

Scheidel, Walter. "The Comparative Economics of Slavery in the Greco-Roman World." *Princeton and Stanford Working Papers in Classics*. November 2005.

———. "The Hireling and the Slave: A Transatlantic Perspective." In *Money, Labour and Land: Approaches to the Economies of Ancient Greece*, edited by Paul Cartledge, Edward E. Cohen, and Lin Foxhall, 175–84. London: Routledge, 2002.

Schlegel, Catherine M., and Henry Weinfield, trans. *Theogony; and, Works and Days*. Ann Arbor, MI: University of Michigan Press, 2006.

Schneider, Helmuth. "Technology." In *The Cambridge Economic History of the Greco-Roman World*, edited by Ian Morris, Walter Scheidel, and Richard P. Saller, 144–74. Cambridge, UK: Cambridge University Press, 2007.

Schwager, Raymund. *Must There Be Scapegoats?: Violence and Redemption in the Bible*. Leominster, UK: Gracewing, 2000.

Scodel, Ruth. "Odysseus and the Stag." *The Classical Quarterly* New Series 44, no. 2 (1994): 530–34.

Scott, Joan Wallach. *Only Paradoxes to Offer: French Feminists and the Rights of Man*. Cambridge, MA: Harvard University Press, 1996.

Seaford, Richard. *Cosmology and the Polis: The Social Construction of Space and Time in the Tragedies of Aeschylus*. Cambridge, UK: Cambridge University Press, 2012.

———. *Money and the Early Greek Mind*. Cambridge, UK: Cambridge University Press, 2004.

———. "Review: Reading Money: Leslie Kurke on the Politics of Meaning in Archaic Greece." *Arion* 9, no. 3 (Winter 2002): 145–65.

Sherman, Heidi Michelle. "Barbarians Come to Market: The Emporia of Western Eurasia from 500 BC to AD 1000." PhD diss., University of Minnesota, July 2008. Proquest LLC (3321933).

Sherratt, Susan. "Feasting in Homeric Epic." *Hesperia: The Journal of the American School of Classical Studies at Athens* 73, no. 2, Special Issue: The Mycenean Feast (April–June 2004): 301–37.

Silver, Morris. "Slaves versus Free Hired Workers in Ancient Greece." *Historia: Zeitschrift Für Alte Geschichte* [Historia: Journal for Ancient History] 55, no. 3 (2006): 257–63.

Smelser, Neil J., and Richard Swedberg. *The Handbook of Economic Sociology*. Princeton, NJ: Princeton University Press, 1994.

Snodgrass, Anthony M. *Archaic Greece: The Age of Experiment*. London: J. M. Dent, 1980.

Sobak. Robert. "Sokrates among the Shoemakers." *Hesperia: The Journal of the American School of Classical Studies at Athens* 84, no. 4 (2015): 669–712.

Sommerstein, Alan H., and Andrew J. Bayliss. *Oath and State in Ancient Greece*. Berlin: De Gruyter, 2013.

Sommerstein, Alan H., and Isabelle C. Torrance. *Oaths and Swearing in Ancient Greece*. Berlin: De Gruyter, 2014.

Spruyt, Hendrik. *The Sovereign State and Its Competitors*. Princeton, NJ: Princeton University Press, 1994.

Star, Chester G. “The Decline of the Early Greek Kings.” *Historia: Zeitschrift für Alte Geschichte* [Historia: Journal for Ancient History]. Bd. 10, H. 2 (April 1961): 129–38.

———. *Individual and Community: The Rise of the Greek* polis *800-500 BC*. Oxford: Oxford University Press, 1986.

Steinmetz, George. *State/Culture: State-formation after the Cultural Turn*. Ithaca, NY: Cornell University Press, 1999.

Strauss, Barry S. “Genealogy, Ideology, and Society in Democratic Athens.” In *Democracy 2500?: Questions and Challenges*, edited by Ian Morris, Kurt A. Raaflaub, and David Castriota, 141–66. Dubuque, IA: Kendall/Hunt Pub. Co., 1998.

Stroud, Ronald S. “The Athenian Grain-tax Law of 374/3 B. C.” *Hesperia Supplements* 29 (1998): iii–140.

Stuurman, Siep. “The Voice of Thersites: Reflections on the Origins of the Idea of Equality.” *Journal of the History of Ideas* 65, no. 2 (April 2004): 171–89.

Tandy, David W. *Warriors into Traders: The Power of the Market in Early Greece*. Berkeley, CA: University of California Press, 1997.

Taylor, Charles. *A Secular Age*. Cambridge, MA: Belknap Press of Harvard University Press, 2007.

Thalmann, William G. “Comedy, Scapegoats, and Heroic Ideology in the Iliad.” *Transactions of the American Philological Association* 118 (1988): 1–28.

———. *Conventions of Form and Thought in Early Greek Epic Poetry*. Baltimore and London: Johns Hopkins University Press, 1984.

———. *The Swineherd and the Bow*. New York: Cornell, 1998.

Thomson, George Derwent. *Studies in Ancient Greek Society*, new ed. London: Lawrence & Wishart, 1954.

van Wees, Hans. “The City at War.” In *Classical Greece, 500-323 BC*, edited by Robin Osborne, 81–110. New York: Oxford University Press, 2000.

———. “The Homeric Way of War: The Iliad and the Hoplite Phalanx.” *Greece and Rome* 41, no. 1 (April 1994): 1–18.

———. *Ships and Silver, Taxes and Tribute*. New York: I.B. Tauris & Co Ltd, 2013.

———. *Status Warriors: War, Violence and Society in Homer and History*. Amsterdam: J. C. Gieben, 1992.

Vélissaropoulos-Karakostas, Julie. "Merchants, Prostitutes and the 'New Poor.'" In *Money, Labour and Land: Approaches to the Economies of Ancient Greece*, edited by Paul Cartledge, Edward E. Cohen, and Lin Foxhall, 130–39. London: Routledge, 2002.

Vernant, Jean-Pierre. *Myth and Society in Ancient Greece*. Sussex: Harvester Press, 1980.

Veyne, Paul. *Did the Greek Believe in Their Myths? An Essay on the Constitutive Imagination*. Chicago: The University of Chicago, 1988. First published 1983 in French.

Visser, Margaret. *The Rituals of Dinner: The Origins, Evolution, Eccentricities, and Meaning of Table Manners*. New York: Penguin Books, 1991.

Walcot, Peter. *Greek Peasants, Ancient and Modern: A Comparison of Social and Moral Values*. New York: Barnes & Noble, 1970.

Wallace, Robert W. "Personal Freedom in Greek Democracies, Republican Rome, and Modern Liberal States." In *A Companion to Greek and Roman Political Thought*, edited by Ryan K. Balot, 164–77. Chichester, UK: Wiley-Blackwell, 2009.

———. "Solonian Democracy." In *Democracy 2500?: Questions and Challenges*, edited by Ian Morris, Kurt A. Raaflaub, and David Castriota, 11–29. Dubuque, IA: Kendall/Hunt Pub. Co., 1998.

Wang, Donni. "Review of *The Making of the Ancient Greek Economy: Institutions, Markets, and Growth in the City-States* by Alain Bresson." *Bryn Mawr Classical Review* 2016.07.35.

Weber, Max. "Objectivity in Social Science and Social Policy." In *The Methodology of the Social Sciences*, edited and translated by E. A. Shils and H. A. Finch, New York: Free Press, 1949. Accessed online March 22, 2013. http://plato.stanford.edu/entries/weber.

Wells, Berit. *Agriculture in Ancient Greece: Proceedings of the Seventh International Symposium at the Swedish Institute of Athens, 16-17 May 1990*. Stockholm: Åströms förlag, 1992.

Welskopf, E. "Free Labour in the City of Athens." In *Non-slave Labour in The Greco-Roman World*, edited by Peter Garnsey, 23–25. Cambridge, Cambridgeshire: Cambridge Philological Society, 1980.

Westermann, William Linn. *The Slave Systems of Greek and Roman Antiquity*. Philadelphia, PA: American Philosophical Society, 1955.

White, Hayden V. *Metahistory: The Historical Imagination in Nineteenth-century Europe*. Baltimore, MD: Johns Hopkins University Press, 1973.

Whitley, James. *The Archaeology of Ancient Greece*. Cambridge, UK: Cambridge University Press, 2001.

Whitman, Cedric Hubbell. *Homer and the Heroic Tradition*. New York: W. W. Norton, 1965.

Williams, Raymond. *Keywords: A Vocabulary of Culture and Society*. New York: Oxford University Press, 1976.

Wood, Ellen Meiksins. *Democracy against Capitalism: Renewing Historical Materialism*. Cambridge, UK: Cambridge University Press, 1995.

———. *Peasant-Citizen and Slave: The Foundations of Athenian Democracy*, corrected paperback ed. London: Verso, 1989.

Woodbury, L. "Pindar and the Mercenary Muse: Isthmian 2.1–13," *Transactions of the American Philological Association* 99 (1968): 527–42.

Woodhouse, William John. *Solon the Liberator: A Study of the Agrarian Problem in Attika in the Seventh Century*. London: Oxford University Press, 1938.

Wright, Erik Olin. *Envisioning Real Utopias*. London: Verso, 2010.

Xenophon. *Xenophon in Seven Volumes*, 7, revised ed. Translated by E. C. Marchant and G. W. Bowersock. Cambridge: Harvard University Press, 1984. Originally published London: William Heinemann, Ltd., 1925.

Zanker, Graham. *The Heart of Achilles: Characterization and Personal Ethics in the Iliad.* Ann Arbor: The University of Michigan Press, 1994.

Zimmern, Alfred. *The Greek Commonwealth: Politics and Economics in Fifth-century Athens*, 5th ed. London: Oxford University Press, (1911) 1952.

Ziomecki, Juliusz. *Les représentations d'artisans sur les vases attiques* [The Representations of Artists on Ancient Vases]. Wroclaw: Zaklad Narodowy im. Ossolinskich, 1975. Cited in Josef Ehmer and Catharina Lis. *The Idea of Work in Europe from Antiquity to Modern Times*. Farnham: Ashgate Publishing Limited, 2009.

CPSIA information can be obtained
at www.ICGtesting.com
Printed in the USA
BVHW011156041019
560237BV00025B/2/P

9 781612 299006